THE ROLE
OF THE ECONOMIST
IN GOVERNMENT:
A STUDY OF ECONOMIC
ADVICE SINCE 1920

Hugh S. Norton

University of South Carolina

McCutchan Publishing Corporation
2526 Grove Street
Berkeley, California 94704

Copyright © 1969
by
Hugh S. Norton

All Rights Reserved

TO MY FELLOW ECONOMISTS

ACKNOWLEDGMENT

I am especially indebted to Charles B. Warden Jr., of the Council of Economic Advisers, who kindly agreed to review certain portions of the manuscript, making many helpful suggestions; to the University of South Carolina for the research grant which made the necessary travel possible; to my associates in the Department of Economics of the University of South Carolina for their many comments and suggestions; to Miss Judy Banks, Miss Janice Bowers, and Mrs. Shirley T. Craft, for their assistance in manuscript preparation; and to my family for their patience and support.

Hugh S. Norton
Columbia, South Carolina

January, 1968

PREFACE

We are accustomed, in the 1960's, to thinking of the economist as an important figure in the government. We take quite for granted that economists are called upon as a matter of course to provide direction for the national economy. But, as a matter of fact, the economist is a rather recent arrival in policy-making circles. As little as forty years ago, the economist had little or no influence in the formulation of Federal policy. This book attempts to trace the progress of the economist from relative obscurity to relative eminence, evaluating the contributions he has made during that progress.

I am indebted for much information, heretofore uncatalogued, to a number of individuals who have taken time and trouble to relate their recollections, to direct me to valuable sources of information, and to make suggestions in regard to methodology. These are:

Stephen K. Bailey, Roy G. Blakeley, Raymond T. Bowman, Philip S. Brown, Arthur E. Burns, Gerhard Colm, Marriner S. Eccles, Corwin D. Edwards, Mordecai Ezekiel, Bertrand Fox, Milton Friedman, Padraic P. Frucht, Alvin H. Hansen, Seymour E. Harris, Gabriel Hauge, Walter W. Heller, John W. Kendrick, Leon Keyserling, Charles P. Kindleberger, Theodore Kreps, Isador Lubin, Charles S. Morgan, Robert R. Nathan, Edwin G. Nourse, Joseph A. Pechman, Winfield Riefler, Walter S. Salant, Arthur Smithies, George Soule, Mrs. Penelope Thunberg, James Tobin, Frederick V. Waugh, Donald Webster, and Lawrence W. Woodworth.

CONTENTS

                                                                        ix

Chapter

Page

CONTENTS

Chapter

Page

1

ECONOMIC PHILOSOPHY AND ECONOMIC ADVICE, PRECEDENTS FOR ADVISERSHIP

Before 1930, the professional economist, i.e., one who earns his living by teaching or interpreting economic data, was rarely encountered outside academic circles. In 1920 there were probably fewer than 1000 professional economists in the entire nation, almost all engaged in teaching. The American Economic Association in that year listed a total membership of 2,301.[1] Then, as now, however, this included nonprofessionals and interested amateurs.

In his informative study of the profession in 1953, Howard R. Bowen notes that there are no reliable data regarding employment of economists in business and government for the early years.[2] In 1931, there were 600 economists reported to be in Federal service.[3] These economists were of all types, employed at various tasks, only a few of which required a high level of economic training. No doubt many of them were empirical economists.

In the past decade, this situation has changed greatly; the economist in Federal service has increased both in numbers and in prestige:

> Today, economists by the hundreds are employed in the Federal Government. Dozens of them are in policy-making or "policy-supporting" positions. The present Director of the Bureau of the Budget—like his two predecessors—is a distinguished economist, so are and have been the last four incumbents as Assistant Directors of the Bureau. The Under Secretary of the Treasury for Monetary Affairs and his immediate predecessor are professional economists, as are the Assistant Secretary of Treasury for International Affairs and

[1]American Economic Association, *Handbook,* 1956, Vol. XLVII, No. 4, June, 1957.

[2]Howard R. Bowen, *Graduate Education in Economics* (Supplement) *American Economic Review,* Vol. XLIII, No. 4. Part 2, Sept. 1963.

[3]See L. D. White, "New Opportunities for Economists and Statisticians in Federal Employment," (Supplement) *American Economic Review,* March 1937.

the Under Secretaries of Agriculture and Health, Education, and Welfare. The second of two professional economists now serves in the recently created post of Assistant Secretary of Commerce for Economic Affairs. Four members of the Board of Governors of the Federal Reserve System are professional economists, as are the Presidents of a number of the Federal Reserve Banks. A number of first-rate economists have helped turn the Pentagon upside down in the past five years. Several professional economists hold or have held major ambassadorial posts as well as Assistant Secretaryships in the Department of State. AID has become an economist's preserve. Both the Treasury and the Federal Reserve have Consultant Groups consisting of distinguished professional economists, whose policy advice is frequently and eagerly sought. More than one economist in private life has survived the shock of finding the President of the United States at the other end of his telephone line. The Council of Economic Advisers finds—sometimes to its regret—that it has no monopoly on professional economic advice in the formation of Administration economic policy. [4]

The economist, often characterized as a man who "never met a payroll," a visionary at best or a charlatan at worst, has now become generally accepted in government circles. A handful have risen to high levels of influence. [5] This study is designed to trace that rise and to discover what factors brought it about.

A Problem of Definition

This study is concerned with economists who were influential in the Federal government either as high-level advisers or as senior analysts. Bowen indicates that there were 3,261 persons employed by the Federal government in 1960 at such tasks that one might be reasonably certain they were trained economists. (There were a

---

[4] Gardner Ackley, "Contribution of Economists to Policy Formation," *Journal of Finance* (Vol. XXI, No. 2, May 1966), p. 170.

[5] A well-known and colorful definition of an economist, widely attributed to the late Bernard Baruch, is: "A man with a Phi Beta Kappa key on his watch chain, and no watch."

total of 8, 692 who had related titles and similar tasks, but many of these were probably not economists in fact.) [6]

This figure must be viewed against additional data in order to get a reasonable picture of the situation with regard to economists' opportunities for employment in the Federal government, since the civil service definition of "economist" is very liberal. In 1964, the National Science Foundation classified (for the *National Register of Scientific Personnel*), a total of 12, 143 persons as economists, using a fairly strict definition.[7] By a more liberal standard, the Bureau of the Census counted 22, 424. Using the N. R. S. P. definition: of the 11, 329 economists who reported their place of employment, 44. 7 percent were employed by educational institutions, and 11. 25 percent were employed by the Federal government; the remainder being employed by state or local governments, nonprofit research groups, and private enterprise (the last accounting for 35 percent). Thus, some 1, 200 economists with sound professional qualifications were employed on the Federal level in 1964.[8]

In summary we have:

Federal government economists of all types (Bowen)	8, 692
Federal government economists doing principally economic work (Bowen)	3, 261
Economists employed by Federal government (N. R. S. P.)	1, 274

Of the economists registered (12, 143), 41. 9 percent were reported to have the Ph. D. degree. Of the 1, 274 in Federal employment, 450 were reported to have the Ph. D. degree, while 254 had a bachelor's degree or less. Thus, roughly one-third held a Ph. D. ; whereas of the economists employed by educational institutions, almost three-fourths held a Ph. D.[9]

Of the 1, 200 economists employed by the Federal government

---

[6] Bowen, *op. cit.*, p. 14.

[7] *American Economic Review*, "The Structure of Economists Employment and salaries, 1964, " Vol. LV, Part 2, Dec. 1965.

[8] *American Economic Review*, "The Structure of Economists' Employment and Salaries, 1964, " Vol. LV, Part 2, December. 1965, pp. 20 ff.

[9] *Ibid.*, pp. 92, 93.

who can be considered professional, many have some graduate training, but relatively few have the Ph. D. Their experience is frequently limited by a high degree of specialization; civil service status
and liberal Federal retirement make them relatively immobile.
Large numbers of them have done substantial work toward the term-
inal degree but have never completed it, in most cases foundering
at the dissertation stage (The "A. B. D. 's").[10] No doubt the expanding
opportunities for economists in government since the early forties
have attracted many Ph. D. candidates away from their studies.
These rank and file economists, though often the workhorses of their
agency, seldom receive top billing.

This, of course, raises the question of what constitutes "high-
level advice, " or being "influential. " Some, like the members of
the Council of Economic Advisers or the personal advisers to the
President are headliners who should obviously be included on a list
of high-level advisers. Others have exercised influence through
executive agencies or regulatory commissions. But in the final analysis, only a handful of economists exercises real influence, mostly
through the Office of the President, the Department of the Treasury,
and the Federal Reserve Board. The Legislative Branch has relatively few. Many economists are employed in the regulatory agencies, but they are in most cases technicians as are the hundreds
who work in the various agencies such as the Departments of Commerce, Labor, and Agriculture. Their services are useful and the
author salutes them, but they cannot in good faith be included as
influential advisers or major contributors to policy.

Stringent standards have been adhered to insofar as professional
qualifications are concerned, relatively the same standards have
been applied to both academic economists and career civil servants.
It is of course recognized that the standards of the economists in
academic life often differ from those in government or business.
The academic economist must put more stress on academic degree
(the Ph. D. is essential for advancement) and upon publication. Many
career economists in government and business meet these requirements but in general they are not so much stressed as in academic
life. In only a few cases are persons included who are not profes-

---

[10] In fact, it has been suggested that a "clearinghouse" be established in
Washington to enable the large number of candidates from various institutions to complete their work.

sional economists by definition. In such cases the individual was of such stature as to require inclusion.

For purposes of this study, the standard employed is generally that used by the National Register namely: (1) a graduate degree in economics, (2) a career as college teacher of economics or professional researcher in economic matters.

Procedure

The problem of drawing a line between the influential economists and the technicians was resolved by selecting a group of more than fifty economists who had been in key positions and asking them to name their more influential associates. Although this procedure ultimately resulted in a list of somewhat more than four hundred names, there was a clear consensus on slightly fewer than one hundred economists who are considered, in the judgment of their peers, as having been genuinely influential. At any given time, perhaps less than a dozen economists are able to wield real influence, occupy positions. The members of the Council of Economic Advisers, the senior staff of the Council and the Joint Committee, senior advisers to the Board of Governors of the Federal Reserve System, senior advisers in the White House or in the agencies, occupy positions where their influence transcends the agency in which they work. In addition to those in official positions, there are at any given time a handful who, though generally based in academic or research institutions, have access to high levels and are thus able to wield influence.

As in most professions, standards of professionalism in economics have been elevated since the 1920's. Many of the New Deal economists would have difficulty in today's competition since many of them were "political economists," trained in the law or in journalism. Such persons are still encountered, but their numbers are diminishing while the number of formally-trained economists is increasing.

Many of the best-known advisers in government move freely between academic life and government. These individuals, being able to hold academic positions of repute, are generally well-qualified in terms of formal training, and, through publication, are usually more visible in the profession than their civil service counterparts. The civil servant is often less flexible and, frequently because of his official position, is inhibited in what he can publish. Furthermore, working up the civil service ladder to a position where one can acquire an independent reputation is a time-consuming proposition for even the most able.

The relative scarcity of economists in government until recent years is evident and is clearly attributable to the fact that American economic thinking was for several generations not oriented toward the function of economic advice.

American Economic Thought and Advisorship

In general, professional economists in the United States, as adherents of the neoclassical tradition, have not been inclined toward public activity. Because the hands-off orientation of this tradition would not lead one into active attempts to influence economic policy, activity in the public area was generally left to pamphleteers and economic journalists. The great American academic figures J. B. Clark, F. A. Walker, F. W. Taussig, remained aloof. The "new school" economists rebelled against classical liberalism after 1870, [11] but their influence on policy was not great; popular political economists or journalists, such as Henry George, were active as writers and sometimes participants in politics. However they usually confined themselves to specific microeconomic questions such as railroad regulation or tax problems.

So long as the doctrine of laissez-faire remained predominant, the passive attitude of the economist was rational. The philosophy of classical liberalism found a hospitable climate in the developing American society, where faith in natural law and the sufficiency of the individual was strongly entrenched. But one would not be quite accurate in saying that the American economy, since colonial times, had been an example of pure laissez-faire. The government did far more than merely maintain law and order; both Federal and state governments were active in programs designed to promote a wide range of economic enterprises especially in the area of transportation. Further, several states undertook farsighted programs with regard to general welfare, such as regulating the labor of women and children. However, after the Civil War, the doctrine of laissez-faire, bordering on "Manchesterism," had its day. Classical economic

[11] Sidney Fine, *Laissez-Faire and the General Welfare State: A Study of Conflict In American Thought* 1865-1901. (Ann Arbor: University of Michigan Press, 1956).

literature was dominant. Ricardo, Say, Smith, Mill, and their American interpreters were the generally accepted authorities. The laws of political economy were considered as immutable as the laws of nature. Nor did these economists who subscribed to the historical school wish to participate in public policy questions.

But by 1870, laissez-faire was subjected to a strong attack. American thinking of the period was much influenced by the social justice and reform philosophies of pamphleteers and popular authors such as Henry George and Edward Bellamy, whose works were read by millions. But these views were premature, sharply contrasted as they were to the ideal of individualism which flourished in the soil of the American frontier. The English philosopher Herbert Spencer and his American contemporary William Graham Sumner articulated the philosophy that expressed the native ideal and thereby influenced a half-century of socioeconomic legislation. Sumner's "forgotten man" (unlike the "forgotten man" of the New Deal) was the "busy ant" who worked hard, paid his taxes, invested wisely, and thereby brought prosperity to society. (In the legal field, the views of the "individualists" were illustrated by Mr. Justice Field and his famous dissent in the Slaughter House cases of 1873.[12] Laissez-faire was enthroned in the law: Mr. Justice Holmes complained in the same case, that, "the Fourteenth Amendment did not enact Mr. Herbert Spencer's Social Statics." But the reaction against this sort of thinking grew in strength after 1880; by 1900, both the new school and the institutional economists were raising fundamental questions about the system as it operated.

However, despite these divergent views, one could not say that economists were directly influential in matters of economic policy in these years; their influence was upon their intellectual heirs who were, as we shall see, primary instigators of the reforms stemming from Woodrow Wilson's New Freedom and Roosevelt's New Deal.[13]

The absence of rapport between the academic economists and their popular counterparts such as George was doubtless a factor in the lack of real policy-making influence. Many economists were disturbed about obvious shortcomings in the classical system; there

[12] See the discussion in Daniel Fusfield, *The Age of the Economist* (Glenview, Illinois: Scott Foresman & Co., 1966), pp. 65, 66.

[13] In Volume 3 of the *Age of Roosevelt, The Politics of Upheaval*, Schlesinger notes that many of the early New Deal figures were influenced as students by the institutionalists.

was growing doubt as to the efficacy of Say's law of Markets and the apparent failure of the system to fit the classical mold of competition. However, aside from discussion of the antitrust laws and the formation of the "public utility" concept of regulating industries, there was little effort devoted to the policy aspects of these questions. Some academic economists such as J. B. Clark and Francis A. Walker, while generally embracing the classical doctrine, were inclined to take a more institutional view than their European contemporaries.[14] Clark insisted on attention to certain social and psychological factors, pointing out that the "economic man" was incomplete as an explanation of economic phenomena. Richard T. Ely and Thorstein Veblen went further in the inclusion of institutional factors. These "holistic" economists were very active, and the split between them and the more traditional representatives of later classicism was intense. Many of the young economists who had studied abroad, especially those who had pursued their graduate work in Germany (H. C. Adams, Simon N. Patten, Richard T. Ely, A. T. Hadley, E. R. A. Seligman), had become advocates of collective utilization of national resources, attracted especially by problems of labor, regulation of the transportation system, and public education.[15] Ben Seligman points out that the interest in historicism was short-lived since the basic mood of the country was "after all, laissez faire."[16] Richard T. Ely and John R. Commons were perhaps the most active in "off campus" activities, serving on various commissions, boards, and other public policy bodies. Others such as E. R. A. Seligman, whose main interest was in taxation, and Thomas Nixon Carver, who did pioneer work in distribution theory, were concerned with public matters. But at the turn of the century, interest in policy matters within the profession was still restricted to a relatively small group.

[14]Both Clark and Walker enjoyed solid academic reputations and were anything but pamphleteers. Both were influential as writers and teachers in general economics. Clark published various works such as *The Philosophy of Wealth* (Boston: Ginn & Co., 1894). Walker was President of Massachusetts Institute of Technology and published numerous books, including a widely-used textbook, *First Lessons in Political Economy* (New York: Henry Holt & Co., 1889).

[15]See Ben B. Seligman, *Main Currents in Modern Economics*, (Glencoe: The Free Press, 1962), pp. 613, ff.

[16]*Ibid.*, p. 616.

The institutional economists went to the heart of the policy problem, rejecting the idea that laissez-faire was an automatic and infallible guide to economic action. No attempt was made by these economists to discover laws such as those applicable to the physical sciences, since in their view such activity was fruitless. Gruchy distinguishes the "holistic" school from the orthodox neoclassical economists in the following way:

> All holistic economists have the same evolutionary, holistic view of the modern economy. All holistic economists have the same dynamic, emergent view of the economic world underlying their general approach to economic studies. They may use different techniques of scientific analysis, such as the historical, comparative, statistical, and case techniques in their interpretation of the American economy as an emergent going concern, but their goal is always the same, to provide a realistic theory of the evolving economic order.[17]

Although the institutional economists were more active than most of their fellows in the realm of policy questions, they cannot be said to have been particularly influential outside their field:

> The institutionalists made a sizable impact on orthodoxy, but they made almost no inroads on the major policy proposals. They served largely as a foil, helping the neoclassicals to sharpen their tools. The formulation, for example, of the theories of monopolistic or imperfect competition is largely the result of institutionalist prodding. But the policy prescriptions remained unchanged: do not tamper with profits, and try to make the real world more competitive. The problems created by the great inequalities that pervaded the society and which were a major concern of the heretics were brushed aside by the orthodox economists as necessary, though perhaps temporary, facts of life.[18]

[17]Allan G. Gruchy, *Modern Economic Thought* (Englewood Cliffs, N. J.: Prentice-Hall, 1947), p. 627. The early roots of American thought are traced by Virgle Wilhite in *Founders of American Economic Thought and Policy* (New York, Bookman Associates, 1958).

[18]B. Hughel Wilkins and Charles B. Friday, *The Economists of the New Frontier* (New York: Random House, 1963), p. 7.

The American Economic Association was organized largely by Richard T. Ely in 1885 with the purpose, among other things, of encouraging research into the "actual conditions of industrial life." (The original declaration by Ely was too strong for even the moderates in its attack on laissez-faire.) It cannot be said to have been highly active in the national affairs; in fact its purposes state "the association as such will take no partisan attitude, nor will it commit its members to any position on practical economic questions."[19] Francis A. Walker of M.I.T. was the first president (thus making it respectable) and the Association was (and is) dominated by academic economists.[20]

Woodrow Wilson's New Freedom was followed by a resurgence of laissez-faire in the 1920's, but the disturbances of the 1930's were instrumental in changing the attitudes of economists toward participation in public affairs. As we shall soon note, their opportunities began to expand with the advent of the New Deal, and under this influence, they began to abandon long-held beliefs that the economist should be merely an observer and never a participant in affairs of state. "Reform liberals" especially began to take a more positive view of economic policy. A brief survey of the outlook of various modern economic schools should illustrate just how far the different views with regard to economic advice have evolved.

Economic Thinking in the 1960's

REFORM LIBERALS

The intellectual heirs of the institutional pioneers are found among the reform liberals. To them the development of natural resources, enactment of minimum wage legislation, coordination of transportation, and other concerns of the New Deal are the embodiment of sound economic policy. Reform liberals distrust, or are at least skeptical of, the mechanism of the market in its uninhibited form,

---

[19]*Handbook of the American Economic Association,* Vol. XLVII, No. 4, June 1957, p. viii.

[20]No nonacademician has served as president of the Association, and the membership is even now overwhelmingly academic.

placing a high value on economic stability and full employment.[21]
Perhaps the best, certainly the most popular, exposition of the
reform liberal viewpoint has been given by John Kenneth Galbraith.[22]
The reform liberals probably reached their peak of policy influence
during the years from 1930–1940, when popular discontent with the
economic system ran high.[23] The economists who came to maturity
during these years of depression were naturally influenced in their
thinking by serious cyclical problems which were so apparent during
that decade.[24] A sympathetic account of the ideas of many of the
economists influential in these years is found in Gruchy's *Modern
Economic Thought.*[25]

Generally speaking, the liberals favor an active governmental
role, employing fiscal and monetary policy as well as direct economic controls (wage–price) to achieve desirable economic ends.
Economic aid to underprivileged groups, control of monopoly, and
quasi–public enterprises are encouraged as means of achieving
their major goal, economic stability. Big business is suspect while
labor union activity is welcomed. Extensive economic planning is
considered most desirable.

[21] The writings of Alvin Hansen illustrate quite clearly the emphasis
placed upon stability in the views of these economists. A leading American exponent of the views of Lord Keynes, Hansen has long been an advocate of positive planning and control. See his *Business Cycles and National Income* (enlarged ed., New York: W. W. Norton & Co., Inc., 1964);
Economic Issues of the 1960's (New York: McGraw–Hill Book Co., 1960);
and *The American Economy* (New York: McGraw–Hill Book Co., 1957).

[22] See, for example, *Economics and the Art of Controversy* (New Bruns-
wick: Rutgers University Press, 1955), esp. Ch. V; *The Affluent Society*
(Boston: Houghton–Mifflin Co., 1958), and his more recent work, *The
Industrial State* (Boston: Houghton–Mifflin Co., 1967). Also see Allen
M. Sievers, *Revolution, Evolution, and the Economic Order* (Englewood
Cliffs: Prentice–Hall, Inc., 1962), Chapters 1, 2.

[23] For a popular account, see Broadus Mitchell, *Depression Decade* (New
York: Holt, Rinehart & Winston, Inc., 1961).

[24] See for ex. Charles J. Hitch, *The Uses of Economics* (Santa Monica:
the RAND Corp., 1960), p. 1.

[25] *Op. cit.,* see esp. Chapters 6, 7, and 8. See also Seymour E. Harris,
ed., *Saving America's Capitalism: A Liberal Economic Program* (New
York: Alfred A. Knopf, 1948); Alvin Hansen, *Economic Policy and Full
Employment* (New York: McGraw–Hill Book Co., 1947); and Gerhard Colm,
Essays in Public Finance and Fiscal Policy (New York: Oxford Univer-
sity Press, 1955).

Liberals often give inadequate attention to the long-run goals of the economic system; where neoliberals tend to oversimplify, liberals frequently seem to be overly complex, mixing social and economic matters unduly. They are apt to put excessive dependence on legislation and regulation as solutions to economic problems. Consequently, many of the more active economic advisers have come from the liberal ranks.

CONSERVATIVES

In general, conservatives view active governmental economic policy with alarm: monetary policy is accepted, but fiscal policy should not be employed except in emergencies. Direct controls should be avoided, although control over monopoly and public utilities is acceptable. Aid to business and individuals should come from private enterprise insofar as possible. While economic stability is desirable, public efforts should be limited. Economic planning is suspect.[26]

Conservatives put considerable stress on competition, with an appropriate lack of government intervention. They are apt to let their economic views be influenced by their political and social views, e.g., a literal interpretation of the Constitution, the "balanced" budget, etc. Conservatives tend to stress rather loosely-defined concepts and slogans such as "sound money," "constitutional government," and on the negative side, "creeping socialism" and bureaucracy." Most conservative economists shy away from active advisory roles, except in wartime when they can perform technical services.[27]

NEOLIBERALS (HIGHLY CONSERVATIVE)

Members of this group generally view both big business and big government with suspicion. To them, economic development is the

[26]See Francis X. Sutton, Seymour E. Harris, Carl Kaysen, and James Tobin, *The American Business Creed* (Cambridge: Harvard University Press, 1956); Russell Kirk, *The Conservative Mind* (Chicago: Regency Press, 1953); Walter Lippman, *The Good Society* (New York: Grosset and Dunlap, 1943); and Henry W. Spiegel, *Current Economic Problems* (Homewood, Ill.: Richard D. Irwin, Inc., 1961).

[27]A definitive work is Clinton Rossiter, *Conservatism in America* (New York: Alfred A. Knopf, Inc., 1955).

province of private enterprise. Stability is important, but only worthwhile when achieved within the framework of private enterprise. Labor unions, if they are to be tolerated at all, should be controlled along with other monopolies. There is limited support for social legislation such as unemployment compensation and social security. [28] Whereas the reform liberals put great faith in planning and distrust the automatic quality of the market, the neoliberals put great faith in the market mechanism and strongly favor individual freedom. [29]

The orientation of the neoliberals does not lead them into the ranks of economists active in government. In general, they are limited to academic pursuits and are critical of governmental institutions. Neither do they have a large popular following. A relatively small group of economists and dissident intellectuals espouse this line of thought. Neoliberals hold as an ideal an economy made up of small units, strongly emphasizing the role of the market. Because, in their view, the market operates as an institution to protect and encourage individual freedom, and market controls are unnecessary and undesirable. Most economists would point out that the neoliberals have failed to grasp the importance of organizations in the modern society. The neoliberals seem to hark back to the economy of the mid-nineteenth century as a model. There is a tendency on the part of neoliberals to oversimplify the problems of the economic and social system. Having such viewpoints, they naturally do not look with favor on the growing involvement of the Federal government in the economy.

---

[28]Oskar Morgenstern, *The Limits of Economics* (London: Hodge, 1937); Fritz Machlup, *The Political Economy of Monopoly* (Baltimore: Johns Hopkins Press, 1964); F. H. Knight, *The Ethics of Competition* (New York: Harper and Row, 1935); Henry C. Simons, *Economic Policy for a Free Society* (Chicago: University of Chicago Press, 1948); David McCord Wright, *Democracy and Progress* (New York: The Macmillan Co., 1948); and John Jewkes, *Ordeal By Planning* (New York: The Macmillan Co., 1948).

[29]Frederick A. Hayek, *The Road to Serfdom* (Chicago: University of Chicago Press, 1944). Also, Ludwig von Mises, *Human Action* (New Haven: Yale University Press, 1949). "The Ultimate Foundation of Economic Science," *American Economic Review*, Vol. LIII, No. 4 (September 1963), pp. 747 ff. See Milton Friedman, *Capitalism and Freedom* (Chicago: University of Chicago Press, 1962).

Changes in Economic Thinking Since 1930

Major changes have taken place in the role of economists and economic thought in the United States: men with professional economic training have found their way into higher levels of business with far greater frequency and these men are increasingly influential in affairs of state. While differences of opinion exist among professional economists, there is less controversy evident than in 1930 or in 1940. One seldom hears of Keynesian and nonKeynesian economists, since Keynes's relevant work has been largely synthesized with the general body of economics. Many of the writers now active were trained during the 1930's and, consequently, were much influenced by the depression years; but the younger writers and policymakers, trained just before or after World War II, have been subjected to a different set of problems. If employment and stability were the catchwords of the 1930's, economic growth and development have been the "status" fields for economists in the 1950's and the 1960's.

Some controversy still exists regarding the role of government in economic affairs, most of it essentially political rather than economic. Except among the dedicated neoliberals, argument centers around the details of the government's role, rather than around whether government should have a role at all. Little doubt exists among professional economists about the basic appropriateness of fiscal policy, minimum wages, unemployment insurance, control over labor relations, issuance of securities, etc., despite disagreement about how these matters should be handled.

Since the 1930's, economic thinking has been influenced by organized groups. The number of these groups has increased in recent years and their number will doubtless proliferate as the impact of public policy becomes more visible. They are, for the most part, fact-finding and educational groups whose reports are designed to acquaint literate citizens with the issues in the modern economy. Perhaps foremost among these is the National Bureau of Economic Research, organized in 1920, and most famous for its work in the area of business fluctuations. Among typical studies it has produced are: Simon Kuznets, *Capital in the American Economy* (1961); *National Wealth in the United States* (1962); and Mitchell's landmark study, *Business Cycles, The Problem and Its Setting* (1927).

A more recent group is the Committee for Economic Development. The CED, broadly based in business, as well as academic, economics, has produced studies such as: *Economic Growth in the U. S. —Its Past and Future*; *Fiscal and Monetary Policy for High Employment*; and *An Adaptive Program for Agriculture*.

The National Planning Association promotes long-range planning and publishes studies of various economic problems. Typical of its work is the study, *Political Economy in American Foreign Policy* (1954).

More akin to the CED is the Twentieth Century Fund, which has produced such studies as George W. Stocking's *Cartels in Action* (1946) and Albert G. Hart's *Defense and the Dollar* (1953). Perhaps best known of the Fund's studies is Dewhurst's *America's Needs and Resources* (1955).

The Brookings Institution has studied many policy areas and has published numerous books and monographs, especially in the areas of traditional regulation such as transport. It is notable that the first chairman of the Council of Economic Advisers came from this organization.

These groups, staffed by capable professional economists, maintain a generally high level of sophistication in analysis and discussion. Their influence is difficult to measure, but it must be fairly substantial. Whatever shortcomings they have, there is no doubt that they do at least focus attention on matters of public policy and create interest in policy discussion.

The relationship between professional economists and businessmen in 1920 was, like that between economists and politicians, almost nonexistent. The professional economist was, almost invariably a pure academician, while the businessmen had no view of the economic system as a whole. By 1940, this situation began to change. As the growing complexity of the business–government relationship made the role of the researcher more important, the economist became a useful person in the boardroom. Economists, for their part, began to be more understanding of business problems; wartime service gave many of them insight into problems of government and a realistic grasp of the practical aspects of public policy.

Several thousand professional economists are now engaged in business advisory activities.[30] Countless seminars, management programs, and conferences which bring the economist and the businessman together are held yearly. These activities have lowered

[30] This group has its own professional association, the National Association of Business Economists, which is increasingly influential.

the barriers between those who teach and observe economic action and those who carry it out, and this has been beneficial to both parties.

It might be noted in passing that the participation of the economist in the English government has always been significant. Since the day of Ricardo, British academic economists have served in influential advisory positions. One might suspect that the British experience had some impact upon the American situation, especially during and after the Second World War. [31]

Clearly, the opportunities are manifold for the modern economist in regard to policy-making. Economists of almost all schools of thought are more anxious to invade the forum of public policy and opportunities are enhanced for economists to perform a meaningful role in the Federal service. In government as well as business, the economist is increasingly popular; his services are more and more in demand. Meanwhile, the economist himself is ever less timid about venturing into the marketplace or putting a hand to the tiller of the ship of state.

[31] In his *Life of John Maynard Keynes*, Harrod gives a good picture of this process in which the academic economist divided his time and talents between the universities and Whitehall. See: Roy Harrod, *Life of John Maynard Keynes* (New York: Harcourt, Brace and World, 1951). See also: Sir Robert Hall, "The Place of the Economist in Government," *Oxford Economic Papers*, No. 7 (June 1955), pp. 119-135; A. K. Carincross, "On Being an Economic Adviser," *Scottish Journal of Political Economy*, No. 2 (October 1955), pp. 181-197; P. D. Henderson, "The Use of Economists in British Administration," *Oxford Economic Papers*, No. 13, (February 1961), pp. 5-26; J. M. D. Little, "The Economist in Whitehall," *Lloyds Bank Review*, No. 44 (April 1957), pp. 29-40; Ely Devons, "The Role of the Economist in Public Affairs," *Lloyds Bank Review*, No. 53, (July 1959), pp. 26-38; G. Hallett, "The Role of Economists as Government Advisers," Westminster Bank Review, (May 1967); Gerhard Colm, letter to Gert von Eynern, *Interdependenzen von Politik und Wirtshaft*, Festgabe für Gert von Eynern, Duncker & Humbolt (Berlin: July 1966).

2

THE PIONEERS, THE NEW DEALERS, AND THE NEW BREED

The dichotomy between professional economists and high-level government officials was virtually complete before the First World War. Only a few individuals such as F. W. Taussig, Chairman of the Tariff Commission from 1917 to 1919, were employed by the government for an extended period. (The work of Arthur T. Hadley in the regulatory field and William Z. Ripley, with his railroad consolidation proposals of 1920-21, however significant, was the result of temporary special commissions or study groups.) Professor Shumpeter illustrates the atmosphere of high-level Federal service in that era:

> To head a new public agency, to shape its spirit and its routine, to create the nucleus of a tradition, is one of the most difficult of all the tasks that can be encountered in public administration. That is so in any country, but it is particularly so in this one where the "old stagers" of bureaucratic work, on whose experience any new agency can draw, are so rare. Not to fail at such a task in American administrative conditions amounts to proving beyond doubt an individual's exceptional force of personality. For the semi-scientific and semi-judicial of that body, Taussig was, of course, the right man and he was by all accounts an unqualified success. His idea of the proper function of the Commission was to stress the factfinding aspect of its duties and to proceed by cautious steps from research to recommendations that he hoped would in time tend to supplant the exparte statements on which legislative action in the tariff area was being based.[1]

Federal Service Opportunities for Economists Before 1935

One reason for the scarcity of economists in Federal service before 1935 was that there was very little for them to do. In 1920, only

[1]Joseph Schumpeter, "Frank William Taussig," *Quarterly Journal of Economics,* Vol. IV, No. 3, (May 1941), p. 209.

two of the now-numerous regulatory agencies existed: The Federal Trade Commission and the Interstate Commerce Commission. The Department of Commerce and the Department of Agriculture did some fairly sophisticated economic work, but much of their analysis was purely statistical.[2] A few economists were employed by the Federal Reserve System and the Department of Labor. Economic analysis of this type, necessary only when the government is involved in the regulation of business; governmental involvement in the economic system was minimal in 1920 and few economists were needed. No call came from Washington, and economists remained undisturbed in their academic halls.

The First World War was a minor turning point. Many economists entered Federal service; Irving Fisher devoted his Presidential Address to the American Economic Association in 1918 to the new opportunities.[3] Although the war brought some economists into Federal service, it did not present the severe economic problems of the total war of 1942-1945. No serious attempt was made to ration goods or to control output on a broad basis; no concept of the relationship of the aggregate economy to the war effort had been formulated. Consequently, little economic analysis was required. At the end of the war, most of the economists returned to academic life.

The Arid 1920's

In the early 1920's several economists served as advisers to agency heads and as members of regulatory commissions, notably the interstate Commerce Commission. However the government did not generally encourage advice and in the years just prior to the New Deal, the influence of economists on government policy was at its lowest point.[4]

[2]One should not underrate the importance of this research, for the efforts of these pioneers to gather and systematize data were indispensable to later, more sophisticated economic analysis.

[3]Irving Fisher, "Economists in the Public Service" (*Supplement*), *American Economic Review*, March 1918.

[4]Many works recount the atmosphere of the period. See the monumental work by Arthur Schlesinger, *The Age of Roosevelt*, Vol. I, *The Crisis of Old Order, and II, Coming of the New Deal* (Boston: Houghton-Mifflin Co., 1957). For the economist who is interested in the blend of thought and policy-making,

In the executive branch, the Harding Administration was not conducive to economic (or other) advice. On at least one occasion Harding did express a desire for professional and unbiased advice in attempting to evaluate conflicting claims regarding a tax bill.[5]

But even the most capable economist would not have had any real influence on administration policy. As Schlesinger indicates, businessmen were in control, and what Harding did personally was of little consequence:

> The Presidency is more than a man. It is an institution, making its own decisions, generating its own momentum, living its own life. No matter how many afternoons the President spent on the golf course, how many evenings at the card table, the business of the Presidency went on. And in Charles Evans Hughes as Secretary of State, in Andrew Mellon as Secretary of the Treasury, in Henry C. Wallace as Secretary of Agriculture, in Herbert Hoover as Secretary of Commerce, Harding had men around him of ability and character.[6]

These leaders in business and industry, except for Hoover and Wallace, in whose departments some analytical work was being done had little or no contact with professional economists. When Harding died and was succeeded by Coolidge, the situation did not improve. Schlesinger sums up the Coolidge philosophy in a devastating passage:

> His speeches offered his social philosophy in dry pellets of aphorism. "The chief business of the American people," he said, "is business." But, for Coolidge, business was more than business; it was a religion; and to it he committed all the passion of his arid nature. "The man who builds a factory," he wrote, "builds a temple . . . The man who works there, worships there." He felt these things with a fierce intensity.

the role of the New Deal economists is well covered in Allan G. Gruchy, *Modern Economic Thought* (New York: Prentice-Hall, Inc., 1947). See Chapters 6, 9.

[5]William Allan White, *Puritan in Babylon* (New York: 1938, The MacMillan Co.) See also Karl Schriftgiesser, *This was Normalcy* (Boston: Atlantic, Little, Brown & Co., 1948).

[6]Schlesinger, *Crisis of the Old Order*, p. 51.

William Allen White, who knew him well, called him a mystic, a whirling dervish of business, as persuaded of the divine character of wealth as Lincoln had been of the divine character of man, "crazy about it, sincerely, genuinely, terribly crazy."

As he worshipped business, so he detested government. "If the Federal government should go out of existence, the common run of people would not detect the difference in the affairs of their daily life for a considerable length of time." The Federal government justified itself only as it served business. "The law that builds up the people is the law that builds up industry." And the chief way by which the Federal government could serve business was to diminish itself; ". . . the government can do more to remedy the economic ills of the people by a system of rigid economy in public expenditure than can be accomplished through any other action." Economy was his self-confessed obsession; it was "idealism in its most practical form;" it was the "full test of our national character."[7]

Unlike Harding, Coolidge did not miss the aid of an economist; he simply did not recognize a need for such services. Although he was disturbed about the level of brokers' loans during 1927, Coolidge, as White makes clear, did not really understand the problem. Dr. Miller of the Federal Reserve Board, who was opposed to the extension of credit, would have been able to enlighten the President but was not invited to do so. Coolidge's luncheon guests in 1927 included J. P. Morgan, Jr., Clarence W. Barron of *Barron's*, and W. H. Grimes, editor of the *Wall Street Journal*, able men, but hardly unbiased on the subject of stock market credit. When the affairs of the money market became too troublesome, Coolidge took refuge in his domestic affairs and the operation of the White House.[8]

Coolidge was the last President able to operate in a highly personal fashion with a small staff. His mode of operation is discussed by Herbert Hoover, who notes the Coolidge observation that, "If one saw ten troubles coming down the road, nine would run into the ditch and only one would have to be dealt with." Hoover comments however that when that one did arrive, Coolidge was completely unprepared to deal with it.[9]

[7]Schlesinger, *op. cit.*, p. 52.

[8]White, *op. cit.*, pp. 350 ff.

[9]Herbert Hoover, *The Memoirs of Herbert Hoover* (New York: The Mac-

Toward the end of the Coolidge Administration, the rise in the stock market was causing considerable unrest in some circles and this matter was brought to the President's attention. Professor Ripley of Harvard had written an article describing the dangers of the situation and Judson Welliver, a Presidential assistant, asked him to come to the White House to discuss it. Coolidge appeared to be concerned at Ripley's alarming analysis, but when the President discovered that the Federal government had no authority, he happily abandoned the question. He likewise ignored Mr. Welliver's strong case for a Presidential statement which all evidence indicates would have been helpful. [10]

The market continued on its disastrous course of Coolidge prosperity. To what extent Mr. Hoover, as Secretary of Commerce, might have used his influence to curb the situation is a matter of conjecture. Although there is little evidence that Coolidge sought the counsel of economists, there was apparently little sound counsel to be found during this period anyway. With few exceptions, academic economists were secure in their ivory towers, applauding the expanding market. [11] No one in authority saw any danger in the stock market, any weakness in the agricultural system, or any value in the labor movement. No one noticed that the celebrated "Coolidge prosperity" was alarmingly superficial. Although brokers' loans reached nearly $4 billion in 1927, Roy Young of the Federal Reserve Board, and a close friend of the President, saw no danger. [12] The religion of business was as supreme in the White House as in the market place. [13]

Millan Co., 1952) Vol. I, pp. 55-56; See also, John Kenneth Galbraith, "The care and Prevention of Disaster," in *The Liberal Hour* (Boston: Houghton-Mifflin Co., 1960), pp. 100 ff.

[10] White, *op. cit.*, pp. 336-338

[11] See Broadus Mitchell, *Depression Decade* (New York: Holt, Rinehart & Winston, 1961), Chapter 1. See also, John Kenneth Galbraith, *The Great Crash* (Boston: Houghton-Mifflin Co., 1961), pp. 99 ff.

[12] H. Parker Willis, "The Failure of the Federal Reserve," *North American review* May 1929.

[13] Irving Fisher, a frequent Treasury adviser in the United States, and J. M. Keynes in Great Britain were among those who attempted without success to find a silver lining in the clouds. See George Soule, *Prosperity Decade* (New York: Holt, Rinehart and Winston, 1961), pp. 308 ff.

Whether professional economists would have had any influence in
the face of the optimistic attitudes of business and financial leaders
is a matter of conjecture. The leading American economists, raised
in the classical tradition, had little to offer. Pioneer work in theory
such as Chamberlain's was essentially microeconomic. The neoclassical economists had concentrated on the tariff question, monetary theory, reforms in the regulated industries, and other areas
having little relevance to the macroeconomic problems facing the
nation.[14] Perhaps the most relevant research effort was that of W.
C. Mitchell at the National Bureau of Economic Research. Mitchell
was also active as adviser during the late 1920's and early 1930's as
was John R. Commons.

Until a generation ago, most professional economists did
not soil their hands with the grimy business of economic en-
gineering, even in business, let alone government. Had they
wished to do so, they probably did not have adequate tools.
Professor Wesley Mitchell, of Columbia University, only gave
the American republic its splendid system of statistics and
measurement after 1920. Alvin Johnson's monumental *Cyclo-
pedia of the Social Sciences* did not appear in print until 1934.
Intellectuals were, in any event, not particularly welcome either
in business board rooms or in governmental offices. Too
often they had not much to say for themselves when they were.
Until the great change, "practical" men were at a premium;
theorists were discounted. And probably theory had not caught
up with developing economic fact.[15]

If this was the attitude of professional economists, it is not surprising that Presidents and senators seeking advice turned to businessmen and financiers. Since there was no formal procedure for
obtaining advice, cabinet officers, general assistants, and friends,
often self-appointed, filled this role. When President Hoover grappled with economic problems, he turned to Secretary Mellon and his
successor, Secretary Mills; academic economists made little contribution. The economists who spoke out after the crash were inclined to make reassuring statements which only impaired confidence

[14]Adolf A. Berle, *The American Economic Republic*, (New York: Harcourt Brace and World, 1963).
    [15]*Ibid.*, p. 85.

in their later analyses. Moreover they failed to suggest specific measures for recovery. Schlesinger comments:

> Nor were the professional economists much help in filling the technical gap. The grand academic figures—Taussig, Ely, Commons, Mitchell, Seligman—were hardly more prepared for depression than the leaders of business and labor. But the economic heretics of the twenties found stimulus, some even vindication, in depression. And, of all the economists of the day, none was quicker in regaining his feet after the crash than William T. Foster of the old team of Foster and Catchings. For the crash, after all, turned out to have been predictable in terms of the Foster system; and, if he knew the causes of depression, he also conceived he knew the cure. [16]

Hoover, His Problems and Advisors

The record discloses few professional economic advisers to Mr. Hoover. Julius Klein, who received his Ph. D. from Harvard in 1913, held several Federal posts and was Assistant Secretary of Commerce, 1929-1933. He was reputed to be close to Hoover, and whether or not his counsel was accepted is not known; but he is said to have given "able and devoted support and advice" during the depression.[17] Walter Stewart, a monetary theorist, investment banker, and sometime college professor, had some influence on Coolidge and Hoover and joined the Council of Economic Advisers during the Eisenhower years. Stewart had served on the War Industries Board during World War I, and in the early 1920's was the first Director of the Division of Research and Statistics for the Federal Reserve Board. Stewart also had an academic career, serving on the faculties of several universities. Another active figure was E. Danna Durand who, as Director of the Division of Statistical Research in the Department of Commerce, served as economic adviser to Secretary Robert P. Lamout.

When the crash came, Hoover's economic advisers tried to reassure the people with optimistic predictions. Frederick Lewis Allen

[16]Schlesinger, *op. cit.*, p. 186.

[17]William S. Meyers and Walter H. Newton, *The Hoover Administration, A Documented Narrative,* (New York: Charles Scribner's Sons, 1936), p. 240.

describes in colorful fashion the spirit of the time and the reluctance
to admit that there was serious trouble ahead:

> For a moment October 30—Wednesday—brought new hope.
> The newspapers were once again plastered with optimism:
> Dr. Julius Klein, the President's personal economic sooth-
> sayer, John D. Rockefeller, John J. Roskob, all beamed with
> confidence about the future. As prices steadied, Richard
> Whitney took advantage of the interval of calm to announce
> that the exchange would be open only briefly on Thursday and
> not at all for the rest of the week. But the flickering hope of
> stabilization turned out to the final delusion. Variety summed
> it up in the headline of its issue on October 30: "Wall St. Lays
> an Egg. " [18]

These statements were not very effective but there were few alter-
natives. Only Professor Taussig bravely and honestly admitted in
a radio address that little was known.[19]
    Hoover had used such talent as was available during his tenure
as Secretary of Commerce. In fact, his reliance on economists
seems to have been greater at that time than it was during the years
of his Presidency. In mid-1921, he assembled a conference on
waste through unemployment. As a result an analysis of the influence of the business cycle on unemployment was undertaken by a
committee under the chairmanship of Owen D. Young, with the assistance of W. C. Mitchell. A second phase, a study of the construction industry was conducted by John M. Gries. Similar work
was done by Edwin F. Gay, an economic historian, and one-time
Dean of the Harvard Business School who had also served in wartime (see "Memorial, " *American Economic Review,* Vol. XXXVII,
No. 3, June 1947), and was later President of the National Bureau
of Economic Research. Although Hoover consulted at length with
business executives, few economists are found in the Hoover record.[20]

[18]Frederick Lewis Allen, *Only Yesterday,* (New York: Harper & Row,
1940), p. 329.

[19]Alvin Hansen, *The American Economy* (New York: McGraw-Hill Book
Co. , 1957), p. 87. Hansen calls this an admission of bankruptcy.

[20]An interesting sidelight: Rexford Tugwell as representative of F. D. R.
lunched with Hoover in late February 1933. Hoover wrote to a friend that
Tugwell "breathes with infamous politics devoid of every atom of patriotism."
Meyers & Newton, *op. cit.,* p. 356.

The New Deal Years

In the early New Deal era the economist became a standard fixture in Washington. The early "brain trusters," Raymond Moley (a political scientist), Adolf Berle (a lawyer), Rexford Tugwell and Gardiner Means (economists), were often in the news. Yet their influence was less as pure economists than as general advisers. It is likely that Roosevelt's experience with neoclassical economists had convinced him that they were unable to give helpful technical assistance, for economists in power in the early Roosevelt years were the descendants of the founders of the "institutionalist" school of economics. Although Gruchy attributes great influence to this group as policy-makers,[21] it is more likely that they exerted more influence as "social architects" than as economists in the technical sense.

Certainly their activities ranged far beyond the collection and interpretation of economic data.[22] There is little evidence that F.D.R. relied on these men for economic advice per se. If he found little help from the neoclassical economists, he apparently found only a modest amount of usable material in the early ideas of Keynes; Harris indicates that Roosevelt and Keynes found little common ground.[23] However, Alvin Hansen, Keynes' leading American disciple, was a powerful force in New Deal circles, and the Keynesian thesis was a fundamental influence upon New Deal economics. Although he felt, after a personal confrontation, F.D.R. was not sympathetic:

> Keynes found others in Washington more receptive. Steered around by Tugwell, he met a number of the younger men and told them to spend—a monthly deficit of only $200 million, he said, would send the nation back to the bottom of the depression, but $300 million would hold it even and $400 million would bring recovery. A few days later he sent Roosevelt the draft of another New York Times article entitled "Agenda for the President." Here he continued his running review of the New Deal,

[21]Gruchy, *op. cit.*, p. 1.

[22]The range of Moley's activities is indicated by his book, *After Seven Years* (New York: Harper & Row, 1939).

[23]Seymour Harris, ed. *The New Economics.* Ch. II, Seymour Harris, "Keynes's Influence in Public Policy," (New York: Knopf, 1947).

saying he doubted whether NRA either helped or hurt as much as one side or the other supposed and again defending the agricultural policies. As usual, the best hope remained an increase in public spending; $400 million, through the multiplier, would increase the national income at least three or four times this amount. In detail, Keynes advocated special efforts in the housing and railroad fields. "Of all the experiments to evolve a new order," he concluded, "it is the experiment of young America which most attracts my own deepest sympathy. For they are occupied with the task of trying to make the economic order work tolerably well, whilst preserving freedom of individual initiative and liberty of thought and criticism." With this, Keynes, pausing only to make astute investments in the depressed stocks of public utilities, returned home.

Newspapermen were quick but wrong to ascribe the increase in spending in the summer of 1934 to Keynes. No doubt Keynes strengthened the President's inclination to do what he was going to do anyway, and no doubt he showed the younger men lower down in the administration how to convert an expedient into a policy. But it cannot be said either that spending would not have taken place without his intervention or that it did take place for his reasons. In 1934 and 1935 the New Deal was spending in spite of itself. The deficit represented a condition, not a theory. What was happening was a rush of spending for separate emergency purposes. "I think that 95 percent of the thinking in the administration is how to spend money," said Henry Morgenthau in a morose moment in the summer of 1935, "and that possibly 5 percent of the thinking is going toward how we can work ourselves out of our present unemployment." Certainly, except for Marriner Eccles, no leading person in Roosevelt's first administration had much notion of the purposeful use of fiscal policy to bring about recovery; and Eccles' approach, with its rough-and-ready empiricism, lacked the theoretical sophistication and depth of Keynesianism. Roosevelt's own heart belonged—and would belong for years—to fiscal orthodoxy. [24]

Before his nomination Roosevelt had cultivated Moley and Tugwell, and others, attempting to find answers to national problems.

[24]Schlesinger, *Politics of Upheaval*, (Boston: Houghton-Mifflin Co., 1955), pp. 406-407.

Many fresh ideas, usable and otherwise, came from this group,
Again to quote Schlesinger:

> The more cautious institutionalists made their headquarters
> at the National Bureau of Economic Research and concentrated
> on working out statistical pictures of economic development.
> But another group in the institutionalist tradition, centering
> at Columbia University, addressed itself to policy issues.
> Two economists—Gardiner C. Means and Rexford G. Tugwell—
> and a lawyer—Adolf A. Berle, Jr.—combined in these years to
> build a fresh and arresting theory of the American economy.
>
> Means, the youngest of the three (he was thirty-six in 1932),
> had long been exploring the area where economics intersect-
> ed with law and where institutions thus set the pattern of ec-
> onomic development. With James C. Bonbright, he publish-
> ed the *Holding Company* in 1932, a first attempt at letting light
> into the mysteries of corporate structure; and the same year,
> with Adolf Berle, Means collaborated in producing one of the
> most influential economic treatises of the time, *The Modern
> Corporation and Private Property.* . . . To their collaboration
> Means brought an original and capacious economic intelligence;
> Berle, a few months the senior of the pair, both the finicky
> precision of a legal technician and the broad perspectives of a
> social prophet. Each felt that the rise of the modern corpor-
> ation had revolutionized the economy—and each concluded that
> it consequently had to revolutionize ways of thinking about the
> public policy. Means developed the implications of this re-
> volution for economic theory, Berle for law and for politics.[25]

Other economists and economic journalists were beginning to
raise fundamental questions about the economic system. Among
these were Hugh Johnson, a retired general (first head of N. R. A.),
Paul H. Douglas, a labor economist from the University of Chicago
(later U. S. Senator from Illinois), George Soule, and Stewart Chase,
economic journalists, and the historian Charles Beard, whose "A
Five-year Plan for America" attracted much attention.[26]

[25]Schlesinger, *Politics of Upheaval*, p. 190.

[26]*Forum*, July, 1931. Among other things, this article mentioned an
"economic council" as a means of solving problems. Beard's article may

Roosevelt, in seeking the nomination, and as a Presidential candidate, had to steer a course between two divergent economic groups. The powerful old-line Democrats such as W. G. McAdoo, Alfred E. Smith, Bernard Baruch, and John J. Raskob, were anxious for him to remain conservative. Douglas, Soule and Senator Burton K. Wheeler, of the more liberal wing, were often critical and of course, Senator Huey Long of Louisiana, far to the left and representing more unorthodox views, viewed F. D. R. as hopelessly conservative.

Just whose idea the use of a "brain trust" was is not clear. Some credit campaign manager James A. Farley, but Judge Rosenman says in his book *Working with Roosevelt*[27] that prior to the nomination, he discussed with Roosevelt some new ideas on current problems:

"Usually in a situation like this," I went on, "a candidate gathers around him a group composed of some successful industrialists, some big financiers, and some national political leaders. I think we ought to steer clear of all those. They all have failed to produce anything constructive to solve the mess we're in today. Now my idea is this: Why not go to the universities of the country? You have been having some good experiences with college professors. I think they wouldn't be afraid to strike out on new paths just because the paths are new. They would get away from all the old fuzzy thinking on many subjects. and that seems to me to be the most important thing."

"What would you have them do—exactly?" he asked cautiously.

This was something new, and he was deeply interested. But he wanted to get nominated and elected—that was the important thing—and he was not sure whether this kind of group would help or hinder.

"I don't know exactly. We'll have to kind of feel our way as we go along. My thought is that if we can get a small group together willing to give us some time, they can prepare memoranda for you about such things as the relief of agriculture,

also be found in *History of Employment and Manpower Problems in the U. S.,* Part V. Committee on Labor and Public Welfare, U. S. Senate, 88th Cong., 2nd Session.

[27]Samuel I. Rosenman, *Working with Roosevelt,* (New York: Harper & Row. 1952), pp. 56 ff.

tariffs, railroads, government debts, private credit, money, gold standard—all the things that enter into the present crisis: the things you will have to take a definite stand on. You'll want to talk with them yourself, and maybe out of all the talk some concrete ideas will come."

After a pause and several puffs on his cigarette, his eyes on the ceiling, he said, "O.K., go ahead."[28]

Following this discussion Rosenman contacted Raymond Moley (a professor of political science at Columbia) who suggested Tugwell, Berle, and Lindsay Rogers as advisers on agriculture, credit, and tariffs. These men were invited to Albany to speak with the Governor and others on the staff. Later this brain trust group met with him in Warm Springs. Rosenman quotes a letter from F.D.R. which indicates the value placed on their services.

. . . Your contribution of Ray and Rex was probably the best that anyone made during the whole campaign.[29]

As Schlesinger notes, the President-elect became less amenable to the suggestions of the brain trust when the pressures of reality became more intense:

"From all sides pressure thus played on the President-elect. Moley was now functioning more than ever as his alter ego—a whole cabinet rolled into one, trying to ride herd on all major issues of both domestic and foreign policy. The campaign brain trust had dissolved. Never again would Moley, Tugwell, Berle, and Johnson meet as a team. And Roosevelt was already displaying disconcerting new habits, especially of asking new people to do jobs which he neglected to tell anybody else about. The comparative order of the campaign had disappeared. "The informality of the whole performance," said Tugwell in retrospect, "gave it a certain nervewracking quality." This especially irritated Moley, who retained the nominal responsibility for coordination and now took out his exasperation in fits of temper.

[28]*Ibid.*, p. 48.
[29]*Ibid.*, pp. 81-82.

Yet Moley found compensations. Thrust into the floodlight by the conference with Hoover, he was becoming an object of national attention. "I had a pleasant chat with Professor Moley," said the irrepressible Huey Long, "I told him that I knew he was a wise man, but that there never was a wise man who did not have to see someone wiser at some time and that I was available at any time he wanted to come. I added that I would not tell a soul about it except the newspapermen." Sam Rayburn of Texas, more direct in his approach, leaned across the aisle toward Moley on the train back from Warm Springs in December and whispered meaningfully, "I hope we don't have any god-damned Rasputin in this Administration." [30]

This was the crux of the problem. Moley, Tugwell, *et al.*, had no direct responsibility to the President *as advisers:* They had various open-ended jobs in the executive branch, where they were in fairly close contact with the President, but their formal responsibilities lay outside their advisory roles. Tugwell became Assistant Secretary of Agriculture; Moley became Under Secretary of State. Both held vaguely-defined positions in which they could presumably be of some help to the President. Rosenman was opposed to administrative assignments, feeling that the brain trust would be best used as purely advisory.

After the election, the President asked me, among others, what I thought should be done about the brain trust. I suggested that it be kept intact for the purpose for which it had been organized and for that purpose only—as a staff to gather materials for study and for speeches, as a group with whom the President could, as formerly, "bat around" ideas from time to time, and who could "bat around" ideas among themselves.

I said that it would be particularly unfortunate if the members of the brain trust were to be given administrative jobs in Washington to which each would have to devote his major time and attention. No matter how large the particular job might be, it would be only a small part of the over-all picture with which the President would have to deal, and these men could be more helpful in advice and discussion within that larger framework. If they were to be genuinely useful, it was im-

[30]Schlesinger, *Politics of Upheaval*, pp. 450-451.

portant, I felt, that they have no personal or departmental
axes to grind. In administrative posts, inevitably they would
each become the spokesman for one small segment of Federal
interest. They would start worrying about the trees when their
job should be to help the President in his concern about the for-
est. . . .

I still think that it was a mistake for the President to break
up the original brain trust and change the functions of its members. Acting together in a consultative and advisory capacity,
they could have been of great help. Acting individually, without the natural restraint and check which came from group discussion, some of the members of the brain trust who did take
administrative positions in Washington in 1933 eventually caused
the President embarrassment in one way or another. Ultimately their paths and the President's separated. The later careers
of Moley, Tugwell and Hugh Johnson, for example, indicate
that there is something about administrative power along the
Potomac that excludes the concept of anonymous helpfulness
which was the basis of the success of the original brain trust.

The only function performed by the original brain trust which
was continued after 1933 was that of helping on speeches. But
the old group never again did that job as a team.[31]

The AAA and the NRA

In the New Deal era, the Agricultural Adjustment Administration
was a breeding ground for economists and economic experimentation. From this group came such influential figures as Louis Bean,
Mordecai Ezediel, M. L. Wilson, and such lesser lights as Howard
Tolley. Secretary Henry A. Wallace had designated the Bureau of
Agricultural Economics as the departmental planning agency, thus
assigning to it a role far beyond its original purview.

During Roosevelt's second term, and definitely by 1939, his close
relationship with the brain trust began to dissolve. Some, like Moley, became anti-Roosevelt and lost all influence. Although others
continued to be influential in various departments, their direct contact with the President was waning and, by the beginning of the Second World War, ceased entirely. However, Isador Lubin, whom
Roosevelt made Commissioner of Labor Statistics, did continue to

[31]*Ibid.*, pp. 87-88.

be a powerful White House adviser. Other survivors of the brain
trust group have remained active in and out of the Federal service.

Tugwell in the early 1960's was in academic life in Puerto Rico
and an active author. Moley was writing in New York City. Berle
was a New York lawyer. Means was in New York. Leon Henderson
(one of the early New Deal economists) was in California. Paul
Douglas was U. S. Senator from Illinois until 1966 when he went to
the New School for Social Research. Lubin was with the Twentieth
Century Fund. George Soule retired and lived quitely in Cambridge.
Tugwell became the "scapegoat" of the New Deal—the symbol of the
impractical professor meddling in others' business, and no doubt
bore much blame not justly his.[32]

Tugwell, in his account of the Roosevelt Administration, gives a
sympathetic description of the administration's efforts to regain prosperity.[33] At this time, advice and counsel poured in from all quarters
as businessmen, labor leaders, and economists, under the lash of the
depression, began to articulate their ideas. The economics of the
New Deal began to take shape. Strangely enough, those who had been
critical of the prevailing system were no more prepared to cope with
its downfall than those who had been its most ardent champions. Until
its demise after the Schechter case in May 1935, the National Recovery Administration, a major New Deal experiment, attempted to
stabilize prices. Economists who played a significant part in N.R.A.
affairs were Theodore O. Yentema, Walton Hamilton, Leon Henderson, Isador Lubin, Charles F. Roos, and Victor S. von Szeliski. The
retired General Hugh S. Johnson, an interesting figure in the New
Deal movement, headed the N.R.A. Johnson graduated from West
Point, served in the cavalry, and during the First World War was
associated with Army purchasing, working closely with the War Industries Board and Bernard M. Baruch. Upon leaving the Army in
the 1920's, he joined George N. Peek as general counsel to the Moline
Plow Co. (he had become a lawyer in his Army days). He interested
himself in agricultural economics, became an associate of Baruch and
an empirical economist. After the Roosevelt campaign, he took over
the N.R.A. task.[34] The NRA was able to engage in considerable ex-

---

[32]See Bernard Sternsher, *Rexford Tugwell and the New Deal* (New Bruns-
wick: The Rutgers University Press, 1964).

[33]*The Democratic Roosevelt* (New York: Doubleday and Company, 1957).

[34]Hugh S. Johnson, *The Blue Eagle, From Egg to Earth* (New York:
Doubleday, Doran, 1935).

perimentation, because economic conditions remained unsatisfactory and there was at least a moderate degree of public support for experimentation with unorthodox ideas. NRA, like AAA, was the base of many economists who were active in New Deal affairs.

The Messiahs

While our concern is with the professional economists, no discussion of economic policy and advice during the depression would be complete without some mention of the quasi-economists who offered unconventional solutions for the nation's economic woes.

Among the more easily classifiable of these were the leftists, including Floyd Olson of Minnesota, Upton Sinclair with his End Poverty in California (EPIC) program, the communists, and the rightists, including Seward Collins, Lawrence Dennis, and William Dudley Pelley. But the more popular of these messiahs do not fit easily into the conventional spectrum: Senator Huey P. Long of Louisiana promoted the organization of a "Share-the-Wealth Society," with the object (means were only vaguely hinted at) of providing each American family not less than $5,000 per year. James A. Farley reportedly said after Long was killed that had he lived he would have received six million votes as a third party candidate.[35]

Dr. F. E. Townsend of California (a retired physician) originated the Townsend Pension Plan, extremely popular among elderly citizens, which would have disbursed the revenues from a two percent transaction tax to people over sixty who would agree to quit work and spend a $200 per month dole as rapidly as it came in. The Detroit priest, Father Coughlin, established a National Union for Social Justice, under which auspices he weekly advanced his monetary theories (plus a dollop of anti-Semitism) over a large national radio network. An engineer, Howard Scott, advanced a specific, comprehensive alternative to free-enterprise capitalism called "Technocracy," based loosely on the theories of Veblen.

These movements attracted a number of followers and, although their political significance was not great, the Roosevelt Administration was forced for a time to follow a policy of accommodation toward Long and Coughlin. There is evidence that Roosevelt incorporated in his program some of the views of these groups to undermine their standing. [36]

[35]Schlesinger, *The Politics of Upheaval*, p. 80.

[36]Whatever the intentions of the legislation, the Social Security Act of August 1935 effectively cut the ground from beneath Townsend.

It is difficult to estimate the influence of these unorthodox economists. In most cases their influence was substantially less than their publicity indicated. They were colorful figures, but their following was limited largely to "born losers" who saw no hope of climbing the economic ladder by traditional means and who, in the stress of the period, were willing to embrace any philosophy which promised to answer their problems. As soon as modest economic recovery began, interest in unorthodox solutions faded and for all practical purposes disappeared completely as World War II began.[37]

Thus, the economist began to carve out a place for himself during the 1930's, but it was not secure, and the use of his skills in government had not been systematic.

World War II and the "New Breed"

Moley, Tugwell, and their associates were political economists, interested in social reform and political development. Their basic ideas were close to the New Freedom of Wilson. When the Second World War began, men with experience in industry came into power; the hard goods of war replaced the soft goods—ideas—of 1933-39. In the post-war era, a new breed of economists appeared, trained during the years of the Keynesian revolution. The younger economists, more specialized and with better professional training than the political economists and journalists, have come to the fore in recent years.

The war was of major importance, but the developments during the New Deal focused attention on the economic policy-making functions of the Presidency. To understand the growing role of the economist, a word must be said about the President's new role in the formulation of economic policy, since the real issues in high-level economic advice generally focus on the executive branch.

[37]As a measure of this eclipse, a check of recent standard textbooks in economic history reveals almost no mention of "technocracy" and other plans of the era.

3
ECONOMIC ADVICE IN THE PRESIDENCY AND THE EXECUTIVE AGENCIES

The Nature of Presidential Responsibility For Economic Policy

By 1940 the immense Presidential responsibility in the area of economic policy had become obvious. Clinton Rossiter commented in 1956:

There are limits, both strategic and physical, to what can be done in the White House, but certainly the alert President stands always ready to invite the managers of a sick industry or the leading citizens of a city plagued by chronic unemployment to come together and take counsel under his leadership. Of course, it is not his counsel but a well-picked government contract or a hike in the tariff or a dramatic recommendation to Congress for which they have come. Fortunately for the President, his position as overseer of the entire economy is obvious to even the most embittered spokesman for special interests, and he can take refuge from their pleas for relief by insisting that he must consider the whole picture before deciding on action in their behalf.

The very notion of the President as Manager of Prosperity strikes many people as an economic and political heresy, especially those who still swear allegiance to the tattered doctrine of the self-healing economy. Most of us, however, now accept the idea of a Federal government openly engaged in preventing runaway booms and plunging busts. We need only think of Mr. Eisenhower's creditable performance in the slack days of 1954—or, for that matter, of his uninspired performance in the harder days of 1958-59—to recognize the central position of the Presidency in this new kind of government. Lest there be any doubt how the President himself felt about the new dimension of government responsibility, let me quote from his message to Congress accompanying the Economic Report for 1953:

'The demands of modern life and the unsettled status of the world require a more important role for government than it played in earlier and quieter times. . . .

'Government must use its vast power to help maintain employment and purchasing power as well as to maintain reasonably stable prices.

'Government must be alert and sensitive to economic developments, including its own myriad activities. It must be prepared to take preventive as well as remedial action; and it must be ready to cope with new situations that may arise. This is not a start-and-stop responsibility, but a continuous one.

'The arsenal of weapons at the disposal of Government for maintaining economic stability is formidable. It includes credit controls, administered by the Federal Reserve System; the debt-management policies of the Treasury; authority of the President to vary the terms of mortgages carrying Federal insurance; flexibility in administration of the budget; agricultural supports; modification of the tax structure; and public works. We shall not hesitate to use any or all of these weapons as the situation may require. '

And this from a Republican President dedicated to the glories of free enterprise! Thus far have we and the Presidency moved in a generation of welfare and warfare.[1]

Much controversy exists as to just what influence the President alone can bring to bear on economic policy since he must share these powers with others, and much Federal economic policy is more or less continuous from one administration to another. Further, social and economic policies intertwine and cannot be separated. Policies which were once highly controversial and partisan tend to become bipartisan and embodied in the socioeconomic structure. Long before a man reaches the White House he has learned the art of compromise and the need to moderate his views. A senator, or more often a representative, may hold unorthodox economic views; a president cannot. Even if his views remained unchanged and specific, the President begins as a candidate and certainly as President-elect,

[1]Clinton Rossiter, *The American Presidency* (New York: Harcourt, Brace & World, Inc., 1956), 35-36.

to face pressures which will act to modify his approach. His appointment or prospective appointments of key cabinet officers, such as the Secretary of the Treasury, Secretary of Commerce, and others directly concerned with economic policy, will be observed closely in an effort to forecast the trend of his economic thinking. Recent Presidents, both as candidates and Presidents-elect, have assembled task force groups to prepare position papers, examine new ideas, suggest staff appointments, and in other ways help prepare for the responsibilities of office. The preparation period often gives the incoming president a good opportunity to examine problems under less pressure than he will encounter later on.

Relatively few Presidential campaigns in this country have been free from hard-fought economic issues, and economic issues have frequently been paramount. In the campaign, of course, the presidential candidates usually deal in platitudes, anxious to present the most acceptable, least assailable views to the general electorate. [2] In the economic area, this means an avoidance of any clear position. The argument at this stage will center around means, not ends, an endorsement of economic growth, full employment, etc. , with each claiming that he can achieve these goals more quickly and efficiently.

In the 1964 campaign, things were somewhat different. Johnson and Goldwater were, on the surface at least, very different in economic philosophy. Goldwater attempted to offer "a choice, not an echo", offering a conservative dismantling of the "welfare state. " What the real outcome might have been had Goldwater been elected in questionable. Most likely Goldwater, like Eisenhower, would have been forced into a more orthodox path than his followers thought. For the President is not sovereign nor does bureaucracy respond to sudden changes. [3]

[2] In the presidential campaigns since 1940, it would require a sharp eye indeed to detect any significant differences in the economic policies of the candidates as expressed in their public statements. This situation probably reached a peak in the Kennedy-Nixon campaign in 1960. See, for example, Theodore White, *The Making of the President*, 1960 (New York: Atheneum House, Inc. , 1961).

[3] See Theodore White, *The Making of the President*, 1964 (New York: Atheneum Press, 1965).

Organization of the Presidency for Economic Policy

While every act of the President will have some economic con-
notation, there are certain specific economic powers attached to
the presidency which, for the most part, relate to appointment of
men with sympathetic views, formation of general policy statements, and issuance of some specific directives.

Four cabinet posts, Treasury, Agriculture, Commerce, and
Labor, relate directly to economic policy; several more, Defense,
Transportation, and Health, Education and Welfare have strong economic overtones. The President appoints the secretaries and generally approves the agency heads immediately under them. The
policy influence actually exerted by these appointees is questionable,
since they, even more than the President, encounter the inflexibility
of bureaucracy. The executive departments are encumbered with
permanent commitments and permanent personnel in policy-making
positions. No secretary of a major department could go far in an
unconventional direction without being pulled into line by long-term
institutional responsibilities.[4] Despite this situation, presidential
supporters will live in hope and his appointments will be carefully
weighed in order to determine the direction of his policies. Aside
from the cabinet posts mentioned above, there are numerous boards,
agencies, regulatory bodies, and similar groups engaged in policy-
making to which the President appoints members, designates chairmen, or gives general guidance. He also receives information from
these bodies, along with suggestions for policy and legislation, such
as; The Council of Economic Advisers (CEA), The Federal Trade
Commission (FIC), The Interstate Commerce Commission (ICC),
The Civil Aeronautics Board (CAB), The Federal Power Commission
(FPC), The Federal Communications Commission (ECC), The Board
of Governors of the Federal Reserve System (FRB), The Tariff

[4] Emmet John Hughes tells how Secretary Humphrey arrived in Washington with the idea that the budget could be cut and taxes reduced, if he
set his mind to it. He found out differently. *The Ordeal of Power* (New
York: Dell Books, 1962). As another example, agricultural policy looked
very much the same under Secretary Freeman in 1967 as it did under Benson in 1964, or Wallace in 1934. No secretary, no matter how bold, can
solve agricultural problems without a much freer hand than he is likely to
get from Congress. Nor is he apt to get cooperation from the "oldheads"
in the department who have seen secretaries come and go.

Commission (TC), The National Labor Relations Board (NLRB), and the Export-Import Bank (EX-IM BANK), some of these bodies have a narrow or specific responsibility, while the policies of others have ramifications in many areas of the economy. In some instances, the President has a large role in determining policy, while in others such as the independent regulatory agencies his role is more detached, both in law and custom.

Even a casual glance makes it clear that, with such a wide variety of areas and the relatively short time which the President can spend on such matters, each area must receive a rather superficial analysis. Likewise, the President has varying degrees of influence over the agencies involved. He has relatively little power over the independent agencies such as the Interstate Commerce Commission, while his power over the Council of Economic Advisers is substantial. In the same manner, he is apt to be much more influenced by the Council, since he has frequent contact with the members, whereas his contact with members of the independent commission is apt to be fleeting at best. Within the limits of his schedule, the President may pursue these matters largely as his interests dictate and as, in his judgment, may be necessary. As a rule the President will let routine matters, especially those concerned with the independent agencies, run their course until some serious problem arises.[5] This is hardly surprising in view of the pressing matters at hand. The extent of the President's involvement, of course, depends heavily upon his understanding of and interest in economic affairs. Little has been shown by past executives. This is in part explained by the fact that many Presidential powers and opportunities are of relatively recent origin, nonexistent before 1932. Even such an aggressive President as Theodore Roosevelt was forced to depend on the initiative shown by private bankers in the crisis of 1907.[6]

The President and the "Establishment"

Because the President and his Cabinet are bound by the policies, programs, and problems inherited from past administration, the

[5]See Hugh S. Norton, *National Transportation Policy, Formation and Implementation* (Berkeley: McCutchan Publishing Corp., 1967).

[6]Nourse points out that T. Roosevelt and Wilson were the first presidents to be aware of the value of economic advice. Personal interview, July 25, 1962.

opportunity to carry out major economic policy innovations is relatively slight. Too much has come before and too much will come
after. Franklin Roosevelt, who probably had as much power and
cooperation as any President expressed his frustration:

> "The Treasury is so large and far-flung and ingrained in
> its practices that I find it is almost impossible to get the ac-
> tion and results I want—even with Henry Morganthau there.
> But the Treasury is not to be compared with the State Depart-
> ment. You should go through the experience of trying to get
> any changes in the thinking, policy, and action of the career
> diplomats and then you'd know what a real problem was. But
> the Treasury and the State Department put together are noth-
> ing compared with the Na-a-vy. The admirals are really
> something to cope with—and I should know. To change any-
> thing in the Na-a-vy is like punching a feather bed. You punch
> it with your right and you punch it with your left until you are
> finally exhausted, and then you find the damn bed just as it was
> before you started punching. "[7]

The President has awesome economic responsibility with limited
economic powers. He can recommend a tax cut but cannot decree
it. He can seek to implement a relief policy, but Congress must provide the funds. He must adjust the domestic economy to the international situation while at the same time preserving internal
stability. He must keep wages high and prices low; he must preserve
prosperity without inflation. He must reconcile high tariffs for the
protection of Colorado cattlemen and low tariffs for New York im-
porters. He must support the demands of labor and listen to the
pleas of management. In trying to accomplish this he can suggest,
cajole, and plead, and use such direct power over Congress as he

[7]Marriner S. Eccles, *Beckoning Frontiers* (New York: Alfred A. Knopf,
Inc. , 1951), p. 336. (Mr. Truman makes the same point in his *Memoirs, 1945, Year of Decisions* (New York: Doubleday & Co. , 1955; Mentor
Ed. , 1965), p. 105.) Eccles' book makes interesting reading in the economics of the period, but especially in that it traces the thought processes
of a pragmatic businessman who became a convert to Keynesian economics
and went to Washington to put his ideas into practice. It is also interesting
to note that a relatively obscure businessman was able to put himself into
a key position and wield considerable influence on policy without the back-
ing of any political organization.

has, but he will probably get nowhere unless the political situation is favorable. Even the strongest President under the most favorable conditions can exercise only limited power.

The Resident Economist

Both before and after the passage of the Employment Act of 1946, there had been economists on the White House staff. Roosevelt, though he apparently lost faith in economists and relied less on the "brain trust" as time passed, did move one from the Federal Reserve System to the White House for service on his personal staff. This was Lauchlin Currie who had been a new deal figure, and junior member of the "brain trust" for some time. Currie had served as Assistant Director of Research in the Board of Governors of the Federal Reserve System, and in 1940, he was taken into the White House as an assistant in economic matters, though he like most Roosevelt assistants apparently bore no special title.[8]

Currie later became associated with the Treasury Department, and in postwar years left government service. Likewise, Isador Lubin was often in the White House and had substantial influence, bearing the title of Commissioner of Labor Statistics.

President Truman, although he had a large staff, had no professional economists. Dr. John Steelman, a political scientist, seems to have attended to economic matters. By Truman's time, the White House staff had grown substantially from the informal days of Coolidge, and had surpassed that of Roosevelt. It became common to have science advisers, military advisers, advisers on problems of minority groups, etc., often on a full-time basis. After the passage of the Employment Act, Steelman acted as a bridge between the Council and the White House. Truman, however, continued until the end of his administration without a staff assistant responsible for and trained to deal with economic matters as such.

Duties of the Resident Economist

Despite the fact that the Council of economic advisers has formal responsibility for advising the President on economic matters, a President may wish to have a personal adviser who can interpret the advice rendered by the Council. In his book, *First Hand Report,*

[8]Eccles, *op. cit.*, p. 333.

Sherman Adams has related the background of the appointment of
Gabriel Hauge as Eisenhower's personal economic adviser.

> I found Hauge at the Eisenhower headquarters at Denver when
> I arrived in August, 1952, to take over my staff duties. He
> came to Eisenhower on the recommendation of the Dewey or-
> ganization, where he had worked under Elliot Bell of the
> McGraw-Hill Publishing Company. Hauge was one of the
> ablest men Dewey had. Previously he had taught economics
> at Harvard and Princeton and had directed statistical research
> for the New York State Banking Department. On the Eisen-
> hower campaign train in 1952, Hauge labored with Robert
> Cutler in what we called a little facetiously "the speech-rescue
> squad," preparing notes for Eisenhower's whistle stop talks
> and revising the final drafts of major speeches. I learned
> then that Hauge's outstanding quality was versatility; along
> with his fine grasp of economics as it applied to public af-
> fairs—he understands, for example, the Federal Reserve
> System, something that not too many people comprehend—
> he could write about and discuss almost anything in the wide
> field of federal government responsibilities with an unusual
> command of the language. Eisenhower was impressed by
> Hauge, too, but after the election I had some difficulty per-
> suading him to add Hauge to our staff. Eisenhower thought
> of Hauge primarily as an economist and he was not sure that
> he needed a personal economic adviser in the White House.
> It was the old question that we had gone over for many an
> hour with the Rockefeller Committee and other experts; should
> the President's staff be composed of specialists in the field
> of banking and finance, for example, or should it be selected
> for well-rounded versatility, depending on Treasury officials,
> the Council of Economic Advisors and such for economic ad-
> vice? Fortunately, Eisenhower was won over in favor of
> Hauge because he decided that this particular economist could
> also be useful as a writer and a general advisor, which in-
> deed he was. [9]

[9]Sherman Adams, *First Hand Report* (New York: Harper & Row, 1961),
p. 55.

Later Hauge participated in the choice of Arthur F. Burns as Chairman of the Council and supported Burns' efforts to instruct the President on economic matters, as well as occasionally helping him to overcome the authority and prestige of Secretary Humphrey.[10]

The principal use of the White House economist is in what Gerhard Colm has called the "fire brigade function,"[11] the task of fielding the various economic issues which land on the President's desk which the Council is too busy to look after or which have a political orientation which would compromise the CEA. Further, the staff economist can often function as Hauge did as general staff adviser, covering a wide range of economic and related issues.

There have been numerous economists who have had White House staff assignments but did not bear the title of economic adviser. Arthur E. Burns, Walter D. Fackler, Charles E. Galbreath, Don Paarlberg, and others have served in this capacity, but their status was apparently more in the nature of general staff than as adviser in the Hauge manner.

Relatively few economists are qualified for this post, for it requires a rare combination of personal and professional qualities. In addition to his professional skills, the White House economist must be willing to operate in a political atmosphere, where his advice may be overbalanced by political considerations, or perhaps ignored entirely. He must also be willing to subordinate his judgment to the President's program and to work in harmony with the rest of the White House staff and the Administration team. Clearly, he must also have a flair for translating economic concepts into lay terms. It has been frequently reported that President Kennedy enjoyed economic discourse and had some interest in methodology, but he was the exception. Aside from the time limitation, no other President is on record as having interest in how the results were obtained. The President must by necessity be highly pragmatic in his approach to matters. The White House staffer is presented with a problem which in most cases requires an answer as soon as possible. Within a few hours or days, he may see the President again to give him the answer or at least recommend a course of action stripped of methodology.

[10]Adams, *op. cit.*, pp. 361, 386.

[11]Twentieth Anniversary of the Employment Act of 1946: *An Economic Symposium,* Joint Economic Committee, U. S. Congress, Second Session, February, 1966, p. 81.

Recent Experience

Although the resident economist can be useful in many ways, even
as a utility man, he might also be a major source of administration
conflict; if he interposes himself between the CEA and the President,
or goes too far in interpreting the CEA's advice, major problems
could arise. A White House science adviser would encounter no
difficulties, since no specific Federal agency or formal group is responsible for science. Likewise, an adviser on problems of minority groups is less likely to infringe on the province of others. The
economic adviser is, however, in direct competition with the Council and perhaps by his physical location and staff position apt to see
more of the President than is the chairman of the Council. A further potential problem stems from the fact that one more voice is
added to those already on the list of persons concerned with economic
policy. Presumably in any major economic matter, the President
would wish to consult with the Secretary of the Treasury, Chairman
of the Board of Governors of the Federal Reserve System, Director
of the Bureau of the Budget, and perhaps others in addition to the
Council. Thus, the White House adviser might be merely another
level of policy clearance which would have to be dealt with.

The confusion might be compounded by the fact that "White House
staff" and "Presidential adviser" or "Presidential assistant" are
very loose terms indeed, often bestowed generously, and sometimes self-adopted. Consequently, an economist on the White House
staff might, if he so chose, vastly overstate his influence and prestige. Numerous names come to mind of those who are reputed to
be the "assistant president," or someone on the staff who is touted
as the "President's right-hand man" sometimes justly so, sometimes otherwise. In the interplay of palace politics, an individual
might seriously undercut the Council. The Chairman of the Council
has a more or less structured job, whereas a "presidential adviser"
might be in a position to "wheel and deal." Many observers have
commented on the fact that Hauge conducted himself in an ideal fashion,
staying out of the limelight and deferring to Burns. Hauge attributes
the success of the arrangement to his close friendship and regard for
Burns, and has expressed doubt that such a relationship would work in
the usual case.[12]

[12]Personal Interview, July 25, 1967.

Informal Advice

Until the Roosevelt era economists were not only absent from the White House staff, but also were seldom sought as informal consultant. Roosevelt entertained Lord Keynes and Irving Fisher, among others and, though they evidently had little influence, they managed to get in the door. Such well-known economists as Robert Nathan, Leon Henderson and Beardsley Ruml at one time or another reportedly had Roosevelt's ear. No academic economists were conspicuously active as informal advisers to Mr. Truman; although President Eisenhower had many contacts with businessmen, his relationships with economists seem to have been limited to those on the staff and in the CEA. Kennedy, on the other hand, though he had no staff economic adviser, was a tireless questioner of economists who crossed his path. Both Schlesinger and Sorensen note instances of his seeking advice from such professionals as Paul Samuelson, Robert Nathan, Russel Nixon and Seymour Harris. "The President paid most attention to Heller and Dillon but he also mixed in his own readings, observations, and sense of the national and congressional mood."[13] Johnson, like Kennedy, has no personal economic adviser but, as we shall see, his relationship with CEA has been close.

How They Got There

Since a President will in the normal course, have few, if any, contacts in the ranks of economists, he will usually have to search for a suitable adviser. Professional eminence and past experience, association with prestige institutions and well-known writings are important qualifications.[14] Many economists, as was the case with the New Deal figures and later Gabriel Hauge, performed yeoman service in the campaign, having been recommended by political advisers. It is interesting to note that, though Eisenhower had been President of Columbia, Burns was apparently not known to him and was recommended by Hauge. When a President is elected he sets up

[13] Theodore C. Sorensen, *Kennedy* (New York: Harper & Row, Bantam Ed.), 1966, p. 443.

[14] Harvard, Yale, Michigan, and MIT have produced many of the recent economists who have functioned on high levels. In "New Deal" days, Columbia was a frequent source. The National Bureau and Brookings have been well represented.

task forces to recruit staff and this method no doubt turns up likely names. In rare cases, the President will have read some of the
economists' writings and been impressed thereby. Kennedy, while
president-elect, asked Paul Samuelson to head up an antirecession
task force, which according to Sorensen had a major impact on policy. It also "redoubled Kennedy's futile efforts to induce Samuelson
to leave the academic calm that he relished and join the New Frontier."[15] Some economists who came to attention through task force
service during the campaign or after the election were John Kenneth
Galbraith, Walter W. Rostow, Carl Kaysen, James Tobin, and Walter Heller.

At the campaign stage, the candidate will be receptive to ideas
and hence an economist with ambition to move in such circles has
the best opportunity of making himself known.

Given their limited numbers, economists have been fairly common
in the White House in recent years, either as occasional visitors or
on specific assignments. Although one might assume that the establishment of the Council would have eliminated the need for outside
advice, this has not been the case. Perhaps the presence of the
Council has stimulated the President's appetite for economic information, or perhaps economic responsibilities have become so one-
rous that the President needs all the advice available. While the
Hauge arrangement worked well, it is doubtful that one would wish
to recommend it. Perhaps Professor Colm's point about the Council acting as a "fire brigade" could be met by enlarging the Council
staff so as to provide a utility man whose job would be to handle the
numerous politico-economic issues which reach the White House for
final disposition.

Nature of Economic Advice and Analysis in the Executive Agencies

Although economists employed in the executive agencies are by
the nature of the tasks involved more likely to be specialists and
analysts than advisers, it is not unheard of for a secretary or agency
head to have a formally-designated economic adviser. In the mid-
thirties, for example, several economists served as economic advisers to Secretary of Agriculture Henry A. Wallace. An economist
in such a position must maintain a much broader outlook than his
colleagues who deal with the specific issues of agricultural economics

[15]Sorensen, *op. cit.*, p. 267.

which are the major tasks of the department, for his function is to evaluate the impact of the department's policies upon the national economy and vice-versa. In a large agency such as USDA, where his work consists largely of coordinating data and drawing conclusions for the secretary, he has little opportunity to acquire a reputation. Furthermore, his connection with agency policy prohibits him from publishing anything even slightly controversial. Unless he has a strong academic background, his professional career and influence will probably be restricted to the agency or to other such agencies.

In the absence of a specific adviser, agencies depend on staff research groups. For this case, communication between adviser and advisee is generally by written memo rather than face-to-face discussion. Thus the secretary may ask his adviser or assistants for a recommendation in order to help him formulate his views. In actual practice this will probably involve various bureaus, divisions, etc., with the actual economic analysis performed participation by numerous economists, passed along the line, and pulled together at the top. Thus economic advice becomes a production line operation and is seldom concentrated in one man. While this process is very systematic and gives each part of the organization a chance to insert its views, it also presents maximum opportunity for hedging and avoidance of a clear position.

Although a surprising number of executive departments operated for years without any formal attempts to use economic analysis, several did recognize the economic implications of their work at an early date. For many departments, refusal to concern themselves with economic matters was completely understandable. Any economic impact was remote; for example, the economic implications of the defense program in 1930 could be safely ignored.

Advisers in the Executive Agencies

The President's executive functions are shared in part by the executive agencies, and the need for sound economic analysis and advice at the agency level is obvious. Cabinet officers have direct responsibility for the administration of vast programs which have great economic impact. Such Departments as Commerce, Agriculture, and Labor, were pioneers in the establishment of research programs and economic advisory activities.

Though there were many economists at various levels in each department, few were really influential as advisers. In most cases those who were influential, were active and known both within and outside the department, but in some cases the nature of the economist's duties or his location would have made it very unlikely for for him to wield influence or become known as an adviser. In some cases no doubt, great influence was never a matter of outside knowledge, since a "headliner" was sometimes generous with credit for his assistants however, in other instances the subordinates went unsung.

A pioneer in economic research was the *U. S. Department of Agriculture,* and early work in the Bureau of Agricultural Economics was of high order.[16] Economists based in USDA who were influential as advisers were Louis Bean, John D. Black (part-time from the Harvard faculty), Nils Olsen, Henry C. Taylor (first head of BAE), and Frederick V. Waugh. Although USDA was and is essentially concerned with agricultural economics, it had wide influence in other areas. Ezekiel and Bean for example, were influential outside the Department. BAE and other USDA groups were training grounds for New Deal economics, under Wallace and Tugwell, and USDA's influence extended throughout the government.

Not surprisingly, the *Treasury Department* has been a center of research into fiscal and monetary problems. The Treasury like other agencies has made use of both career staff and consultants. Many from both ranks have served with distinction, but few have been really influential as policy makers, such as Harry D. White, Harold M. Groves, Dan T. Smith, John J. Williams, Frank Southard, and more recently, Robert V. Roosa.

The *Department of State* with international economic responsibilities has like other departments, produced many skilled specialists, but few economists of real influence as advisers. Among them, one would include Herbert Feis, Henry J. Wadleigh, Willard Throp, and more recently, Walt W. Rostow.

The *Department of Commerce* with widespread responsibilities in many economic areas has done pioneer work in research especially in national income accounting. Like State, Commerce has produced many technical specialists, but few influential on the policy level. Among these, one would include, Julius Klein, Richard V. Gilbert, and Robert R. Nathan.

[16]See Mordecai Ezekel, "Henry A. Wallace, Agricultural Economist," *Journal of Farm Economics,* Vol. 48, Fall 1966, pp. 289 ff.

The *Federal Reserve Board* from its inception in 1914 has been a leader in research and many distinguished economists have served. More than most agencies, the FRB has made use of academic economists for special studies. Because the Board is to some extent an advisory agency, an economist high in its organization will have more opportunity to become an influential adviser than his counterpart in other organizations. Consequently, the Board must be regarded as a prime source of influential economists, including E. A. Goldenweiser, Sherman Maisel (member of the Board of Governors), Winfield Riefler (whom Eccles credits with the idea of the Federal housing finance system), Woodlief Thomas, Robert Triffin, H. P. Willis (founder of the Division of Research and Statistics at the Board), and more recently, Ralph A. Young.

Although the *Bureau of the Budget* is a key group it has remained small. Consequently relatively few economists of renown have been associated with it. Those who have rendered outstanding service and have had substantial policy influence are David Bell, Gerhard Colm, Grover Ensley, and Arthur Smithies. Both Colm and Smithies, with distinguished academic careers, have made substantial contributions to the literature of the Budget process. Bell later served as Director of AID, and Ensley served as Staff Director of the Joint Economic Committee. There has been some cross-over between the Budget staff and CEA, since the two groups work in close harmony.

In the *Labor Department,* another pioneer in research function, were Ewan Clague, Thomas Holland, Edward Whitte, Arthur Altmyer, Isador Lubin, and Arthur M. Ross. Perhaps best known to the public for its work on labor statistics, such as the BLS cost of living index, labor does a great deal of high-quality research on all aspects of the economy having some relation to labor matters, and its economists have often been influential beyond the Labor Department.

Something of a latecomer insofar as high-level economic research is concerned, The *Defense Department* has nonetheless become the source of significant research especially into the performance of the aggregate economy. It must also be noted that the department in addition to its own "in-house" research, sponsors a vast amount of economic research throughout the nation. Economists notable in the Defense Department are Alain Enthovan, and Charles S. Hitch, later President of the University of California.

In the Justice Department where the antitrust division has long been engaged in high-level economic research, one finds: John M.

Blair (later with the Senate Antimonopoly Subcommittee), Corwin D. Edwards, and Louis Paradiso.

Other influential economists in the executive branch appear in appendix A. Though the various executive agencies have been quite successful in conducting significant research in their special fields, the work underway is of necessity oriented around the mission of the agency. However, the research activities conducted by some departments are very broad in scope. Thus, for example, the USDA carries on a great deal of research work in transportation and marketing, only distantly related to agriculture per se. Consequently, the areas of research interest are often much broader than the name of the agency would indicate. Except on the highest level, economist in a Federal agency is not likely to be in a position where his work will receive much outside, or perhaps even inside, recognition. There is seldom much interchange between academic economists and those employed by a Federal agency. Some agencies, such as CEA and the Board of Governors of the Federal Reserve System, provide internships for young scholars, and others bring in mature scholars for task force duties and special research projects. Unfortunately this interchange is not as widespread as it might be since it does raise many practical problems.[17] A large percentage of academic economists have had their "Washington years," but most of this service has been routine. Unfortunately, most of the agencies which really need interchange of ideas seldom get it.

Many young economists shy away from Federal service except for really challenging assignments such as in CEA. Also, as academic salaries increase, the attraction of Federal jobs, which were very much sought after in the 1930's, diminishes. Opportunities in business, research organizations, and other areas in addition to academic life have increased substantially since the mid 1930's. Nonetheless, the usefulness of a stint of Federal service both to the economist and the government agency is great and more adequate arrangements for movement to and fro should be made.

The Economist in the Second War, The Positive Image

As a prelude to understanding the economist's new role, it is necessary to mention briefly the part played by the economists in

---

[17]Coming and going and constantly acquainting newcomers with the policies of the organization makes it difficult to carry on long-term projects. Academic economists find it difficult to get leave, etc.

the Second War. In all honesty it cannot be said that the economist really distinguished himself (except perhaps as a technician) in governmental operations in the 1930's. The depression stoutly resisted the prescriptions compounded by the economic advisers. When the Second War began, however, specific economic problems presented themselves and generally the economist was more successful and began to establish a reputation for expertise.[18] Problems of material shortages, price control, allocation of goods, etc., were more concrete and narrowly-defined than had been true of their depression counterparts and thus lent themselves to analysis, expecially by the neoclassical economists whose microeconomic tool kit was appropriate for these tasks.

While vast numbers of economists were employed in wartime agencies, again only a relative handful were in really significant positions. When the Second War began the agencies concerned with mobilization proliferated rapidly. A large number of economists were called from academic pursuits to take over tasks of advice or analysis in the wartime agencies such as the Office of Price Administration, War Production Board, the Office of Strategic Services, and the Board of Economic Warfare. Also, a number of economists who had already made a reputation in government were recruited to man the wartime agencies temporarily. After the war ended, other temporary organizations were established and operated under similar conditions. These were generally short-lived, and there was much coming and going, but some of the temporary wartime service lasted for years.

Most of the economists in the war agencies did a workmanlike job but, under the circumstances, few were able to wield long-term influence. Some such as Henderson (who directed the Office of Price Administration) had been figures in the early new deal years; but others such as Walter Heller and Gardner Ackley were at an early point in their careers. Many economists now in middle age had just completed their professional training at this time, and unlike their older associates often began their careers in Federal service.[19]

[18] John Kenneth Galbraith, a widely-read economist, notes that much of the growing acceptability of economists stems from this service during the Second World War in Federal agencies. See *American Capitalism, the Concept of Countervailing Power* (Boston: Houghton-Mifflin Co., 1952).

[19] Ackley for example received his Ph.D. in 1940, and was in O.P.A. and O.S.S. from 1941 to 1946. Most earlier economists were in academic life for many years before undertaking government service. But many of the "new breed" had government service first and academic pursuits came afterward.

In the postwar years most economists who did wartime service returned to their peacetime pursuits, but many remained in Federal service, becoming members of CEA, the Bureau of the Budget, and other agencies.[20]

Economists who served in such agencies as the Office of Strategic Services, War Production Board, Board of Economic Warfare, or Office of Price Administration shifted after the war to the Agency for International Development, Central Intelligence Agency, and other new organizations. The role of the academic economists was especially important in these agencies, since many of them either remained in the Federal service or returned at frequent intervals for temporary assignments. Although these economists were highly useful, their role was essentially technical.

Theodore White notes that the Harvard economists, Edward S. Mason who served as Chief Economist in the Office of Strategic Services, brought to Washington several young associates who later served in key positions, among them W. W. Rostow, Carl Keysen, Charles P. Kindleberger, Moses Abromowitz, and Kermit Gordon. In commenting on the role of the scholar in politics in the mid 1960's, White holds that the "back-room politician" is being pushed out by the "back-room scholar."[21]

The importance of this wartime era is greater than it appears at first glance, for several reasons. In the first place, young academic economists of high professional training became acquainted with government service and it is unlikely that they would have done so under normal circumstances. Secondly, they were given an unusual opportunity to demonstrate their abilities under fluid conditions. In the war emergency, the government was able to tap resources of talent and information both in the U. S. and abroad which would have been otherwise unavailable. In addition, these men were able to operate on a level of authority that would have been impossible in peacetime; and as a consequence, many experienced men were available for significant advisory activities when the opportunities expanded in later years.

[20] No doubt many economists who would have otherwise gone into academic life found Washington jobs to their liking and, having put in some years of Federal service, were reluctant to leave for many reasons, practical and otherwise. A Federal employee who has accumulated more than ten years of service and who has advanced into the higher grades may have a great deal to lose by leaving.

[21] Theodore H. White, "The Action Intellectuals," *Life,* June 9, 1967.

It seems fairly clear that except for the war years, professional economists played a minor role in executive level advisership until the formal tie was established in 1946. Although they were increasingly active in the departments and independent agencies, few of them were close to the President or to Cabinet officers. The reason can be discovered in the nature of the presidential office and the men who occupied it, and in the orientation of professional economists.

The presidency is by its nature a pragmatic and demanding office, leaving the President no leisure to pursue methodological discourse. Few presidents have had any substantial acquaintance with academic people. Until the 1930's, the economist was seldom encountered outside the academic institution.[22] From 1920 until the employment act of 1946 was passed, Roosevelt alone sought out economists. But he was by no means always satisfied with the result and probably never really understood modern economics, or enjoyed dealing with economic problems.[23] Only a few of the executive departments and to a degree in the regulatory agencies, did the economist carve out a niche for himself before the Employment Act was passed.

Of the Presidents considered, none was (for different reasons) able to use professional advice in the way the adviser would have liked to see it used. Harding knew not where to look. Coolidge was not aware of its need. Hoover, Roosevelt, and Truman were, in somewhat different ways, strong men who made decisions largely on the basis of their own ideas, Hoover less so perhaps than the others. Few men who reach high levels in government are at home with abstractions. Last, but not least, until the years after the Second World War, economists had little of value to the high-level government official. Neoclassical economists, most often micro-oriented, were not helpful to a man faced with the problems confronting Hoover and Roosevelt.

The nature and over-all quality of economic advice to the President or other high officials depends on a number of factors. Among these are the type and variety of economic problems which he faces

[22]Indeed, before 1870, he was rare even on the campus. See John B. Parrish, "Rise of Economics as an Academic Discipline: The Formative Years to 1900," *Southern Economic Journal,* Vol. XXXIV, No. 1, July, pp. 1-16.

[23]Most historians (e.g., Schlesinger) note that F. D. R. remained a personal conservative in economic matters and had no real interest in the subject.

and the manner in which he is expected to have the answers to all problems, his direct responsibility for guiding the economy would have been much less in the public mind than now.[24]

"Hard times" were expected to occur from time to time and, while complaints were lodged against the President who happened to be in power, he was not really expected to be able to do much about them. Since 1930, and especially since the Second War, the public has become more sophisticated and more demanding.

The activities of the professional economists did encourage participation in affairs of state. Few were interested in practical matters and fewer still had any concept of the aggregate economy. Those who did enter the public policy area confined themselves to special segments of the economy, like agriculture, railroads, and tariffs, and were apt to be interested either in broad socioeconomic matters on the other.

As the responsibility of the President as economic leader and guardian of the economy has grown, so has his ability to meet it. This responsibility is of course shared with the Congress, but the President, by custom and within the framework of the Act of 1946, must make the basic moves. No modern President could operate with the detachment of Coolidge, nor could he bear his responsibilities without the complex machinery, including advisery agencies, which he has at his disposal.

By the end of the Roosevelt years and the Second World War, the general notion of economic advice was well accepted with certain very important limitations. The complexity of the economy and the high degree of government participation in the war years had brought about substantial change in public thinking and had convinced many skeptics that some professional advice was essential. Economists had demonstrated a degree of expertise during the war years which was to stand them in good stead. There were, however. many reservations. Those who still opposed the New Deal and all its works (and there were many, especially in business), tended to distrust

[24] How much this public awareness is due to the great success of the democratic party in pinning the depression label on Hoover is hard to say but interesting to speculate about. The modern Presidency with the televised press conference, sophisticated economic questions, etc., is no doubt a major element.

planning, economists, brain trusters, and other aspects of the New Deal.[25]

Despite this residue of distrust, there was general acceptance of the need for some organization which had the ability to coordinate and analyze economic policy and analysis at various levels of government. At the end of the Roosevelt Administration, there were still in existence the numerous wartime agencies which had the task of advising Federal officials in the formulation of postwar economic policy. Economic advice was well organized in the Federal Reserve System, the Departments of Commerce, State, Agriculture, and Labor. Elsewhere, it was less impressive. In the White House at that time, it was almost nonexistent. So far as this writer has been able to determine, no one with economic training had a significant position in the White House by the time of Roosevelt's death in 1945. Domestic economic problems had, of course, receded into the background after 1940. When Mr. Truman became President he had a personal interest in budgeting and was reputedly good with figures, but had little use for economists. Like Roosevelt, Truman faced economic problems which were dealt with by general assistants whose backgrounds were generally legal or in the case of John Steelman and David Stowe, academic, but not economic. Thus, at the war's end, there were several hundred economists stationed at various points throughout the government, mainly in the executive agencies, but no one on the White House level was in a position to tap these sources and synthesize and analyze the information they produced. This fact was the basis of the Employment Act of 1946, which helped to change the status of the economist.

[25]In the late war years for example, the National Resources Planning Board fell into such political ill grace that Nourse, CEA's first chairman, refused to accept its former quarters for fear of association, even though CEA was desperate for space.

[26]See Nourse, *Economics in The Public Service, op. cit.,* pp. 376-377.

4

THE EMPLOYMENT ACT OF 1946 AND ECONOMIC ADVICE, THE COUNCIL UNDER TRUMAN

It is necessary to survey briefly the events leading up to the passage of the Employment Act of 1946, in order to lay a foundation for the evaluation of the administration of the Act by the Council of Economic Advisers and the Joint Economic Committee.

The Act of 1946, which established economic advice on a formal basis, was the product of many years of thought. There is no need to retrace here the ground so well covered by others leading up to the passage of the Act itself. Not surprisingly, the passage of the legislation was greeted with less than universal acclaim. One must recall that more than twenty eventful years have passed since that time, public policy has been greatly altered, and the economic philosophy which prevailed at that time has changed greatly in the intervening years. In retrospect it seems very likely that only the widespread fear that postwar unemployment would be a serious problem was responsible for the passage of the Act.

Although there was considerable interest among economists and labor groups, there was little indication of involvement on the part of the general public, nor was there much understanding of the implications of the Act. There had been, however, widespread fear that the large number of returning veterans would find a unemployment comparable to, or perhaps worse than, that prevailing before the war began. Consequently, there was intense interest in any plan which would prevent such a catastrophe. On the other hand, there was suspicion of government control and an understandable desire to free the economy from wartime controls as rapidly as possible. Out of this dichotomy came the Act. In summary of the forces which preceded the legislation, Bailey says:

A major policy bill does not burst like a mature Athena from the head of Zeus. The Full Employment Bill had a gestation period of at least six months, and as we have seen, its ancestry dates back a long way. If we are searching for the moment when the idea of a separate Full Employment Bill came into existence, we should probably have to choose that instant of time in August, 1944, when the Patton amendment to the

Kilgore bill was first brought to the attention of Senator James E. Murray of Montana. Although Patton had submitted his amendment to a wide variety of Congressional leaders as well as to President Roosevelt and Vice-President Wallace, it was Senator Murray who assumed responsibility for having the proposal printed in the form of an amendment to the Kilgore bill and circulated for comment to various government agencies—although he made it clear that he did not intend to call action upon it at that time. Granted the logic of events in the Senate fight over reconversion policy, it was obvious to Murray that the Patton amendment would have no chance of becoming part of the pending [reconversion] legislation. His real interest was in the fact that the National Farmers Union proposal had placed the full employment issue on a new plane of permanent federal obligation, far transcending the limited reconversion concepts which had dominated the thinking of most of Congress for a year or more.

In this general awareness by Senator Murray and his War Contracts Subcommittee staff that limited reconversion legislation was not enough and that the Patton amendment had created a new frame of reference for thinking about postwar employment problems, the Full Employment Bill of 1945 had its real beginning.[1]

At any rate, the ideas embodied in the Act became facts and the era of informal presidential economic advice came to an end. However the new era did not mean that the economic adviser had decisively emerged from the twilight zone he had so long occupied. Much doubt still remained whether the economist was able and willing to assume the new office to which some at least had long aspired.

The Philosophy of the Economist and the Role of the Adviser

By his nature, the economist may have some difficulty in adjusting to service as an economic adviser within the framework of the Employment Act of 1946. Perhaps the most obvious problem is what Nourse has called his "superindividualism" which causes him to elaborate his own system of economic analysis and even to devise

---

[1]Stephen K. Bailey, *Congress Makes a Law* (New York: Columbia University Press: 1950). See also, Nourse, *op. cit.*, Chapters 1-6.

his unique terminology in contravention to the scientific method. Further, the economist may be reluctant to play the role of anonymous adviser required of one who serves on a high political level. If he accepts such service he must resign himself to the fact that his advice (though scientifically sound) may be ignored or distorted for political purposes. He may find that he is unable to defend his professional integrity from political attack. He must be ready to see his carefully-crafted gems of analysis brushed aside by those who have no knowledge of or appreciation for his science. Most serious of all, the high-level adviser must be able to separate his technical analytical skill and his value judgments. For most economists this is a difficult task. By their nature, economists and executives are bound to differ. Economists, especially those based in academia, are trained to be observers, not participants. The economist's scientific sense cautions him against projecting his personal views into the situation. A man who reaches the presidency or is in the cabinet is by contrast a man of action and decision and has no hesitation about injecting his personal viewpoints. Thus, although the Act of 1946 put the economist in a position to bring his skill into the public service, it also imposed a severe test upon him.

The work of the adviser in government proceeds on two levels. On the first, the adviser supplies specific information to his superior, essentially an exercise in technical skill, of which the work of the Tariff Commission is an example. The staff of the Commission, after careful, technical analysis of complex factors, makes these facts known to the President or other responsible officials. The task of the economist ends when he has made the facts known to his superior, a line official, who must then act.

On the second level, the economist goes a step further, and using the facts *advises* his superior on a course of action. On the first level technical skill is a requirement. On the second, judgment and personal rapport between adviser and advisee, are also required. In short, high-level advice is more of an art form than a scientific exercise. Most well-trained economists can operate successfully on the first level. Competence on the second is more rarely found.

The well-trained economist is skilled in the manipulation of data and concepts and is able to perform such technical tasks as national income analysis and translation of data on consumption and other functions into reasonable accurate forecasts.

In recent decades economics as a science has made great progress. It has become much more analytical and its content more uniform;

tools and concepts have become much more standardized and precise. But on the higher levels of advice, the problem of analysis remains acute, and the unmeasurable variables increase in number. Although research bureaus and Federal agencies employ numbers of competent economic technicians, relatively few combine the qualities necessary for successful service on the higher levels of government. Generally, these matters had been given little thought in 1946.

The Transition Period

When the Employment Act of 1946 was enacted, professional economists observed with great interest the probable new course of economic policy. It was hoped that uncoordinated Federal economic policies would be brought under more or less unified control and that a sense of direction would be provided. The Act made it, for the first time, a specified Federal responsibility and policy to maintain a framework of full employment and to devote the resources of the Federal establishment to economic stability, saying in Section 2:

> The Congress hereby declares that it is the continuing policy and responsibility of the Federal Government to use all practicable means . . . to coordinate and utilize all its plans, functions, and resources for the purpose of creating and maintaining, in a manner calculated to foster and promote free competitive enterprise and the general welfare, conditions under which there will be afforded useful employment opportunities . . . and to promote maximum employment, production, and purchasing power.[2]

The function of the Council created by the Act was the preparation of an economic report which would be transmitted, with or without comment by the President, to the Joint Economic Committee of the Congress (originally called the Joint Committee on the Economic Report). The Joint Economic Committee would then make to the whole Congress such reports or recommendations as it saw fit. The CEA report (including that portion written for the president), was to be made public in order that the recommendations, or at

[2] Public Law 304, 79th Congress (1946).

least those printed in the report, would be in the public domain, although of course discussion leading to the report between the CEA and the president was private.

The early years of the Act were as one might expect somewhat uncertain. Mr. Truman, who had been somewhat less than enthusiastic in his support, did appoint the members after some delay, the Joint Committee was formed, and the new era began. However, a period of confusion did occur since there were White House assistants who had been involved in economic matters who were now uncertain as to their relationship *vis-a-vis* the CEA and the President.

Truman, Feeling the Way

Perhaps the leading White House adviser who overlapped the council years was Dr. John Steelman. Steelman (a political scientist) was involved with many high-level matters on the economic and social front, and in the early days there was no clear line between his duties and those of the council. Mr. Truman apparently did not have a clear idea of the purposes of the Employment Act. In his second press conference after becoming President, he stated that he was not familiar with it.[3] However, in this hectic period (May 1945) it can be understood that he was beset with more pressing problems than the "Full Employment Bill." On September 6th, Mr. Truman sent to the congress a statement covering twenty-one points of needed legislation, including the full employment legislation.[4]

The actual assistance given the Act by the Administration during its consideration by Congress was spotty, beginning with the unfortunate testimony of John Snyder (the Chief of the Office of War Mobilization and Reconversion, and later Secretary of the Treasury). Snyder was apparently unsympathetic toward the bill or, at best, only mildly interested. However, in October, Mr. Truman made a strong personal appeal via radio, taking the case of full employment directly to the people.[5] Bailey comments on responsibility for passage of the Employment Act:

[3]Bailey, *op. cit.*, p. 161.

[4]*Congressional Record*, 79th Cong., 1st Sess., December 14, 1945, p. 12267.

[5]*Op. cit.*, p. 235.

Certainly President Truman cannot be held responsible. It is true that he attempted to provide political leadership through his messages to Congress, his radio appeals to the public, the testimony of members of his Cabinet before the Senate and House Committees, his conversations with key Congressional leaders, and his appointment of a Cabinet committee under Fred Vinson to press for passage of a strong bill. It is true also that he signed the final compromise Act. But the forces which shaped and modified the legislation were far beyond his control, and it is almost certain that if he had vetoed the conference bill he would have got nothing in its place. [6]

It should be mentioned here that many writers have noted the President's general coolness to the professional economist. But Mr. Truman was a highly pragmatic man of modest formal education, and it is not surprising that he found little common ground with academic professionals. For example, although they were almost the same age, it is hard to imagine two people more different temperamentally than the cool, precise Dr. Nourse and the President. Whatever his feelings, Mr. Truman appointed the council members in July 1946, and it began to function. [7] Mr. Truman quite obviously took the appointment task seriously and was careful to keep politics at a minimum in appointment. The members were Edwin G. Nourse, John D. Clark, and Leon Keyserling. All three men were well-trained, respected, and experienced in government affairs. Nourse and Clark were professional economists, Keyserling was a lawyer and, as Senator Wagner's assistant, had been a figure in the drafting and passage of the Wagner Act in 1937. [8]

A word about these appointees will be appropriate. At the time of his appointment Nourse was sixty-three years old. A highly-respected economist, he had been associated with the Brookings Institution for many years, had received his Ph. D. in economics from the University of Chicago in 1915, and had spent some years in academic life in the early years of the century.

[6] *Op. cit.*, p. 237.

[7] The full story of these early days is recounted in Nourse, *Economics in the Public Service* (New York: Harcourt Brace & World, 1953).

[8] Leon Keyserling, "The Wagner Act: Its Origin and Current Significance," *The George Washington Law Review*, Vol. 29, Dec. 1960, No. 2, pp. 199 ff.

Keyserling, then thirty-eight years old, was a lawyer by profession, having graduated from Columbia in 1931. He studied economics at Columbia on a parttime basis and joined Rexford Tugwell in Washington in the early 1930's serving on the legal staff of the Agricultural Adjustment Administration. From then until 1946 he served in a number of Federal agencies, as a staff member of the Senate Committee on Banking and Currency, and as General Counsel of the National Housing Agency. It was generally known that he was Senator Wagner's choice for the Council. In 1944 he had attracted attention by winning second prize ($10,000) in the Pabst Postwar Planning Essay Contest with a paper which stressed economic growth as an important economic goal.[9]

Although less well-known, perhaps the most personally interesting of the trio was John D. Clark. A lawyer, he had in middle life resigned a vice-presidency of Standard Oil of Indiana to earn a Ph.D. in economics in 1931 from Johns Hopkins University. Later, he had become involved in Wyoming politics and was an associate of Senator O'Mahoney. At 62, he left the post as Dean of the College of Business at the University of Nebraska to accept an appointment on the Council. In general press reaction to the appointments was favorable though somewhat guarded.[10]

Personnel and Organization of the Truman Council

Serving the council as staff was a capable group headed by Gerhard Colm who acted in general as chief of staff. Colm stood very high among his professional associates and had long experience in both academic life and government. Fifty-three in 1950, he had left Germany in the early 1930's and, after a short stay at the New School for Social Research, had served in the Department of Commerce and in the Bureau of the Budget. He left Budget to become

[9]A word about this Pabst Essay Contest is of interest. (W. C. Mitchell and Beardsley Ruml were among the judges.) Of the seventeen winners, eight were government economists (in 1943). These were: Herbert Stein, (1st prize, $25,000), Leon H. Keyserling, Grover Ensley, Mordecai Ezekiel, Joseph M. Gillman, Leo Grebler, Everett M. Hagen, Albert G. Hart, and John H. G. Pierson. These essays published by the Pabst Brewing Company make very interesting reading indeed.

[10]Nourse, *op. cit.*, pp. 110 ff.

senior economist in the Council in 1946, where he remained until 1952. He was later to join the National Planning Association as Chief Economist, and was for some years an adjunct professor at George Washington University.

Serving with Colm on the staff were several other economists: Benjamin Caplan, who had had experience in the War Production Board and OPA; labor economist John C. Davis, veteran of the War Manpower Commission and other agencies; Walter Salant, also of OPA and other groups, one of the pioneers of the early period of the Act of 1946; housing and public works expert, Robinson Newcomb, who had served in the National Recovery Administration, Departments of Interior and Commerce, WPB, and The Federal Works Agency; an agricultural economist, Frederick V. Waugh, who had been in various jobs in agriculture since 1928; for a brief period Donald Wallace, a veteran of OPA, and later on the Princeton faculty; and an academic economist, Edgar M. Hoover of the University of Michigan, who had been in brief service with NRPB, OPA, and the WPB in the early war years, was essentially an academician and returned to academic life in 1954. It will be noted that unlike some to serve in the future the staff consisted largely of veterans of government service.

In the second line of support were several staff assistants: Hamilton Q. Dearborn, Joseph L. Fisher, Burton H. Klein, Susannah E. Caulkins, and Mary W. Smelker, all with long government experience. A political scientist, Bertram Gross, who was instrumental in the passage of the Act in 1946, served as assistant to the Chairman and later as Executive Secretary; the chief statistician, Frances James, completed the team. Like the staff, these were Washington-oriented people, with long Federal service. Several of them were not professional economists in the academic sense and, except for Fisher who had varied teaching assignments and later became President of Resources for the Future, they had had government careers. A later addition was Charles Schultze, a professional economist and academician who became a council member and later Director of the Budget. Several part-time people served: Edward Hollander, Carl Shoup, Wilson Wright, and Robert Warren. Later, two new staff members, John P. Lewis and Karl Arndt, arrived to find the staff in turmoil because of the Korean War. Arndt was to work with Clark on monetary policy. Lewis, who had written a doctoral dissertation on price policy in full employment, was apparently chosen because his work came to the favorable attention of Colm. (Lewis

served later in the Kennedy years as a council member before joining the faculty at Indiana University in 1964.)

It seems fair to say that Nourse was almost universally well regarded by his fellow economists. Keyserling though well known was
considered to be the politician of the group. Clark was little known
by his fellow economists. Colm was outstanding on the staff level.

Two others later served on the Truman Council, Roy Blough and
Robert C. Turner. Blough, forty-nine at the time of appointment,
held a Ph.D. from Columbia University, and was a tax expert who
had worked in the treasury and been a faculty member at the University of Chicago. Turner, with a Ph.D. from Ohio State in 1937,
was born in 1908, and after a brief academic stint, spent many years
in Federal service, serving in the WPB, OPA, OWMR, and on the
White House economic staff.

The original appointees were widely different in philosophy and
background; indeed, Mr. Truman notes in his memoirs that he felt
their difference to be an advantage.[11]

The Nourse Period

From the first it was apparent that the exact role of the Council
was not clear. The most serious uncertainty centered around the
issue of advice as opposed to advocacy. That is, to what degree
should the Council merely advise the President and to what degree
should it justify and perhaps even promote the President's policies.
The core of this problem was the fact that the report was to be made
public. When programs and predictions are made public and widely
distributed, the question arises how much these policy positions
bind the administration in future action. The Council also faced the
troublesome question of what and how much information should be
made public. The Council soon became divided on the issues. Nourse
was of the opinion that they should stick closely to the task of giving
economic advice; Clark, and especially Keyserling, were of the
opinion that their advice should cut across advisory lines and include
social and political aspects.

Mr. Truman, a highly pragmatic man, apparently took little interest in the methodology of economics or in the internal problems

[11]"I was well advised in their selection by the very fact that they were
not all of one mind," *Memoirs* (New York: Doubleday & Co. , 1955) Signet
Ed. , p. 544.

of the Council. In general, he supported the Clark-Keyserling view. Keyserling maintained that Nourse was unable to adjust himself to the problems of the White House and could not understand that the President did not have time for "economic bull sessions" as was the custom at Brookings.

Nourse became more and more frustrated with the situation and shortly before he resigned, he said:

> The events of recent weeks have confirmed my belief that it is useless to try to go on in my post under present conditions. The physical and nervous strain is so great that several times I have seen my breaking point just around the corner. Further, the President's handling of the Midyear Report shows how little real opportunity there is for having our work adequately considered in actual policy making. Although the President said when we submitted our draft materials, "I want to study these very carefully and discuss them fully when I get back" (from a weekend cruise), he never consulted with us thereafter, nor did he sit in with the Cabinet-Council—it was a couple of Steelman's assistants who had the chance to talk to him.[12]

In another context he said:

> Some cynical people have alluded to the Council as "the Three Wise Men of Economics," standing at the President's elbow to give him smart answers to economic riddles or to tell him just what to do in every economic crisis or situation as it arises. Now I do not regard myself as 33 1/3 per cent of the Three Wise Men. I do not claim that the Council is composed of the three greatest economists in the United States or even that it includes any one of that sacred three. As I understand the matter, we have, by the vicissitudes of politics, been entrusted with the task of organizing an agency through which, over the years, the Chief Executive of the United States may see the economic situation and problems of the nation in their entirety and through professional eyes. It is the responsibility of this agency to process for his consideration the materials which should be of most use to him in

[12]Nourse, *op. cit.*, p. 280.

laying out his policy and following his course of action with reference to the national economy. . . . I conceive this agency as the doorway through which the best thinking of systematic economics (not forgetting the lay brothers) may be brought into clear and effective focus at the point of executive decision as to national economic policy and action.[13]

The Nourse view was clearly that of one who thought of himself as an adviser to the President, and whose role was confidential. He did not see himself as being an active participant in the President's program, involved in day to day affairs or in promotion of the program. In his view the Council was to operate in a detached fashion, giving the President technical advice.

Keyserling and to a lesser extent Clark did not embrace the Nourse view, and soon made it clear that they did not see anything improper in the council's active participation in the President's program, nor was Keyserling opposed to testifying before Congress as was Nourse.

Keyserling stated his philosophy thus:

It is clear that the members of the Council are employees of and advisers to the President, and that they are not employees of and advisers to the Congress in the same sense. But this does not mean, in my opinion that the members of the Council cannot or should not testify before, cooperate and consult with, and in a sense give advice to, committees of the Congress just as this is done by heads of other agencies in the executive branch, and even other agencies in the Executive Office of the President such as the National Security Board, who are appointed by the President and confirmed by the Senate under statutes defining their functions and responsibilities, and who are employees of the advisers to the President in the sense that they work under his direction as members of his "official family" and may, of course, be dismissed by him. . . .

In addition, it has been the almost universal custom and entirely appropriate for such officials (Cabinet Secretaries) to appear before congressional committees and to make analyses and give advice in the fields in which they operate under

[13]Nourse, *op. cit.*, pp. 393-4.

statute, even when this has not been preceded by a Presidential message covering the specific matters before the committee. In appearing before committees of Congress in this role,
I cannot see where the Council of Economic Advisers is doing
any different or appearing in any different light from what is
done by heads of other agencies working in different fields.
And I have never seen any valid reason why the members of
the Council, in view of the statute under which they operate
and the nature of their role, should follow a contrary course
or differentiate between themselves and heads of the other
agencies to whom I have referred above. [14]

One staff member who was close to the situation holds that Nourse
was apt to object to liberal advice as political, and to regard conservative advice as entirely within the legitimate purview of his position. Keyserling complained, with some justice, that Nourse made
speeches to conservative groups, while objecting to Keyserling's
similar activities before liberal groups. However, Keyserling has
also maintained that the differences between Nourse and himself
were not on economic theory and methodology, but on political organization and procedure. Keyserling has said that the differences
should have been settled by the President instead of telling the Council members to work things out among themselves. [15] Nourse agrees
but holds that some basic economic differences were present. [16]

It seems plain in retrospect that Nourse and Truman were hardly
destined to be entirely compatible. Aside from age, they had little
in common. Nourse had spent nearly all his professional life in the
Brookings Institution. Truman was, aside from his coolness towards
economists, a man faced with daily crises. It seems likely that,
although the President had regard for Nourse's professional reputation, they would never have been easy in each others company.

This incident points up the dilemma of the economist-adviser in
a situation of advocacy. It can be argued that, in fact, it would be
impossible for an adviser in this context to disassociate himself.
One can imagine the political capital which the opposition could make

[14] *Monetary Policy and the Management of the Public Debt,* Hearings before the Subcommittee on General Credit Control and Debt Management,
82nd Cong., 2nd Sess., March 1952.

[15] Personal interview, March 15, 1967.

of an adviser who refused in public to endorse the President's program. The difference of opinion in the CEA was of course widely known and much discussed among economists. Another C.E.A. member has considered the problem carefully:

> . . . What the individual in an inconsistent position like that facing the Council may do is to carry on as well as he can, thinking and speaking as independently as possible but being discreet and cautious, never abandoning his standards of integrity by saying what he does not believe to be true. Almost inevitably in the end, the inconsistency of the position will become too clear and he will be obliged either to withdraw from some aspect of his work or resign his position. I have no criticism of any economist who is not willing to put himself into such an inconsistent position, or who, being in it, prefers to retire. That is clearly the most comfortable choice and the most unequivocal position. But unless economists are willing to carry on in the Council under the conditions I have outlined, I doubt if we shall be able to achieve through the Council the various goals we would like to see achieved. Perhaps we should look on Council members as expendable, each carrying forward the work as far as he individually can and then retiring in favor of others who can carry it farther before they, too, drop by the wayside. I suggest that even the institution of the Council itself is expendable and that sooner or later it will be cut down politically to be replaced by some other organization carrying forward the same functions in somewhat different ways. [17]

In general, although many economists disagree and their numbers are growing, the economist has cast himself in the role of a ship's navigator, aiding those in office by advising on how to reach a given goal and avoiding active participation in choosing that goal. The economist has feared that his own value judgments and preconceptions would intrude upon his professional duty as an unbiased adviser.

A closely related question is to what degree should the Council restrict itself to broad economic advice? Should the economist give

[17]Roy Blough, "Political and Administrative Requisites for Achieving Economic Stability," *The American Economic Review*, Vol. XL, No. 2 (May, 1950), pp. 177, 178.

advice which obviously conflicts with political reality? Or should
he temper his recommendations in the forge of practicality? Should
he present various policy choices and let the President or the Congress (by means of the Joint Economic Committee) decide what is
practical? Clearly, what a President needs most from the Council
is professional economic advice, not political counsel. But an economist who gives impracticable advice would certainly not succeed as
an adviser. Thus, the economist who wants his counsel to prevail
must be *a political economist*. As the Council was without prece-
dence, particularly in its early years, those who served were forced
to formulate their own procedure for meeting these philosophical
problems in such a way that they satisfied their personal code of
ethics.[18]

Keyserling, the Expansionist Philosophy

The departure of Nourse completed the first phase of the active
operation of the Council. The original team had worked together
with reasonable harmony and had performed extremely useful service
for three eventful years which, in view of the newness of the tasks,
was remarkable. Nourse's resignation precipitated a mild crisis
in the affairs of the Council. The Nourse view of the proper conduct
of the Council had substantial support in the Congress and among
economists, especially those in academic life. At the annual meeting
of the American Economic Association in December 1949, a session
was devoted to an analysis of the administration of the Act. The
general tone of papers presented was critical of the Council for being
too politically oriented. Professor Paul Strayer in a paper entitled
"The Council of Economic Advisors: Political Economy on Trial,"
said:

> The Act itself can be considered a step in the right direc-
> tion. However, the decision to give the Council of Economic
> Advisers three members rather than one made certain that it
> would be divided on many issues to the detriment of its influ-
> ence. The actual differences among the members of the Coun-
> cil have been well known and have undoubtedly hurt it within
> the executive branch and in the public eye. However, the de-

[18]Seymour Harris, "The Gap Between Economists and Politicians,"
New York Times Magazine, April 14, 1965.

cision to place the Council in the President's office was a wise one. Only as the Council can use the authority of the President can it hope to get either the notice it requires or can the development of balanced plans and programs be hoped for. The Council has made some progress in this direction but much more is required.

Much has been made of the issue whether Council members should appear before Congressional committees in support of the President's program. On this issue there has been misunderstanding on both sides and the relations between the Council and Congress have suffered accordingly. The development, in the first days of the Act, of the practice of the Joint Committee on the Economic Report publishing two reports representing majority and minority views did much to discourage co-operation and gave support to the feeling that little would be gained and much lost by Council members' appearance before even this Committee. On the other hand, the inclusion of all types of economic programs in the President's Economic Report invited such reaction on the part of the Joint Committee. The recent hearings conducted by the Sub-committee on Monetary, Credit, and Fiscal Policies of the Joint Committee on the Economic Report have raised the level of the debate in this Committee and give hope for the future. Certainly the continued gulf between the Council and Joint Committee cannot continue if positive action is to be taken.[19]

Also, Nourse's departure intensified an organizational question raised by the Hoover Commission in 1949 when it recommended that the Council be replaced by an office of Economic Adviser, with a single head.[20] This problem was to arise later, as we shall see. However, the immediate problem was to find a new chairman.

Some controversy exists about Keyserling's candidacy to succeed Nourse as chairman. As vice-chairman Keyserling would be

[19]*American Economic Review,* Vol. XL, No. 2 (May, 1950).

[20]Commission on organization of the Executive Branch of Government (Hoover Commission) General Management of the Executive Branch (1949, p. 17).

a natural candidate for the chairmanship. Although Truman reportedly assured Keyserling that he would be appointed, six months elapsed before this was done. Keyserling was apparently sensitive to the fact that he did not have the Ph.D. in economics; like many government economists, although he had done graduate work in economics at Columbia and had had many years of practical experience in Washington agencies, he did not possess the badge of the academic economist.[21]

Nourse notes that a list of thirteen prominent economists had been compiled by Dr. John Steelman, to which he (Nourse) added "three or four" as possible candidates. None of these to whom the post was offered accepted; some declining "pretty brusquely" according to Nourse.[22]

At any rate, Keyserling took over formally as chairman on May 10, 1950, and Professor Ray Blough of the University of Chicago assumed duties as the third member. Thus began an active period. Keyserling, who had been a disciple of Rexford Tugwell in his student days and an expansionist during his early years in the New Deal, at forty-two was twenty-one years younger than Nourse and a dedicated New Dealer deeply involved in social problems.[23]

The new Chairman immediately became active on many fronts. Keyserling had numerous Washington contacts, and he did not hesitate to use them. Flash says of this period:

There is no doubt that Keyserling was the energizing force behind the Council's operations. Staff members of the period who have been interviewed agree that Keyserling ruled with a strong hand, that he drove his staff and could be demanding and impatient, but through delegation could also give them a sense of participation. In his leadership, Keyserling did not adhere to any formal patterns of giving assignments or holding staff meetings but passed out work as it came along, sometimes in a continuing manner and sometimes on a crash emergency basis. Sometimes assignments would be direct;

[21]See Flash, *op. cit.*, p. 27.

[22]Nourse, *Economics in the Public Service, op. cit.*, p. 286.

[23]His post council has made this clear. After leaving the council in 1952, Keyserling became a practicing lawyer and consulting economist in Washington, and was later founder and Chairman of the Conference on Economic Progress.

at other times they would be made through Colm. Consequently, most of the infrequent staff meetings centered on particular projects and involved only those who were working on them.

Under such circumstances, there was an interpenetration between objective economic analysis and policy questions. In applying technical competence, both Keyserling and his staff expected that the staff as well as the Council would think, research, write, and otherwise operate in terms of policy considerations. True, staff members would not take ultimate responsibility for policy recommendations, but they were expected to think in these terms. [24]

Under Keyserling's aggressive leadership, the Council took part in the argument over direct controls after the onset of the Korean War, and much of 1950 and 1951 was spent on these issues. The Council was active, along with the Office of Defense Management, in preparation for the Korean War and in the struggle toward stabilization of the economy under wartime conditions. All of this activity was in addition to the regular work of the Council.[25]

Perhaps the most significant activity aside from the regular Council work was its part in the famous accord between the Treasury and the Federal Reserve Board. The financial burden of the Korean mobilization effort had reopened the long smouldering dispute between the Treasury and the Federal Reserve Board. At issue was essentially whether the Federal Reserve Board would continue to support the government bond market, at the expense of what it viewed as its freedom to pursue an active monetary policy. The Treasury, supported by Truman and the Council, took the view that the Board should support the bond market.[26] In mid-1950 the Board withdrew support from certain Treasury issues which brought

[24] Flash, *op. cit.*, pp. 32-33.

[25] Nourse told the Author, "perhaps Keyserling pushed too hard, perhaps I did not push hard enough." Personal interview, July 28, 1967.

[26] This issue is thoroughly discussed in the monumental study by the Joint Committee (then the Joint Committee on the Economic Report), *Monetary Policy and the Management of the Public Debt.* (Washington, U.S. Government Printing Office, 1952).

about an open conflict between the two. Truman was strongly supported by his Secretary of the Treasury (Snyder) and on the Council
by Keyserling and Clark.

This issue of inflation control versus expansionist economics was
made to order for Keyserling. When, in late December 1950, the
Federal Reserve Board announced that reserve requirements would
be increased in January and February, the conflict between Treasury and the Board became a major issue. Treasury bills had increased from 1.09 percent in January to 1.38 percent by the end of
the year (1950). Yield on nine to twelve month issues averaged
1.44 percent in the fourth quarter of 1950, as compared to 1.09
percent for the corresponding quarter of 1949, and open market
rates had likewise increased.[27]

At this point, the President met with the Open Market Committee
and subsequently issued a press release indicating that the issue
had been resolved to his satisfaction.

> I was given assurance at this meeting that the Federal Re-
> serve Board would support the Treasury's plans for the fi-
> nancing of the action in Korea. This assurance was given en-
> tirely voluntarily. At no time during the conference did I at-
> tempt to dictate to the Board or tell them what specific steps
> they ought to take. I explained to them the problems that faced
> me as Chief Executive, and when they left I firmly believed
> that I had their agreement to cooperate in our financing pro-
> gram. I was taken by surprise when subsequently they failed
> to support the program.[28]

Unfortunately, the Board took a different view and the veteran member, Marriner Eccles, released to the press his view of the meeting
which conflicted sharply with Mr. Truman's; Eccles maintained that
no such commitment had been made.[29]

Although FRB Chairman Thomas B. McCabe wrote Mr. Truman
a letter straightforward but conciliatory in tone, the Council was
concerned about the issue, having mentioned some months before

[27] *Economic Report of the President*, January, 1951, p. 142.

[28] Truman, *Memoirs*, *op. cit.*, p. 62. See also Eccles, *Beckoning
Frontiers*, *op. cit.*, Ch. 6.

[29] *New York Times*, February 3, 1951, p. 2.

the need for eliminating uncertainty saying "the consequences of leaving the issues in suspense will be most dangerous."[30] It is an interesting exercise in bureaucratic byplay that Blough, as a newcomer to the council who had not associated himself with the Keyserling-Clark position, played an unofficial role in the settlement. Although Blough had served in Treasury, he was also more acceptable than either Keyserling or Clark who were on record as critical of the Board. Thus although the Council had no direct role in the accord, it was able to play a minor role through force of personality. Flash notes that Keyserling was upset by the exclusion of the Council since he regarded it as a matter of economic policy upon which he should have been consulted.[31] This incident is interesting in that it is typical of the general Keyserling approach, namely, that there were few if any economic policy incidents from which CEA should be excluded.

Keyserling's activist orientation was again evident in the mobilization decisions as the Korean War progressed. He viewed with alarm the partial mobilization efforts and, always, the interventionist, attempted to break into the policy-making process via the Office of Defense Mobilization. He also tried to have the Council designated as economic adviser to the Office of Defense Management, as it had to the National Security Resources Board before the Chinese intervention in Korea.[32] Also, he attended ODM staff meetings as Council representative and in other ways tried to project the CEA into the situation. Keyserling took the view (not without merit) that the mobilization effort would have an influence toward inflation when superimposed on an economy already operating at full capacity. In the *Report* for January 1951 and in a special report to the President, Keyserling warned of inflationary pressure. However, as the military situation in Korea reached a stalemate and as domestic measures took hold, the price pressure relaxed. It thus became administration policy to stretch out the mobilization program.

---

[30] *Monetary Policy and the Management of the Public Debt,* U. S. Congress, Joint Committee on the Economic Report, 82nd Cong., 2nd Sess., Doc. No. 123, Part 2, p. 816.

[31] Flash, *op. cit.*, p. 49.

[32] Hearings on the Independent Offices Appropriations Bill for Fiscal Year 1952, 82nd Congress, 1st Sess., pp. 90-91, U. S. Congress, Senate Committee on Appropriations.

To Keyserling the expansionist this decision was anathema since he felt that to reduce the anti-inflation pressure would reduce the drive for expansion, i.e., that fear of inflation would become a rationale for not expanding. The President had multiple noneconomic factors to consider and many advisers to listen to; and a combination of calculated military risks, budgetary and debt considerations made it inevitable that the Council would lose influence. As they acquired economic staff resources, ODM, OPS, and the Economic Stabilization Agency became less dependent on the Council; ODM took over the area of mobilization policy which Keyserling had coveted. As Flash notes, this was the President's intention, "In mobilization matters, it had relative to the Council pre-empted the economic advisory function."

Throughout his tenure, Keyserling had espoused the doctrine of expansionist economics, but at this time his stock in trade was not very salable. The theme runs through his entire performance, and Truman applauded this orientation as a basis for his "Fair Deal," but was unable to follow beyond a point.[33] Flash quotes David Bell on the issue:

> The President let Nourse go and promoted Keyserling because Keyserling fitted better the economic tone the President wanted for his Administration. A 5 percent annual increase in GNP would not have been a natural way for Mr. Truman to have described his objective, but what Keyserling was driving at appealed to his understanding, convictions, and hopes for the nation.[34]

Thus, when other factors became more important, the Keyserling theme had to be played in a minor key.

The Keyserling Council and staff by and large agreed with his policies, and the emphasis on expansion was a major factor in extending the Council's influence into other agencies and facets of governmental policy. However, it seems clear that the rise (and

---

[33]Nourse says, "The president continued to make protestations as to the value of the Agency. But it seemed to me that he valued it only as a dignified 'front' for his policies. As soon as we ventured to challenge any of them, he retreated behind his presidential prerogative and 'put us in our place.'" Nourse, *op. cit.*, p. 370, (footnote 4).

[34]Flash, *op. cit.*, p. 96.

subsequent fall) in the Council's fortunes was in large part an accident of timing. The theme of expansionist economics as played by the Keyserling trio was short-lived. Truman was essentially a fiscal conservative and, as an adjunct to the "Fair Deal," he accepted the CEA view of expansionist economics but was in the long run unwilling to give it free rein, especially in the face of other complex domestic and international problems.

Keyserling was an aggressive chairman who headed an agency not yet five years old. Various accounts make it clear that his personality did not make him universally liked. He did not hesitate to articulate his views (One source says that "Keyserling was apt to mount his verbal bicycle and peddle furiously!") or to push the Council into areas of influence.

Not surprisingly, because of his apparent inclination toward expansion, and his undoubted attachment to the "Fair Deal" ideology, he became a figure of controversy and so, of course, did the Council. Several powerful and conservative members of Congress had never accepted the Council, and they were no doubt happy to find a rallying point against it. Few doubted Keyserling's ability as an economist nor his skill as an advocate. However, his detractors felt that he was expanding the Council into political areas, beyond its intended scope.

As the Truman administration neared its end, the Council even more than the rest of a dying administration shared in its loss of influence.

It is instructive to compare the Nourse-Keyserling philosophies. Nourse rejected the view that the council should play an active part in advocating the Truman program. To what degree this reluctance was based on adherence to a view of his role as advisor, or on his general lack of strong interest in the ultimate aims of the "Fair Deal" is impossible to say. On the other hand Keyserling found a program which he could endorse wholeheartedly, and he very likely viewed the chairmanship as a vehicle for promoting his views. Perhaps he would have been equally or more at home as a presidential assistant or as a U. S. Senator. Nourse in contrast was a professional economist and career scholar, who did not view himself as a part of the administration, taking part in or promoting policy. Perhaps it was inevitable that the Council would become involved in broad policies, and Keyserling's fault may have been that he went too far too fast, given the climate of the times. To what degree the attempt to reduce the CEA budget resulted from factors far beyond Keyserling (and given its source, such a prospect is likely) is a matter of dispute; however, Keyserling must bear some blame.[35]

The Truman period can be viewed with great interest. The six-year period represents the pioneer years of the Council and the formative period of formal economic advice on the presidential level.

Mr. Truman was never willing to use the Council beyond a limited degree. Nourse complained frequently that the President did not take sufficient notice of its advice or spend enough time on Council affairs. Keyserling, although he was deeply involved in many issues, was often upstaged by others, particularly after the Korean War became a major issue. It seems obvious that Truman was never really sold on the merits of the Keyserling expansionist economics, remaining a traditionalist in economic matters. In the end, Keyserling disturbed the uneasy peace between the Council and the conservative element of the Congress by his insistence upon the expansionist theme.

After two decades of observation, it seems likely that both Nourse and Keyserling were in a sense, victims of excessive rigidity. Each took extreme viewpoints, and neither would make basic alterations in his mode of operation. It must, of course, be kept in mind that no precedent existed. The incoming Republican Chairman, Arthur F. Burns, was able to chart a course somewhat between their positions and emerge successfully.

A major element in successful advisorship is clearly rapport between the adviser and advisee. All evidence suggests that Nourse was never able to achieve an easy relationship with Truman.[36] It is likely that Nourse was at a disadvantage because of his age and the fact that he already had a firm reputation built on a long career

[35]Many of those interviewed by the author pointed out that both factors were at work, and that a residue of distrust of such agencies was present. Yet as one observer noted, the Democrats were in control of Congress and the Republicans who instigated the move were obviously able to obtain Democratic support for their views. Consequently, a sizable share of the blame is attributed to Keyserling.

[36]Personal factors were no doubt of major importance. For example, many close observers have commented on the fact that Kennedy and Heller were able to achieve a close personal relationship, having many characteristics in common. Neither Keyserling nor Nourse could fit closely into the group of Truman cronies of those years!

when he came to the Council, and most importantly because he began a new and demanding line of work, the outlines of which were ill-defined. Nourse also suffered from the fact that not only Keyserling, but also Clark were often in basic disagreement about procedure. Yet Nourse, in establishing procedures and techniques, made a major and long-lasting contribution.

Despite all the problems, one is reminded of the talking horse; it is not so much what he says, but the fact that he can talk at all which is remarkable. The Truman-Nourse-Keyserling Council worked and for the most part worked well. The precedent for economic advice was established and survived a very eventful six years. Let us pause briefly and recall what had taken place. By the end of the Truman years the Council had become an operating body. Nourse, the first chairman, had taken a view detached from the political goals of the administration. Keyserling, his successor, had operated the Council in an aggressive fashion. A combination of Keyserling's personality, the Korean War, distrust of the Council among conservatives, and other factors had brought the Council into controversy. These events took place as the Democratic era of two decades came to a close, and an apparently conservative Republican administration came into office. Thus, the future of the Council was in grave doubt.

The Eisenhower Council, Changing the Guard

With the advent in 1952 of the first republican President since Hoover, the question of the future of the Council became acute when the Eisenhower Administration took office. As we have seen, the Council had lost considerable prestige in the eyes of Congress in the last days of the Truman Administration. Some observers have indicated that it was congressional antipathy to the Keyserling view which led to the crisis which we will now consider.[37]

In some Congressional quarters opinion of the value of the Council had been lukewarm at best. More conservative elements especially in the House had been mildly critical from the first, and the professional economizers looked upon the Council as an organization of limited usefulness compared to its cost, even though the cost was modest. (In the Nourse years the Council Budget was $350-400

[37]For example, a letter to the author from Neil H. Jacoby, January 19, 1966.

thousand.) In the latter days of any outgoing administration the Congress is apt to attempt to eliminate or reduce the scope of any programs of which it disapproves. In this instance, the Council was included among various agencies in a move to reduce expenditures. Fortunately, this attitude was not universal, and by legislative strategy those senators who were favorable towards the Council managed to overcome a move to reduce its operating budget by twenty-five percent. This was done by applying the full sum to three quarters of the year, thus enabling the Council to operate at full capacity for that long, but creating a serious problem for the incoming administration.[38]

Burns, Industive Economics

The status of the Council was unclear when the new administration opened for business. At best the Eisenhower Administration was not expected to be sympathetic to the idea of the Council, and the economy-minded Chairman of the House Appropriations Committee, John Tabor of New York, refused a request for $75,000 to provide funds to the end of the fiscal year.

Amidst this confusion, Dr. Arthur F. Burns arrived to serve as Chairman of the Council. It was Tabor's idea, also shared by others, that the Council should be replaced by a single economic adviser with a small staff, and he stood ready to approve an appropriation of $50,000 for the operation of such an office. Tabor was apparently under the impression that the President was in favor of such a move. However, at this point, Eisenhower and his assistant Sherman Adams made an appeal to the Chairman of the Senate Appropriations Committee, Styles Bridges, to provide funds to carry the Council through the fourth quarter. The President told Bridges that he intended to rebuild the Council and improve its status. Following this, the Senate voted $60,000, which was reduced to $50,000 in conference and given not to the Council but to the President for an adviser, in line with the Tabor idea.

[38] The move to reduce the budget of the Council was made by Representative Rees of Kansas. It was opposed by a group of Senators who devised the method of dealing with it: Maybank, S. C.; Ellender, La.; O'Mahoney, Wyo.; Saltonstall, Mass.; and Taft, Ohio. Both Saltonstall and Taft were Republicans; all others were Democrats.

Meanwhile, the President announced Burns' appointment and noted that the "Fair Deal slate would be wiped clean. " In his book, *First Hand Report,* Sherman Adams has written a revealing account of Burns' arrival at the White House and the circumstances surrounding the Council as the new administration began.

The unpalatable theories of Leon Keyserling were too fresh in their recollection to stimulate any enthusiasm for restaffing the agency. Indeed, some of them would have been happy to have the Council abolished altogether. Having the President's office budget in mind, I was inclined at first toward cutting the Council down to one man, whereupon I listened to a stern lecture from Gabriel Hauge on the reasons [for continuing the C. E. A. and recommending Burns]. . . .

When I took my first look at Burns, on the day he came to my office before I was to take him in to meet the President, I had a sinking sensation. If somebody had asked me to describe the mental image I had of the type of New Deal official we were in the process of moving out of Washington, this was it—a glassy stare through thick lenses, peering out from under a canopy of unruly hair parted in the middle, a large pipe with a curved stem: the very incarnation of all the externals that were such anathema to Republican businessmen and politicians. I wondered if we would both be thrown out of Eisenhower's office. But I swallowed hard and invited the professor to follow me in.

If Eisenhower had any misgivings, he kept them to himself. To me, Arthur Burns turned out to be a pleasant surprise. He and Eisenhower got along fine. They shared the same outlook and philosophy. Far from being the abstract and impractical professor, Burns had his feet planted solidly on the ground and had no difficulty in more than holding his own in arguments at the Cabinet table with such hard-headed protagonists as Humphrey and Dodge. As soon as the 1954 downturn began to appear, Eisenhower set aside ample time at Cabinet meetings so that Burns could discuss the economics of the situation. These periods lasted often as long as thirty minutes and Eisenhower listened to him with fascination. The President was particularly impressed by the importance that Burns placed on the time factor in his analyses of business

conditions. Going back, as he often did, to his Army experiences, in one such exchange on the role of time in the economy, Eisenhower remarked that a commanding officer in combat could recover lost men and lost weapons, or a strategic
position on high ground, but he could never recover lost time.
One morning, after Burns finished a detailed outline of contributions that various government departments could make
toward strengthening the economy. Eisenhower said to him
admiringly, "Arthur, my boy, you would have made a fine
chief of staff overseas during the war." [39]

Personnel and Organization

Despite the fact that he had been confirmed as a member of a
group which did not then exist, Burns began to assemble a staff and
to formulate policies. Since many of the Council staff members had
departed in the previous uncertain period, Burns was forced to re-
build the staff under a handicap, but fortunately a cadre to professional staff was available. [40] Unfortunately, the period of confusion
during which the matter of the future status of the Council was being
decided did not facilitate Burns' search for adequate personnel. Furthermore, there was some feeling among economists that the general atmosphere of the Republican administration would not be amenable to economic analysis. Burns was anxious to assemble a core
of highly-qualified economists who shared the general views of the
new administration.

Burns was forty-nine at the time of his appointment, had been
Professor of Economics at Columbia University and long associated
with the National Bureau of Economic Research as a student of Wesley C. Mitchell. He had received the Ph. D. from Columbia in 1934.
Neil Jacoby, then forty-four, came to the Council from the University of California at Los Angeles. He had obtained his Ph. D. from
Chicago in 1938. The senior member, Walter W. Stewart, who was
sixty-eight, had been an advisor to Hoover with long government

[39] Sherman Adams, *First Hand Report* (New York: Harper and Row,
1961), pp. 155-156.

[40] Old Washington hands are adept at dealing with situations where an
agency disappears or is subjected to a drastic cut in appropriations. Thus,
they may fade from view having landed in old line agencies where they have
contacts, but reappear when the fortunes of the agency take a new turn.

service, and was an authority on gold and foreign exchange. He had taught at the Universities of Missouri, Michigan, and Amherst College, and had been an investment banker. For some years prior to his appointment, he had been at the Center for Advanced Study. In the area of high-level advice, Stewart was by far the most experienced Council member.

Five more members served on the Council before the end of the Eisenhower administration. A word about these members may be helpful here. Joseph S. Davis joined the Council in May 1955, serving until late 1958. Davis, who was sixty when appointed had served in many capacities since obtaining his Ph. D. from Harvard in 1913 and was essentially an agricultural economist and expert on food supply.

Raymond J. Sauliner, who became Chairman in 1956, had been appointed a member in 1951, having first served on the staff, and was the only person to rise from staff to chairman. He served as Chairman until the end of the administration. Sauliner was an expert in the mortgage and finance area, had been in the Treasury, and earlier was a professor of economics at Barnard College, to which he returned when his service ended.

Paul McCracken, who served from late 1956 to early 1959, had received his Ph. D. from Harvard in 1948. McCracken had been a professor at the University of Michigan, and returned there after his council tour ended.

Karl Brandt, fifty nine, was like Davis an agricultural specialist and had spent many years at Stanford after obtaining his Ph. D. from the University of Berlin in 1926.

Henry C. Wallich of Yale served from May 1959 until the end of the Eisenhower administration. Born in 1914, he received his Ph. D. in 1944 from Harvard and had done much work in monetary policy, finance, and international economics.

On the staff level, the first to be hired was Asher Achinstein from the Library of Congress. He was soon joined by Melvin G. de Chazeau from Cornell University and Louis Shere of Indiana University. By October, the ranks had been increased by the addition of Clarence Long, on leave from Johns Hopkins University, and William H. Nicholls, on leave from Vanderbilt University. Albert Koch was borrowed from the Federal Reserve System to work on monetary policy and Collis Stocking from the Office of Defense Management also joined the Council at this time. The staff was completed by the addition of Robinson Newcomb, a holdover from the Nourse-Keyserling era, Robert Triffin of Yale, on a part-time basis (international money matters), Albert Riefman, borrowed from the State Department, Irving H. Siegel, on leave from the Twentieth Century Fund, and Charles Schultze from the University of Maryland. These newcomers were supplemented by the holdovers, Fisher, David Lusher, and Miss James, who were charter staff members, from the original council.

Burns' operating philosophy was noticeably different from Keyserling's. He indicated a desire to play a role more in the Nourse tradition. The issue of his relationship to the Congress arose at the time of his confirmation, when he told Senator Sparkman, "My own personal inclination would be to stay out of the limelight, make my recommendation to the President, indicate to him what the basis of the recommendation is, . . . and then having done that, to remain eternally quiet."[41] Although Burns did not take so extreme a position as Nourse, he apparently agreed that his usefulness would be diminished if he responded to all questions from a political group. In Burns' view, there were several areas in which he could cooperate without impairing his advisory relationship to the President. He recognized that Council members were more than advisers; they were also "administrators" of the Employment Act. Thus, it would be proper for Council members to advise Congress in this regard. A second area in which Burns was willing to testify was with reference to a technical matter, such as derivation of data. Thirdly, he was fully willing, of course, to testify on matters relating to the Council per se, such as defending its budget requests.[42] On the fourth issue, (testimony dealing with economic conditions and policy), Burns notes two major dangers in testifying:

First, in some cases the President had to adopt policies that he didn't like and that I didn't like. He had to do it for reasons of overall political policy, but his heart was bleeding

[41]U. S. Congress, Senate Committee on Banking and Currency. *Hearings on the Confirmation of Arthur F. Burns as Chairman of the Council of Economic Advisers*, 83rd Congress. 1st Session quoted in Corine Silverman, *The President's Economic Advisors*, Inter-university case program, #48, University of Alabama Press, 1959, p. 16.

[42]Nourse agrees with these points saying, "I only wish I had been smart enough to differentiate these cases as explicitly as Burns has done from the fourth issue, the one on which I took my stand." . . . (See Silverman, *op. cit.*, p. 16.)

over it. What should I do before a committee of Congress
in such a case? Should I criticize the President when I happen to know that he shares my views? Would that be fair?
On the other hand, how could I say to a congressional committee that something is sound when I believed otherwise?

The other major danger in testifying is that once an adviser takes a strong position in public, he is apt to become a
prisoner of that position. I wanted to give the President the
fullest benefit of my knowledge and thought. Hence I wanted
to be free to advise the President one way one day, and yet
be able if necessary to go in the next day and say, "I've been
thinking it over. What I told you yesterday was wrong. I
overlooked some important points. What really ought to be
done is thus and so."[43]

Despite these pitfalls, as time passed Burns frequently gave
testimony on semipolicy matters, although he often requested permission to testify in executive session. As Miss Silverman notes,
in both Republican and Democratic congresses, Burns was able to
make this precedent effective:

Burns established his policy. He would express his pref-
erence to the congressional committee's dealing with economic issues. If the committee in question accepted his pref-
erence, that was all to the good. However, if the committee
insisted on different terms, Burns would accept those terms.[44]

Miss Silverman quotes Burns on the issue subsequent to his return
to private life.

Keyserling took an extreme position and in the process
ignored a vital distinction. Cabinet officers are directly responsible to Congress. Their responsibilities are largely
defined by Congress. But the Council is not an administrative
agency. It is advisory only—advisory to the President by law,
and advisory to the Presidency by practice.

Nourse also took a rigid position. To the extent that the
Council had duties defined by law it is responsible to Congress

[43]Silverman, *op. cit.*, p. 17.
[44]*Ibid.*, p. 17.

and must answer to it—that is why I placed no conditions on
my testifying on proposed changes of the Employment Act or
on the statistical gathering functions of the government or on
the defense of the Council's budget.

But I want to add this: if there had only been the type of
Council that Keyserling envisaged, I never would have accepted
the appointment. I would have taken it for granted that the
Council Chairman must, as a practical matter, support the
President's views at public hearings, and I would not place
myself in that position. But because there had been a Nourse
I could conceive of there being a practical alternative and
could try to find it. So Nourse did more than make my job
easier by taking the position he did; because there had been a
Nourse my job was possible.[45]

As a result of the congressional reappraisal of the council at the
beginning of the new administration and subsequent consultation with
the Bureau of the Budget, a change was made in the organization of
the Council. Re-organization Plan #9 read as follows:

The functions invested in the Council of Economic Advisers
by section 4(b) of the Employment Act of 1946 (60 Stat. 24),
and so much of the functions vested in the Council by section
4(c) of that Act as consists of reporting to the President with
respect to any function of the Council under said section 4(c),
are hereby transferred to the Chairman of the Council of Economic Advisers, provided for in the last sentence of section
4(a) of the said Act, is hereby abolished.[46]

The essence of this plan was that the chairman was designated
the operating head of the Council, to be responsible for reporting to
the President as well as for making staff appointments. Thus, the
stress which had resulted from having three members with equal
power, with no real executive power vested in the chairman, hopefully might be eased. It is difficult to say to what extent this reorganization plan was responsible for the Burns mode of operation
and to what extent his own personal preferences were influential.

[45] *Ibid.*, p. 18.
[46] *Plan to Reorganize the Executive Branch* (Hoover Commission Report),
1949.

Several observers have commented on the fact that Burns was inclined to "play the game close to his chest," and to take little account of staff views. Although Burns was able to gain frequent access to the President and was successful in introducing him to the rudiments of economics, there is some doubt as to his real influence on policy issues *vis-a-vis* Secretary Humphrey. There can be little doubt that Humphrey was the strong man of the cabinet, at least in domestic affairs. One close observer told the author, "While Burns was successful in the game of words and phrases, Humphrey played the power game." However, another participant pointed out that any secretary of the Treasury is in a very powerful position. However, Secretary Humphrey was especially powerful, and the fact that Burns won a number of issues speaks very well of his position in the administration. Under Burns' leadership the young Council was holding its own in company with the strongest cabinet post in the government, despite the fact that Humphrey had accepted the job on Eisenhower's assurance that, when the talk was about money, he would be consulted.

Inside the Council Burns generally operated a tighter ship than had Keyserling and took more hand in actually supervising work which came to him for final analysis, personally pulling it into final form. On the other hand, Burns had been determined to re-establish the reputation of the Council and he managed to reach his goal despite the generally conservative "hard-headed" atmosphere of the administration. In contrast to both Keyserling before him and Heller after him, Burns had strong ideas about staff function: "I believe that the staff functioned primarily to advise me; it was not supposed to go about selling programs."[47] Consequently, staff members did not become involved in policy matters but were given assignments which were essentially requests for data or information, often stripped as far as possible of policy overtones.

Burns, however, did create an innovation in the operation of the Council which gave him good channels to other areas of the Federal establishment. He suggested to the President that Eisenhower establish the Advisory Board on Economic Growth and Stability (ABEGS). This group under Burns' chairmanship, with representatives from Treasury, Agriculture, Commerce, Labor, Federal Reserve, and the Bureau of the Budget as well as the White House, proved to be a valuable organization.

[47]Quoted in Flash, *op. cit.*, p. 165.

Burns was new in Washington as was Jacoby, and while Stewart had a vast fund of experience on the Federal level most of it was years in the past. Outside contacts made at first through ABEGS and then in other ways involved the staff in some degree of policy operations. Typical was David Lusher's "Tuesday group," an informal gathering of professional economists on the operating levels of the Budget Bureau, Treasury, Commerce, Labor, and the Federal Reserve. Further, Burns used his former National Bureau connections to sponsor a conference on antirecession policy at Princeton University which published a series of papers. Thus, the Council utilized its various channels of information in much the same manner as had previous councils, regardless of the somewhat centralized nature of its internal operations.

Although Burns was the only member who spoke in public for the Council and testified before Congress, he was careful not to endanger his advisory relationship with the President, and he managed to operate in close harmony with the President's personal economic adviser, Gabriel Hauge. Hauge occupied a unique position *vis-a-vis* the Council as we saw in an earlier chapter, for in the Truman years, no professional economist (but many advisers) had been on the White House staff. Likewise in the Kennedy years as we shall see, Heller was anxious that no one in the White House have the role of economic adviser. Hauge with a Ph.D. from Harvard (1947) had combined a career in teaching, research, and government service. He left a position as assistant to the Chairman of the McGraw-Hill Publishing Company to join the White House staff in 1952, leaving in 1960 to join the Manufacturers, Hanover Trust Co., where he later became President. Hauge's attendance at the President's Monday morning briefing conferences served to increase his grasp of economic affairs. Although this seems at first to be an overlap with Burns' functions several factors must be kept in mind.

First, Hauge constituted a link with the White House, although clearly he could have been a barrier if other circumstances or personalities had prevailed. Second, and perhaps of overriding importance, Hauge was able to field a wide range of economic problems which landed on the President's desk, matters regarding farm policy, import quotas, and tariffs which demanded top-level attention. Hauge could usually extinguish these "brush fires" without involving the time of the Council.

In addition to ABEGS and other conduits of information, Burns made use of task forces to examine specific problem areas. Although as Burns became better oriented in Washington, ABEGS suffered some eclipse, he has retained his view of its usefulness and has recommended that the idea be formalized in an economic policy board to relate to economic matters in much the same way that the National Security Council relates to matters of defense.

While Burns was working out his mode of operation and rebuilding the Council, he was also occupied with the economic problems which began to beset the administration. By April 1953, a noticeable weakening was taking place in four of the National Bureau's eight leading economic indicator series. Other economists had warned of a decline shortly after the first of the year. Despite this the administration, committed to a reversal of the "spending policies of the Democratic party," had begun to follow a restrictive budget policy in its planning for fiscal 1954. Unfortunately, an economist's dilemma was that, in contrast to these indicators, G. N. P. was rising, unemployment was down to 2.7 percent, and industrial production was holding to the high level established in March. Further, the administration had taken steps to encourage economic activity and to inject a greater degree of free enterprise spirit into the business community. Eisenhower reduced the Truman budget of $72.9 billion (fiscal 1953) to $64.4 billion (fiscal 1954), urging agencies to make further reductions, in preparation for fiscal restraint in 1954 and 1955.

In May, the Open Market Committee began a policy designed to ease pressure on bank reserves;[48] in July, reserve requirements were reduced. Through this period Burns apparently played only a minor part. However by August warning signs had begun to multiply and the Council, now fully in operation, was aware of the implications. Burns requested Achinstein, Lusher, and Saulnier to prepare an analysis of possible anticyclical moves which might be made if matters continued to deteriorate. The item of major concern to Burns and his associates was the accumulation in business inventories, coupled with a decline in sales. ABEGS and other task force groups were asked to undertake studies of measures encouraging stabilization and economic growth to be pursued in the event of a slow-down in economic activity.[49] In late September, 1953, the *New*

---

[48] Care was taken not to attribute this action to a potential recession, but to point out increased tension in the financial markets.

[49] *Economic Report of the President*, January, 1954, p. 123.

York Times reported that the warnings of the Council had been reported to Secretary Humphrey, who expressed alarm and sought advice from Burns. Meanwhile Burns urged the staff to consider the effects of various measures upon which action might be taken within a short period.

Both because of the Eisenhower program and the desire to stimulate the economy, proposals were made for various programs, including tax reform and reduction, housing and welfare, and improvements in unemployment insurance. The Council was involved to a degree in all of these matters, although its contribution was largely indirect. Flash sums up:

> What these men did do was not to provide ideas but, as Burn's statement emphasizes, to produce the necessary encouragement and support for what others had proposed. In short, they served an essential catalytic function. With particular expertise available at both the presidential appointee and staff levels, the Council used the power of its acceptance in the Eisenhower Presidency and of its role as spokesman for economic conservatism to gain favor for a series of proposals, not of tremendous importance in the overall program, not of priority in terms of Republican objectives, but of importance to the particular department representing the interests of labor. In a current period of growing unemployment, the Council minimized the New Deal social welfare aura by stressing adequate unemployment insurance as "a valuable first line of defense against economic recession [helping] . . . to curb economic decline during an interval of time that allows other stabilizing measures to become effective." That these particular proposals would probably not become effective in time to help the immediate situation did not negate their long-term value.[50]

However, these measures were merely preliminary to the main event in which the Burns Council participated, the recession of 1953-54.

[50]Flash, *op. cit.*, p. 117.

Recession in a Republican Administration: The Council in Action

A recession early in the first Republican administration since 1932 was a political disaster beyond contemplation. Immediate action was essential. Using sound strategy, the 1954 *Economic Report of the President* emphasized a positive tone of confidence and reassurance, as if no serious economic disturbance were probable. The performance of the economy had never been brighter, according to the *State of the Union Message* and the *Economic Report* of that year:

> The upsurge of production and employment, which has been sustained with but brief interruptions in the United States for about a dozen years, continued in 1953. New records were established in industrial activity, employment, and the disbursement of incomes. Unemployment reached the lowest level of any peace-time year in recent decades. The average level of prices was remarkably steady. The fruits of expanding production and enterprise were shared widely. Perhaps never before in their history have the American people come closer to realizing the ideal of high and expanding employment, without price inflation, than in 1953. But some sections of industry, notably farming, failed to participate in the widespread prosperity. The index of consumer prices inched a little higher in spite of some decline in food prices. And economic activity, taken as a whole, receded somewhat toward the close of the year.[51]

Despite the optimistic tones of the Economic Report, there was considerable feeling in various quarters that the situation, especially with regard to unemployment, was more serious than the report indicated.[52] Substantial soul-searching went on within the higher levels of the administration and Eisenhower himself was fully aware of taking a calculated risk in awaiting the turn of events.[53] During

[51]*Economic Report of the President,* January, 1954, p. 76.

[52]See, for example, the comments of Walter Reuther, *Hearings on the January,* 1954, *Economic Report of the President,* Joint Committee on the Economic Report, 83rd Congress, 2nd Session, pp. 722, 730.

[53]Robert J. Donovan, *Eisenhower: The Inside Story,* (New York: Harper & Row, 1956).

this period, the President and Burns were in frequent contact. Likewise, Burns maintained constant contact with ABEGS, departmental and cabinet officials and other concerned parties. There was much talk about the "arsenal of weapons" to be used in economic stabilization. The *Economic Report* mentioned such tools as debt management policies, agricultural support policies, tax policies, and public works.

While public works had wide appeal to the public, Burns was well aware of the weakness of public works as an anticyclical device. Although it is common to speak of a "shelf of public works," off which projects can be pulled, dusted off, and put into effect, the actual process is something quite different because the essence of the problem is timing. Professor Saulnier, who succeeded Burns as Chairman, has noted that, in any event, increased Federal spending is not likely to do much good unless there is at the same time, an atmosphere which is conducive to private spending:

> I think we may conclude . . . that if the atmosphere is not favorable to an expansion of private spending, an increase in Federal expenditures, even a large and rapidly accelerating increase, will not necessarily produce an appreciable and continuing rise in overall economic activity.[54]

As a result of his experience as chairman, Professor Saulnier has formulated an appropriate strategy of economic policy, given the various constraints which must be taken into account. First priority is given to a tax policy which will be such as to "carry the highest potentiality for stimulating increased private investment expenditures."[55]

(1) Allow for a direct reduction in corporate income tax rates in order to stimulate the flow of funds available for corporate expansion.

(2) A Program designed to promote high levels of business investment expenditures should also permit a reduction in the rates on upper and middle income brackets. This would

---

[54] Raymond J. Sauliner, *The Strategy of Economic Policy* (New York: Fordham University Press, 1963), p. 44.

[55] Saulnier, *Strategy of Economic Policy, op. cit.*, p. 62.

make investment funds more generally available and less costly.

"Quite apart from its beneficial impact on the large companies that provide the bulk of employment in our economy, a joint program of this type would give long-needed help to our country's numerous small and medium-sized business concerns, a substantial part of whose net earnings are absorbed every year in federal income taxes. Having served for four years as Chairman of President Eisenhower's Cabinet Committee on Small Business, let me say that in my judgment this is the most effective and genuinely constructive way open to us for assisting small business. We can supplement this by such measures as loans, assistance in obtaining procurement contracts, help in gaining access to research results, etc., but nothing can take the place of a reduction in the tax burden as a way to help small business. And it is vitally important that we give effective and constructive assistance to these concerns. The task we face in the remainder of this decade of providing jobs for a rapidly increasing number of young people."

(3) Various measures of tax reforms should accompany these adjustments in order to minimize revenue loss. However, care must be taken not to endanger investment incentives by such a process. Many opportunities exist to fund revenue losses resulting from tax reduction. These (e.g., reasonable user charges for Federal facilities) must be further explored.

(4) It would be futile to attempt to stimulate the economy via tax reduction and concurrently to impede progress with unduly restrictive monetary policy. Thus, there must be close coordination on these fronts.

(5) In order to use monetary policy aggressively, we must make progress in solving the imbalance of payments.

(6) Likewise, labor-management policies must be such as to improve the profit margins of industry and enable some reduction in prices to be made.

(7) Finally, Sauliner suggests that it might be appropriate to reactivate a group such as A BEGS to serve as a clearing house of information with particular reference to such matters as government credit programs.[56]

These reflections were far in the future when, during 1954, the Burns Council grappled with the recession problem.

Despite major shortcomings, public works were widely discussed by the Council and by others in the administration. The increased expenditures for highways and the Federal and Highway Act of 1954 were supported on these grounds. Further, two staff members, George A. Deming and John S. Bragdon, public works specialists, were added to the CEA staff. But no additional public works were undertaken to facilitate countercyclical policy despite apparently strong sentiment in the cabinet.

Tax Policy

The administration's proposals for tax reform had been under attack as being too favorable to upper income brackets and business interests, and the administration agreed that the long-run effects of the proposals would be to enhance the revenue position of the Treasury. However, congressional reaction was adverse and the administration was sensitive on this score. Burns suggested without success to the cabinet that depreciation allowances be liberalized (an action not requiring congressional approval). An immediate problem did have to be faced, however, in that the expiration of certain excise taxes and a reduction in corporate income taxes were scheduled to go into effect April 1. For tactical reasons, the Administration was forced to choose between two proposals, a ten percent cut in excise taxes or an increase in exemptions of personal income taxes. Secretary Humphrey was strongly opposed to the latter, and the former alternative was adopted. On economic grounds, the reduction in excise taxes was expected to increase consumer spending, bringing the multiplier effect into play. In sum, a loss of $1 billion was substituted for a gain of $3 billion. While the excise cut was predicated on the basis of avoiding an increase in the deficit (a prime Humphrey goal), it was accepted as a countercyclical move.

[56] *Ibid.*, p. 64.

Monetary Policy

In this area, which was not complicated by such crucial political aspects as those surrounding tax reform, action was taken more quickly. In July, the Federal Reserve Board reduced the reserve requirements for member banks, and continued the policy of open-market purchases which had been underway for some time. In the spring of 1954, the Board reduced the rediscount rate, then made a further reduction in late June, moving from 2 to 1-1/3 per cent over the period.

Burns and the officials of the Board were in close contact during this period since the Council was obviously interested in monetary policy as a means to recovery. The independence of the F. R. B. makes it difficult to evaluate the precise role of the Council in the general easing of credit, but it clearly deserves a degree of credit for the moves. Likewise, the Council made efforts to ease credit in the field of housing, expediting the work of the Veterans Administration and the Housing and Home Finance Agency.

These steps, combined with an acceleration of Federal expenditures, were generally successful in stalling off the impending recession, making Burns something of a hero in the administration. Unusual interest attached to the Burns Council since it served an administration not originally thought to be receptive to economic advice. Despite his triumph, Burns was never a match for Humphrey in over-all influence in the administration; however, Burns deserves great credit for establishing the Council on a firm basis.

In his Fairless Memorial Lectures in 1965, Burns, reflecting upon the limitations of various measures available for formulating economic policy, noted:

. . . fiscal policy does not encompass all of governmental action. Important though fiscal policy is, it must still be fitted in with other matters of large governmental concern—that is, policies involving gold, the labor market, corporate mergers, education, defense, foreign trade, and so on. These policies too have their influence on the state of confidence and prosperity. Indeed, the effectiveness of a particular fiscal policy will always depend on what other policies have been recently pursued or are currently being pursued. An expansionist fiscal policy, for example, may come to naught if

credit is simultaneously being restricted. Or to give a historical example, the proposal that President Roosevelt made
in early 1937 to enlarge the membership of the Supreme Court
would have caused little stir outside of legal and academic
circles had it been made by President Hoover in early 1929.
As it was, this proposal followed a mass of legislation that
deeply disturbed the business community, and it came at
a time when a wave of sit-down strikes posed a threat to property rights. In these circumstances, it was widely feared that
the Supreme Court proposal was a step toward abridgment of
constitutional safeguards of private property. I doubt if any
fiscal policy that was plausible at the time could have prevented
the collapse that occurred in business confidence and investment.

As these remarks suggest, it is unrealistic to expect the
"new economics" to protect government officials from making
mistakes in their efforts to manage prosperity. In fact, by
helping to bend governmental policy toward inflation, the new
fiscal theory will at times promote mistakes, just as the older
theory of balanced budgets did by bending governmental policy
at times toward deflation. To be sure, the new theory requires that the government should reduce spending or increase
taxes, if aggregate demand keeps growing faster than productive capacity once full employment has been achieved. In
actual life, however, inflationary pressures do not wait until
this point is reached. They usually emerge much earlier—
that is, when the presence of a gap between productive capacity and actual production still requires, according to the
theory, an expansionist fiscal policy. The theoretical system
of the "new economics" cannot deal with this early type of
inflation because it falls outside the system. Hence, the adherents of the theory are forced to resort to improvisation—
which may be guidelines for wages and prices today, and something else tomorrow. The steel price episode of April 1962
should suffice to remind us that here too is a source of possible misadventures.[57]

[57]Arthur F. Burns, *The Management of Prosperity*, **Fairless Memorial
Lecture, Carnegie Institute of Technology** (New York: Columbia University
Press, 1966), pp. 58-59.

There is widespread agreement that Burns played a successful and highly important role as tutor to the President. Flash considers this to be "perhaps Burns' greatest contribution."[58] But actually, Burns' most significant contribution was probably his success in reviving the Council and removing it from the area of partisanship into which it had fallen in the late Truman-Keyserling period. Further, he managed to accomplish this feat in an administration not initially sympathetic to the Council and its objectives. As will be apparent later, the Burns-Saulnier Councils, although serving a Republican President, did not differ markedly from their Democratic counterparts insofar as active policy is concerned. There is, however, a rather distinct difference between the Truman-Eisenhower years in which the Council was somewhat grudgingly accepted, and the Kennedy-Johnson era in which the Council was accepted wholeheartedly, and the economist gained greater prestige with the so called "new economics" becoming widely accepted.

[58]Flash, *op. cit.*, p. 122. It seems questionable as to how much of this economic education really "took" in view of Mr. Eisenhower's article in the *Saturday Evening Post*, early in 1963. In this article entitled "Spending Into Trouble" the former President did not demonstrate much understanding of aggregate economics as espoused by Burns.

5
THE NEW ECONOMICS IN ACTION
KENNEDY AND JOHNSON

In 1960 when John F. Kennedy assumed office after a Republican interlude of eight years, several unique factors were evident relative to economic policy and advice. The first president born in the twentieth century, Kennedy was elected by the smallest popular vote margin in history. An activist and an intellectual, Kennedy began to make full use of the Council's policy-making potential and appointed Dr. Walter Heller of the University of Minnesota as the Chairman. This appointment was announced at the same time as the most important cabinet appointment.

Heller, then forty-five years old, was a prototype of the "new breed" economist and, typical of many economists of his generation, he had served almost equally in academic life and in public service. There is ample evidence that Paul Samuelson, perhaps the outstanding young American economist of the postwar years, was Kennedy's first choice. Samuelson was reluctant to leave academic life and felt that he would prefer an informal relationship, and often served the President in that capacity. Although he points out that an informal advisor may have only modest influence, he and Heller were in general agreement on the issues. [1]

Whatever the background, Heller was appointed, and the choice proved to be a happy one. He had received his Ph.D. from the University of Wisconsin in 1941, had served in the Treasury Department and OPA during World War II, as well as in the U.S. military government in Germany, and had returned to the University of Minnesota as Professor of Economics where he was at the time of his appointment. The other two members of the original Council were Kermit Gordon then forty-four of Williams College and a scholar of high repute; and James Tobin of Yale. Tobin, forty-two, a specialist in econometrics and economic statistics, stood high among his professional colleagues, having been awarded the coveted John Bates Clark Medal, awarded infrequently to an economist under forty in recognition

---

[1] Letter from Professor Samuelson to the author, June 10, 1966.

of his distinguished contribution to the field.[2] Despite his self-characterization as "ivory tower," Tobin had also had considerable government service, serving in OPA and as a consultant to the Federal Reserve Board.

Both Gordon and Tobin left the Council in 1962, Gordon to become Director of the Budget and Tobin to return to academic life. Gordon was replaced by John P. Lewis of Indiana University who had been a Council staff member under Keyserling. Tobin was replaced by Gardner Ackley, of whom more will be said later. This triumvirate continued until the Kennedy Administration ended in November 1963.

The Kennedy Philosophy

Schlesinger points out that Kennedy had received his highest grade (and only B) in his freshman year at Harvard in the introductory course in economics (under a young instructor, Russell Nixon, later an economist for the A.F. of L.-C.I.O.). The course made no deep impression on him. Indeed, he remembered his grade as C, or so at least he liked to tell his economists in later years.[3] Nevertheless, it was fortunate that this early exposure to economics came in the later days of the New Deal, when the Keynesian revolution was having its first effect. This saved him from being taught that government intervention in the economy was wicked per se and that a balanced budget should be the supreme goal of economic policy. Unlike F.D.R., he never had to unlearn classical maxims in order to meet contemporary problems.

His experience as a young Congressman watching the fluctuations of the economy in the late forties confirmed an incipient Keynesianism. Thus, just after the election in 1952, when Sylvia Porter, the financial columnist, asked him on the television program, "Meet the Press," whether he now expected inflation or deflation, he replied,

[2]It was on the occasion of his appointment that J. F. K. made his celebrated remark: Tobin had been reluctant to accept for several reasons, pointing out his orientation toward theory, saying to the President, "I am afraid that I am only an ivory tower economist." Kennedy replied, "That's the best kind, I am only an ivory tower President."

[3]Arthur Schlesinger, Jr., *A Thousand Days* (Boston: Houghton Mifflin Co., 1965).

"Deflation is going to be the more serious problem, particularly if efforts are made which General Eisenhower and Senator Taft and others have talked about of reducing our federal expenditures. Once we begin to balance the budget or begin to reduce our national debt, then deflation obviously is going to be the major issue." The proper policy, he continued, should be ". . . to build up sufficient consumer purchasing power to absorb our increased productivity." He was prepared to do this either through maintaining government expenditures or cutting taxes, ". . . anything to put enough consumer purchasing power in the market, and obviously that's both ways." If unemployment continued, ". . . then I'd be in favor of unbalancing the budget, not enough to cause a severe economic dislocation but enough to keep a reasonable level of prosperity." If we went into a recession, ". . . one of the steps to meet the recession obviously is going to be government expenditures, as it was in the thirties."[4]

He made good use of his diverse economic advisory resources, to quote Schlesinger:

To this combination of influences, Kennedy added his own devouring curiosity about the way things worked. If at the start of his administration he was sometimes unsure of technical detail, he readily acquired an excellent command of economic analysis. In addition, he had shrewd economic intuitions, though perhaps more on national than on international problems. "He was the most perceptive of critics," Walter Heller later said—"he could pick out a sentence or a paragraph and see its weakness. Even though he might not have understood the analytic bases for its weakness, he had the feel for it, and this was uncanny." His approach to economic and social policy, in short, was that of an experimentalist and activist, restrained by politics and prudence but unfettered by doctrinal fetish or taboo.

As President, he meant to assure himself a wide range of intelligent advice. Having chosen Douglas Dillon as Secretary of the Treasury, he chose Walter Heller as chairman of the

[4]Seymour E. Harris, *Economics of the Kennedy Years* (New York: Harper & Row), p. 24.

Council of Economic Advisers. "I need you both," he told Heller, "for a proper balance in economic matters." Diverging institutional interests created in any case a balance, or at least a tug of war, between the Council, charged by statute with working, "to promote maximum employment, production and purchasing power," and the Treasury primarily involved in taxation, the management of the debt and the protection of the dollar. But Kennedy was further pleased by the personal contrasts: the economics professor vs. the investment banker; the liberal vs. the moderate; the man who worried about deflation vs. the man who worried about inflation; the Democrat vs. the Republican.

Dillon, if to the right of Heller, was by no means an economic conservative. He understood the value of academic advice, restored the economists to the Treasury Department, from which they had been driven out by George Humphrey, made Seymour Harris (on Kennedy's suggestion) his economic adviser and encouraged Harris to set up a panel of outside consultants, whose meetings the Secretary regularly attended. Harris, who had a realistic grasp of the political problems of economic policy, became an effective bridge to the Council. Nevertheless, both Dillon's personal background and the institutional predilections of the Treasury inclined him to a particular solicitude for the business community. He was also an exceptionally skilled operator within the bureaucracy, ready to pull every stop and cut many corners to advance the Treasury view, always (and justifiably) confident that his charm could heal any feelings hurt in the process.

Heller on the other hand, had the knack of composing breezy memoranda on economic problems— some hundreds in three years—and Kennedy read them faithfully. Both Heller and Dillon were urbane and articulate men; and much of the debate between them was conducted in the President's presence. The directors of the Budget also made significant contributions to the dialogue. David Bell was himself a professional economist, and Kermit Gordon, who succeeded Bell at the end of 1962, had been on Heller's Council. The Treasury, the Council and the Bureau soon constituted an informal national economic committee known as the "troika," meeting every two or three months with Kennedy for discussions of the economic outlook.[5]

Sorensen points out that Kennedy had little real interest in high finance or in his father's business affairs. He attempted to keep his household finances in balance as a Senator but, as a man of great wealth, money had no real meaning to him. Little evidence exists that the President's father made much impression on his (the President's) economic policy, although many have suggested it. Sorensen makes the point that Kennedy, though largely unschooled in formal economics, but able to learn and to judge people, was able to absorb diverse viewpoints and come to logical conclusions. Sorensen also states that Kennedy's views on Federal finance and budgeting were much more conservative than many of his supporters had believed.[6]

In his book, *Economics of the Kennedy Years*, Harris notes that, in terms of economics, Kennedy was the most sophisticated President who has served in recent years. He indicates that by background and training Kennedy was inherently conservative, although he became more Keynesian in his thinking as his administration progressed. Harris says: ". . . after the first eighteen months of the Kennedy Administration the President underwent a fundamental change. He had become convinced that deficits would stimulate the economy, that with large amounts of unemployment they would not bring on inflation, and that there were some objectives much more important than the balanced budget."[7]

He was of course led to think in terms of regional economic problems in his congressional years:

The special character of his New England problems led him in the fifties to think less about fiscal and monetary and more about structural remedies—in other words, direct attempts to strengthen New England's position in the national economy. His membership on the Labor and Education Committee encouraged the structural approach. (Though he sought appointment to the Joint Committee on the Economic Report,

[5]*Ibid.*, p. 623.

[6]Theodore C. Sorensen, *Kennedy* (New York: Harper & Row, 1965), p. 440.

[7]Harris, *op. cit.*, p. 28.

which dealt with fiscal and monetary issues, he did not make it until 1960.) In general, he looked for programs which he thought would at once benefit New England and the nation, like redeveloping depressed areas (he served as floor manager of Paul Douglas's first area redevelopment bill in 1956) or raising the minimum wage (and thereby reducing the South's competitive advantage) or repealing the Taft-Hartley Act (and opening the way for the unionization of the South). On occasion, he would vote against what Massachusetts considered its local interest, as when he supported the St. Lawrence Seaway. On other occasions, he was ready to help New England at possible expense to the general welfare, as when he favored special protection for textiles or, for a while, opposed farm price supports on the ground that they worsened New England's terms of trade with the rest of the country.[8]

As President he was forced to broaden his outlook. Harris lists two major items among the economic accomplishments of the Kennedy Administration: an increase in Gross National Product (GNP) of almost $100 billion and a generally successful effort to stabilize prices. Many of the Kennedy economic policies were not fully successful. Unemployment remained a problem and the balance of payments situation was not satisfactory, although some progress was made with the problem as it stood at the close of the Eisenhower Administration.

In terms of the economic policy role of the President, Kennedy faced some classic problems: (1) the aggregate demand resulting from the Second World War and the Korean War had been largely satisfied; (2) his margin of victory in 1960 was so thin it hardly constituted a mandate for basic economic change; (3) the balance of payments problem made expansion policies difficult to pursue since it limited the role of fiscal policy; (4) the alliance in Congress between Republicans and the Southern Democrats (largely because of civil rights) made for relatively little control in the Congress; (5) his relationship with the Congress was not as sound as it might have been; and (6) he and the business community were mistrustful of one another, especially after the "steel price incident" in April 1962.

This incident deserves some attention since it was to be of great

8Schlesinger, *op. cit.*

future interest. The President had obtained agreement from the United Steel Workers upon a wage settlement which in the eyes of the Council would not disturb price-wage relationships. The "Guide Posts" which were to become widely known in later years were not then widely understood although they were introduced in the *Economic Report* in January 1962. After the contract was signed, the major steel producers announced price increases which, in the Council's view, exceeded the proper amount. Kennedy lacked the emergency powers of seizure that Truman had exercised a decade earlier in a similar situation, but had recourse to public opinion. He denounced the steel companies, and began a vigorous campaign to force a price reduction, in which his strategy involved several points: (1) evidence that the steel price increase was unnecessary for the welfare of the steel industry; (2) an attempt to encourage a split in the industry in which the smaller major firms such as Inland and Kaiser held the price line; and (3) stress upon the adverse effects on the steel industry in the international market if prices increased. Within seventy-two hours, the companies had reversed themselves.[9] There is some question as to the relative influence of the pressures involved. McConnell suggests that the marketplace played a major part in the re-evaluation, and no doubt this is true. However, the power of the Presidency, backed by the analysis of the Council, was what really brought about the reduction. This incident stirred up considerable controversy and influenced the President's relationship with the business community for some time.

Perhaps more than any President (with the possible exception of F. D. R.) Kennedy asked for and acted upon the advice of academic economists. The members of the Council appointed by Kennedy— Heller, Tobin, and Gordon, later Ackley and Lewis—were all adherents, generally speaking, of the postwar Keynesian views of fiscal policy. All of the original members of the Council were, like the President himself, born in the twentieth century and trained in the years of the Keynesian revolution.[10]

[9]Both this incident and the Truman steel incident are discussed in detail in Grant McConnell, *Steel and the Presidency* (New York: W. W. Norton & Co., 1963). For a brief version, see "The Steel Price Controversy 1962," *Problems of the Modern Economy,* Edmund Phelps and others, eds. (New York: W. W. Norton, 1966).

[10]Heller, Gordon, and Tobin were all in graduate school in the early or late 1940's, at the peak of academic Keynesianism.

Harris notes that Heller was able to bring the President around to his view on modern economics, [11] whereas Keyserling, Burns, and Saulnier in the Truman and Eisenhower years were dealing with Presidents who already shared their views. [12] By every account, Kennedy was more sophisticated and discriminating in his relationship with those who advised him than Roosevelt who, although he made use of academic types, did not apparently take their advice very seriously and was not always to be relied upon in his judgment of professional orthodoxy.

Kennedy was a natural to attract the able academic economist. In Roosevelt's day, there were few capable professionals with experience in high-level affairs. Moley, Tugwell, Henderson, et al., were not of the professional calibre of Heller, Ackley, or Samuelson. In the Kennedy years, need and availability coincided; economists of ability and experience were available and the administration was anxious to use them. But it should not be thought that the Kennedy administration was a haven for the pure theoretician who had no pragmatic views. [13] Kennedy was first, last, and always a hardheaded politician, appreciating capable performance and intolerant of vague concepts, fuzzy thinking, or a general lack of competence. [14]

Many young and distinguished economists in and out of the administration were also known to have influence on the Kennedy philosophy. Paul Samuelson, John Kenneth Galbraith, Carl Kaysen, and W. W. Rostow were frequent consultants. Seymour Harris, a Kennedy adviser, organized a group of economists who met at irregular intervals with the Council, the officials of the Treasury, and the Bureau of the Budget. George L. Bach, Carnegie Institute of Technology; Philip W. Bell, Haverford College; Roy Blough, Columbia University; Harvey E. Brazer, The University of Michigan; Gerhard Colm, National Planning Association; Richard N. Cooper, Yale University;

[11]Harris, *op. cit.*, p. 20.

[12]Jacoby disputes this contention, holding that Eisenhower needed "education" and his views were shaped by the Council, especially Burns. (Personal correspondence with the author, Jan. 1966.)

[13]The volume of economic memoranda which was passed to Kennedy was immense. Heller notes that more than three hundred economic memos went to J. F. K. in the thousand days of his presidency. Walter W. Heller, *New Dimensions of Political Economy* (Cambridge: Harvard University Press, 1966), p. 29.

[14]Most all sources, e.g., Sorensen, Schlesinger, make this point.

James S. Duesenberry, Harvard University; John G. Gurley, Stanford University; Gottfried Haberler, Harvard University; Alvin H. Hansen, Harvard University; Seymour E. Harris, University of California, S.D.; Albert G. Hart, Columbia University; Hendrik S. Houthakker, Harvard University; Harry G. Johnson, The University of Chicago; John H. Karenken, University of Minnesota; Peter B. Kenen, Columbia University; C. P. Kindleberger, Massachusetts Institute of Technology; Hal B. Lary, National Bureau of Economic Research, Inc. ,; John Lintner, Harvard Graduate School of Business Administration; Fritz Machlup, Princeton University; Lloyd A. Metzler, The University of Chicago; Raymond F. Mikesell, University of Oregon; Franco Modigliani, Massachusetts Institute of Technology; Geoffrey H. Moore, National Bureau of Economic Research, Inc. ; Richard A. Musgrave, Princeton University; Alice Rivlin, The Brookings Institution, Carl S. Shoup, Columbia University; Warren L. Smith, The University of Michigan; Arthur Smithies, Harvard University; Robert Solow, Stetson University; Daniel B. Suits, The University of Michigan; James Tobin, Yale University; Robert C. Turner, Indiana University. Others who participated upon an occasional basis include: Edward M. Bernstein, E. M. B. , Limited; Joseph A. Pechman, The Brookings Institution; Walter S. Salant, The Brookings Institution; and Paul A. Samuelson, Massachusetts Institute of Technology.

Harris gives Heller great credit for being Kennedy's teacher of modern economics; he also has substantial praise for Secretary Dillon. He notes that the budget, under Eisenhower an instrument for keeping spending down, became in the Kennedy years, "What it should be, a plan to help achieve stability and growth."[15]

The Great Debate Over Expansion and the New Economics

Perhaps no incident more clearly illustrates the role of economic advisership than the now famous debate over expansionist policy which went on in the Kennedy Administration in the early 1960's on the issue of economic growth and the continuing problem of unemployment. Among economists, two basic schools of thought contended. The first group, of which Heller was a member, was of the opinion

[15]Harris, *op. cit.*, p. 28.

that there was a lack of aggregate demand for goods and services. Citing the experience of the war years, these economists argued that the need was for public spending, public works, and other such activities which would increase aggregate demand. The second school (less popular among economists) held that there was unemployment due to structural deficiencies in the economy, that is, there were large numbers of people who, because of lack of training or obsolete skills, were unable to participate in the modern economy. The obvious remedy to these observers was a policy of preparing the unemployed through programs of training and relocation. [16] Those who endorsed the structural view also argued that increased spending would not only fail to solve the problem, but also it would further aggravate it, by contributing to inflationary pressures. The Council, viewing the tax burden as a drag on the economy, was in favor of increasing demand by means of a tax reduction. John Kenneth Galbraith, an economist close to Kennedy, opposed this route on grounds that it would merely increase spending for personal consumer goods of which as he had argued in his well-known book, *The Affluent Society,* there was already a more than adequate supply. In Galbraith's view, the real need was for increased spending in the public sector, which had been far outstripped by private affluence (the doctrine of social imbalance). A tax cut was in many ways desirable, but political problems complicated the picture. These divergent views were articulated by various advisers and the President considered them carefully; but, as President, he was forced to temper professional advice with practical politics. Others outside the administration lent a hand; for example, Paul Samuelson met with the President at Hyannis Port and made a plea for a cut. [17] The President was not fully convinced however as Schlesinger says:

> . . . but in the President's mind what was theoretically desirable had to be tempered by what was politically feasible. His campaign had emphasized discipline and sacrifice; his victory had been slim; his Congress was conservative; and,

[16]These arguments are well summed up by Robert Theobald in his book, *Free Men and Free Markets* (Garden City: Doubleday & Co. , Anchor Ed. 1965). An excellent statement of both cases is the address by Gardner Ackley, *Vandeveer Memorial Lecture,* Southern Illinois University, October 26, 1966. (Mimeographed).

[17]Heller, *op. cit.,* p. 32.

at least in the mind of the business community, his party had a reputation for fiscal irresponsibility. As Kennedy told Heller in December 1960, "I understand the case for a tax cut, but it doesn't fit very well with my call for sacrifice." Nor did it fit very well with the need, increased by the shaky balance-of-payments situation, to appear, though a Democrat, a defender of the dollar. The science, so called, of economics had to return to its honorable antecedents and become the art of political economy.

Paul Samuelson, heading an interregnal task force, adjusted his recommendations to fit the presidential and congressional mood. While a believer in deficits and inclined toward social spending, he refrained from recommending investment in the public sector, apart from defense, and mentioned a temporary tax cut only as an emergency weapon. As for the use of monetary policy—the traditional Democratic remedy of lower interest rates—this, he thought, was seriously limited by the international payments problem. All this left structural measures, along with defense spending, as Samuelson's main recommendation and the administration's main resort.

Kennedy's special message to Congress on February 2 therefore concentrated on the extension of unemployment insurance, area redevelopment, the increase of the minimum wage, housing and community development, acceleration of procurement and construction and the like. More novel though hardly more radical was a proposal for special tax incentives to investment. The message even catered somewhat to congressional fears about the budget, promising balance "over the years of the economic cycle." Later messages through the spring called for other institutional measures. And Congress proved responsive to the structural approach. Within six months it passed an area redevelopment bill, an omnibus housing bill, a farm bill, a rise in the minimum wage, the liberalization of social security, temporary unemployment benefits, benefits for dependent children of unemployed parents and a program to combat water pollution—a record of action on the domestic front unmatched in any single sitting since 1935.

Still, this was a program of welfare, perhaps a program to end the recession, but not a program of economic expansion. Kennedy himself restlessly continued to seek the answer to the

5 per cent growth rate. A few weeks after his special economic message, when an Americans for Democratic Action delegation called on him, he singled out Robert R. Nathan, a Washington economist from New Deal days, and asked him the usual question. Nathan replied that the President could get his 5 per cent growth rate, but the price would be a deficit of $5 billion a year for the next ten years. The President said skeptically that would be great if only Nathan would organize the political support for such a policy.

As Kennedy told Walter Lippmann and me at luncheon a few days later, most economists were evasive when he tried to pin them down as to what exactly government could do to stimulate growth, but Nathan had been frank; and an addition of $50 billion to the national debt would of course be very little compared to the extra growth and revenue which could be thus induced. Only the systematic creation of annual deficits, he said, was the one thing which the political situation, short of a depression, precluded his doing. "I don't want to be tagged as a big spender early in this administration," he said on another occasion. "If I do, I won't get my programs through later on."[18]

This was, in the true sense, an exercise in the art of political economy. Many factors were to be taken into account. Harry F. Byrd, Sr., then senior Senator from Virginia and long-time Chairman of the Senate Finance Committee, was unalterably opposed to a tax cut at this time. Even more important, Congressman Wilbur D. Mills, Chairman of the House Ways and Means Committee, was opposed to a cut unless it incorporated a basic reform of the tax situation.[19] While the Kennedy forces were not opposed to a reform, they felt that it would be a long-term proposition—much too long for any immediate economic gains. Flash notes:

As Nossiter and many other commentators clearly recognized, Kennedy was restrained by other noneconomic factors.

[18] Schlesinger, *A Thousand Days*, *op cit.*, pp. 628-629.

[19] One notes with interest that, in late 1967, the CEA was hard-pressed by Mills to prove the case for a tax increase (surcharge), which the Administration sought.

Mills was strongly opposed to immediate reduction because of the lack of clear indications of recession and because such a step would deny an essential sweetener for the structural reforms in which he was primarily interested and which had yet to be presented to Congress. Further, Mills felt that imposition of the tax cut without accompanying reduction in expenditures would increase the risk of inflation. Without Mills' support, no tax legislation was possible. The slow and tortuous progress of the 1962 revision dulled any remaining optimism that a bill could be passed quickly. Furthermore, to push the tax cut would jeopardize other priority legislation by risking a fight within Congress at a highly inappropriate time. Although Dillon favored cuts in the next year (the nature and extent of them yet to be determined), he was strongly opposed to any immediate cuts for reasons paralleling those of Mills. The likelihood both of a sizable deficit instead of a modest surplus for fiscal 1963 and a congressional refusal to enact a postal rate increase for additional revenue made the prospect of further deficits stemming from a tax reduction all the more unwelcome. [William McChesney] Martin's distaste for deficit financing and the power of the Federal Reserve to react to its use by raising interest rates were an additional restraint. A few enlightened sophisticates might not be worried about deficits, but the general public was, and in an election year this was an important consideration. Kennedy wished to meet the criteria of fiscal responsibility as applied by the general public and by the business community both at home and overseas.[20]

Although this controversy was perhaps the most illustrative example of economic advice at work in the administration, other serious economic problems were troublesome.

Unemployment continued to be of concern, and the problem of gold outflow was far from solved. The argument over attacking unemployment or recession continued over most of the early Kennedy Administration. As the Kennedy Council took over, unemployment had reached almost 7 percent. Within days after the Council was organized, the special message of February 7 on a "Program for Economic Recovery and Growth" was in preparation. This message,

[20]Flash, *op. cit.*, pp. 246-247.

coming only four days after the *State of the Union Message*, was largely the work of the Council and provided an excellent opportunity to demonstrate the ability of the CEA to the President, and enabled the Council members to separate the strands of their own thoughts.

Within a brief period, the Council also participated in messages on gold and the balance of payments, national resources, and the Federal highways program while at the same time laying down the outlines of its own testimony before the Joint Economic Committee on March 6 (i. e., its support of the President's emergency program).

Although the economic downturn with which the Council was concerned was mild, countercyclical operations centered around the diminishing rate of economic growth as seen in the increased frequency of recession and the ominous weakness of recovery after each downturn. The basis of action on this front was a report (indeed a classic of economic advisorship), commissioned by Kennedy while President-elect, and made by a task force committee under the chairmanship of Paul Samuelson. Entitled *Prospects and Policies for the* 1961 *American Economy,* and largely written by Samuelson, the report nonetheless reflects the views of other highly-respected professionals. In addition to Samuelson, those who served were Gerhard Colm, Henry Fowler, Otto Eckstein, Joseph Pechman of the Brookings Institution, and Tobin and Heller, future members of the Council. This group had worked informally (much of it between sessions of the American Economic Association meeting) for some time in preparing the report. The tone of the report was generally expansionist. But the President was not anxious to embark upon a major program of federal expenditures because, as we have seen, he did not wish to gain the reputation of fiscal irresponsibility.

Having in mind the controversy between Nourse and the Joint Committee and Burns and Senator Douglas in regard to testifying, Heller took steps to avoid difficulty. In a presentation early in March, the chairman pledged cooperation with the Committee, but included significant sentences (emphasis added):

> In Congressional testimony and in other public statements, the Council must protect its advisory relationship to the President. *We assume that the Committee does not expect the Council to indicate in what respects its advice has or has not been taken by the President, nor to what extent particular proposals, or omissions of proposals reflect the advice of the Council.*

Subject to the limits mentioned, members of the Council are glad to discuss, to the best of their knowledge and ability *as professional economists, the economic situation* and problems of the country, and the possible alternative means of achieving the goals of the Employment Act and other commonly held economic objectives. In this undertaking, the Council wishes to cooperate as fully as possible with the Committee and with Congress *in achieving a better understanding of our economic problems and approaches to their solution.*[21]

Heller clearly recognized that testimony, in addition to being of substantial value in congressional relations, also gave him an invaluable launching pad for economic ideas. He recognized the educational value of the Council's role in putting forth new economic ideas. For example, he brought his ideas on fiscal policy into sharp focus in his testimony on the role of stabilizers. Typical of his educational role was his comment on the balanced economy:

The success of fiscal and budget policies cannot be measured only by whether the budget is in the black or in the red. The true test is whether the economy is in balance. Only an economy which is realizing its potential can produce the goods and create the jobs the country needs. If at the end of this year the unemployment ratio is still near 7 per cent, our fiscal policies would have to be viewed with great concern, even if there is little or no deficit in the budget. On the other hand, if we have succeeded in reducing the unemployment ratio and expanding output significantly by year's end, we will be on our way to the goals of a stronger economy and the restoration of budgetary strength.[22]

These were relatively bold forays into advanced economic policy; and, in stating them in public, Heller was pushing beyond the thinking of the administration, although some of these ideas had been presented in a Joint Economic Committee study.[23] Heller recognized the value

[21]U. S. Congress, Joint Economic Committee, *Hearings on January* 1961 *Economic Report of the President, and Outlook,* 87th Cong. , 1st Session,
[22]*Ibid. ,* p. 361.
[23]U. S. Congress, Joint Economic Committee, *Study of Employment, Growth, and Price Levels.* This study was led by Otto Eckstein and James W. Knowles in 1959.

of the platform provided by the opportunity to testify, a policy which Burns had established and Ackley was to follow. Kennedy, of course, helped to set the tone in June 1962 in his famous Yale Speech on economic myths which Heller justly claims marked a new era in American economic policy. [24]

The Heller Technique

The Heller Council employed a different mode of operation from the Burns Council and was highly informal in its internal organization. The young and generally inexperienced staff members were not entirely suitable for high-level representation of the Council, leaving the burden on the older members, especially Heller. Further, it has been agreed by the President and Heller at the time of his appointment that there would be no Kennedy counterpart of Gabriel Hauge, the White House resident economist and leg-man under Eisenhower. While this assured Heller that the Council would be *the* economic authority, it was to prove troublesome. A White House economist is able to undertake many tasks for the President on semipolitical matters, usually short-term and urgent. With no such talent available, Heller and the other CEA members were engaged in many errands for the President which took time and effort from other matters.

Gerhard Colm commented on this matter during the Twentieth Anniversary Symposium, noting a weakness:

. . . the Council has had to act frequently as a fire brigade for the President, particularly for the implementation of the price-wage guidelines. I believe that it is essential for a policy in support of economic growth to inject the public interest into the process of price and wage determination in a more orderly manner. I don't want to support exactly the wage-price guidelines as formulated at present. I also don't want to advocate price and wage controls in peacetime. I would favor, however, the establishment by law of an office for price-wage-productivity analysis which would work under the general direction of the Council of Economic Advisers but would have its own operational responsibility. This office

---

[24]Heller, *op. cit.*, p. 37. This speech, perhaps the best J. F. K. ever gave, was a classic of economic understanding, put forth with Kennedy's characteristic grace and wit.

would establish, on request of the President, special committees for crucial industries to study the effect of proposed price and wage actions on economic growth, productivity, and price stability. The President could bring these findings, if he wished, to the attention of Congress.[25]

It may be well that the fire brigade function is the price paid for Council involvement; there is no doubt that the Heller Council was involved.

Unlike the Burns Council, intra-Council discussion of issues, wide staff participation and flexibility were encouraged; consultants and part-time experts were used, especially at report-writing time. In general, the Council staff was a three-level structure: the career staff; the academic economists who served for a year or more; and the consultants, often former Council or staff members, on call to deal with special problems.

In the second group were academic economists, mostly young, often only recently out of graduate school. These staff people were highly mobile, often moving back into academic life, or into research organizations such as the RAND Corporation.[26] This group was young, dedicated to the New Frontier philosophy, and oriented toward quantitative economics; it was supplemented by somewhat more senior men with substantial Washington experience.[27]

In external relations, the Council was somewhat more formal and maintained close contact throughout the government with other groups related to its concerns. Secretaries Goldberg and Wertz, for example, pressed hard for a solution to unemployment. Chairman Heller, Treasury Secretary Dillon, and Budget Director Bell were closely allied in the "Troika," a group which often expanded to

[25] *Twentieth Anniversary of the Employment Act—An Economic Symposium,* (Joint Economic Committee, 89th Congress, 2nd Session, Feb. 23, 1966, Washington, D. C.), p. 81.

[26] Typical of this group were Sidney G. Winter, Jr., Richard E. Attiyeh, Barbara R. Bergman, Richard Nelson, Arthur Okun, Lee Preston, Lloyd Ulman, Vernon Ruttan, Robert M. Solow, Charles A. Cooper, Richard N. Cooper, and George L. Perry.

[27] Henry Brifs, Burton Klein, Charles Schultze, Robert Triffin, Paul Samuelson, Kenneth Arrow, Martin Bronfrenbrenner, and James Duesenberry (who was to become a Council member under Gardner Ackley).

include William McC. Martin of the Federal Reserve. Apparently there was more personal rapport among this trio than had been the case among their counterparts in the Eisenhower years. Heller moved early to establish good congressional relations, and similarly he did not overlook the importance of nongovernmental groups. Contacts were maintained with the Brookings Institution, the Committee for Economic Development, the National Planning Association, and other similar organizations.

As was true in previous administrations, economists associated with other agencies and some outside the Federal establishment were influential in the Kennedy government: David Bell, Director of the Agency for International Development, who held a Harvard M.A. and was lecturer and research associate in the Graduate School of Business at Harvard before joining the New Frontier; Willard W. Cochrane, Director of Agricultural Economics, USDA, formerly professor of agricultural economics at the University of Minnesota, a Ph.D. from Harvard; Philip H. Coombs, Assistant Secretary of State, formerly professor of economics at Amherst College; Charles J. Hitch, formerly with the RAND Corporation and Assistant Secretary of Defense; Robert V. Roosa, a respected monetary scholar, Ph.D., University of Michigan, Undersecretary of the Treasury for Monetary Affairs; W. W. Rostow, Chairman, State Department Policy Planning Council, formerly professor of economic history at M.I.T., a Yale Ph.D. and Rhodes scholar. This group in part carried over into the Johnson administration when the Kennedy years ended.

Lyndon Johnson, New Deal Economics in New Economics Form

When John Kennedy was succeeded by Lyndon Johnson in November 1963, there was immediate speculation about the future of the Council and of the academic adviser in the high levels of the administration. Liberal Kennedy supporters had not been pleased when Johnson was selected for second place on the ticket in 1960; Johnson, a pragmatic politician, had little of Kennedy's appeal for the academic type but Chairman Heller remained in his position until 1964, when he returned to academic life. One might suspect that he was more at ease with Kennedy than with Johnson, but there is no evidence to confirm such speculation.[28] Contrary to what had been thought, Johnson not only continued the relationship with the Council, but also increased its participation.

Upon Heller's resignation, Gardner Ackley became chairman. Ackley (forty-nine in 1964) received his Ph.D. from the University of Michigan in 1940. After service in OPA, OSS, and other wartime agencies, and in academic life, Ackley had joined the Council as a member in 1962. John P. Lewis was appointed in May 1963, overlapped the Kennedy and Johnson administrations, and remained as a Council member through August 1964.

Otto Eckstein became a member in September 1964. Thirty-seven when appointed, he had also received the Ph.D. from Harvard in 1955 and, after teaching at Harvard, joined the Council, having served as staff director of the Joint Committee Study on *Growth, Employment, and Price Levels*.

Arthur Okun, youngest to serve on the Council, was thirty-six at appointment in November 1964 and had been granted the Ph.D. from Columbia in 1956. After teaching at Columbia, Okun had served as a Council staff member and returned briefly to Yale before being promoted to membership.

It is interesting to note that the original Council averaged age fifty-four, with both Nourse and Clark over sixty; the 1966 group averaged forty at appointment, with both Eckstein and Okun under that age. Corresponding to their ages, the latter group was long on education and short on wide experience. While in the original group only Nourse was a professional economist of national reputation, of the 1966 trio, only Ackley had substantial government experience, and none had broad business experience. These differences and their implications will be commented upon in later chapters.

Under Johnson, the Council has taken a more active part than previously in the conduct of national economic affairs, especially those relating to price-wage relationships. The increasing participation has not been without its price; the Council has found itself increasingly on the day-to-day firing line, forced to defend policies based on estimates of a highly fluid situation.

Further, the Vietnamese War has made any rational budgetary policy very difficult to pursue. The Council has shared with the

---

[28]On the contrary, Heller makes it quite clear in *New Dimensions* that he and L. B. J. got along well, and that Johnson recognized the value of economic advice.

Treasury and the Bureau of the Budget the congressional displeasure over the rather obvious "budgeteering" techniques of the Administration used to attempt a balance of sorts. All of this has been greatly complicated by the Administration's reluctance to reduce the scope of Great Society programs.

The Guideposts, Administration or Advice?

The famous economic guideposts, intended to serve as informal guides to wage-price decisions and given formal expression in the President's Economic Report in January 1962, were a major policy effort, and deserve more mention.[29] Few economic pronouncements have in recent years evoked more controversy than these, which were obviously little more than a compromise between full price-wage controls such as those prevailing under such wartime conditions as full employment, and complete price-wage freedom which marks the traditional peacetime economy (whenever that may be).

Historical Aspects of Guidepost Policy

Except for the National Industrial Recovery Act and similar attempts to keep prices and wages from falling, the experience of the United States in wage-price control has been restricted to efforts to restrain the inflation which results from the extraordinary economic activity of wartime. During the First World War, rather mild and generally unsuccessful efforts were made to control prices. These efforts, largely restricted to negotiation with industry by the War Industries Board, were conspicuously unsuccessful. Bernard Baruch has noted in his autobiography the problems stemming from a refusal to recognize the magnitude of the problem.[30] Weak as these efforts were, they represented a substantial departure from the past, when wars were fought without any attempt to control the economic effects.[31]

---

[29]A book devoted to these matters was published by the University of Chicago Press in 1966. The book embodies the results of a conference of well-known economists, and is edited by George P. Schultze and Robert Z. Aliber. See *Guidelines, Informal Controls and the Marketplace* (Chicago 1966).

[30]Bernard Baruch, *The Public Years* (New York: Holt, Rinehart & Winston, 1960), p. 54.

[31]See Emanuel Stein and Jules Backman, Eds., *War Economics* (New York: Farrar and Rinehart, 1942), Chap. VI.

During the Second World War more sophisticated and more effective machinery for price-wage control was established. During the prewar defense build-up, a span of almost two years during which the U.S. was acting as a supply base for the entire Allied effort, prices rose very little in comparison to output, due to the large excess capacity in both plant and manpower which had existed since 1932. Employment and industrial output were able to expand greatly without any real strain on the price system. In May 1940, President Roosevelt established a National Defense Advisory Commission whose functions included a watch on inflationary tendencies in the economy. At this early date, and later when the Office of Price Administration was established, price problems were isolated and were generally handled informally. Neither congressional nor public opinion was ready to embrace outright price controls. The first formal price schedule (on used machine tools) was issued in February 1941, and by the end of that year, nearly fifty schedules had been issued. Another fifty-eight were issued by the time the Price Control Act was passed in January 1942. Selective price controls continued until it became obvious that piecemeal measures would not be adequate. In April 1942, the OPA issued a general freeze order; from this time on, price increases could be undertaken only with OPA approval.

For some time, wage stabilization attracted little attention; in general, emphasis was put on dispute settlement. Shortly after Pearl Harbor, the President commended a labor-management group which agreed to a "no strike, no lockout" pledge for the duration. This trend was then formalized with the appointment of the War Labor Board to settle disputes, including wage disputes, referred by the Secretary of Labor. In the course of its operations, the Board adopted the "Little Steel Formula" (July 1942), which entitled workers who had not enjoyed a 15 percent increase since January 1, 1941, to make up the difference. The formula was based on the estimated 15 percent rise in the cost of living between January 1, 1941 and May 1942. With the adoption of this general principle, the whole wage structure was brought within the purview of the National War Labor Board. Executive Order 9250, which prohibited wage increases without the approval of the Board, was issued on October 3, 1942. The character of these controls is expressed by Arthur M. Ross:

The character of wage stabilization was affected by several important decisions made early in the period. First, some flexibility was preserved through continuation of the Little Steel formula, the inequity principle, and permission to eliminate substandard rates. Second, control over fringe benefits was looser than the limitation of hourly wage increases. Unions therefore were able to concentrate on benefits long enjoyed by white collar workers and executives such as vacations, paid holidays, and sick-leave allowances. Third, wage control was kept separate from price control. Wages were not automatically adjusted for changes in the cost of living, nor were the wage decisions of the Board normally influenced by possible effects on prices. Likewise, except in a few cases, wages were disassociated from manpower considerations.[33]

Due to fringe benefits and other allowable loopholes, there was considerable wage drift and, at war's end, there was immediate pressure for withdrawal of wage-price controls. Executive Order 9599 was issued by President Truman in August 1945, allowing price increases. Widespread strikes in key industries proceeded to put pressure on wage-price controls throughout the economy. By June 1946, the line had been broken and formal decontrol soon followed. It seems very doubtful if wage-price controls would have stood up anyway under the "demand pull" inflationary pressures present at the time. Between 1946 and 1947, the consumer price index rose 15 percent, whereupon President Truman attempted without success to have price and wage ceilings reimposed.

Unlike World War II, the Korean War brought an immediate increase in prices as a wave of consumer buying struck. A curious situation then developed. After a somewhat serious delay, during which prices and wages rose rapidly, Congress enacted price-wage controls in the Defense Production Act, September 10, 1950. Almost at the same time, consumers evidently realized that World War III was not after all impending, and consumer buying, as well as inventory accumulation, began to taper off. It is generally agreed that the controls were too little and too late, although they had some psychological effect. Again, Ross sums up:

Looking back on the situation, it may be concluded that direct controls over wages and prices were needed at the out-

[32]Arthur M. Ross, "Guideline Policy, Where We Are, and How We Got There," *Guidelines, op. cit.*, pp. 116-117.

set of the Korean War because of the substantial increases and realignments in output, drastic changes in economic expectations, vivid memories of World War II shortages, and great uncertainty over the meaning of the new situation. Controls, however, were established too late and continued too long on a comprehensive basis. They could have been removed when the major economic shifts had been accomplished, the community had become psychologically adjusted to the Korean War, and fiscal and credit policies had had time to become effective. Specifically, they could have been eliminated by the fall of 1951 except for price ceilings on a few scarce materials.[33]

Little or nothing was heard of a need for inflation control for a decade after the conclusion of the Korean War.

The first formal mention of the guideposts came in the President's Economic Report in January 1962. They were not, however, a completely new idea. In 1952, the Truman Council had held that wage increases should be limited to productivity gains, then considered to be in the range of two to three percent. The Eisenhower Council endorsed this proposition (at least in general terms) on several occasions.

Rationale of the Guideposts

The guideposts attempt to restrain wage-price increases within the framework of economic freedom. Wage-price stability can be approached in three ways: (1) Judicious use of fiscal and monetary policy may along with careful budgeting make it unnecessary to apply any direct or indirect controls to wage-price relationships. (2) A program of either selective or comprehensive wage-price controls may be put into operation. (3) Guideposts may be established to provide a general direction and magnitude of movement for wages and prices. Each of these techniques has advantages and disadvantages which must be considered, and for which politico-economic trade-off procedures must be worked out.

Budgetary-fiscal-monetary policies sufficiently effective to avoid serious wage-price fluctuations during periods of expansion, such as that from 1963 on, would involve many aspects of policy politically

[33]*Ibid.*, p. 119.

impossible of enactment in normal times. Either selective or general outright control would be equally unpopular except in serious crises such as full-scale war or catastrophic depression.

Wage-price guideposts have several advantages, although it is doubtful if they balance the disadvantages. The guideposts based on productivity increases do provide a clear directive for those segments of the economy (of which there must be a few) sincerely attempting to avoid an unduly inflationary situation. They also act to serve notice that the executive branch is aware of the importance of avoiding inflationary situations, although it lacks any formal method of combatting them. Further, the guideposts focus attention on the wage-price relationship, thus highlighting its importance in inflation control. And, finally, they are better than nothing at all, the only other likely alternative. By any measure, these advantages are weak and unimpressive, but the real measure of the guideposts is not how good they might have been, but did they work, that is, without them would there have been more inflation; did they do more good than harm?

In attempting to evaluate the guideposts' effectiveness, one is torn between two sets of evidence. It is argued on the one hand, that they were so weak as to be meaningless, on the other, that they were highly detrimental to various segments of the economy and thus must have been fairly effective. The major arguments against them can be summarized as follows:

(1) They were ineffective since everyone knew that, if they were really to be useful, direct price-wage controls would have been used instead.

(2) They were unfair since they were applied only in conspicuous situations.

(3) Their theoretical basis, namely, productivity increases, is not practical since productivity cannot be accurately measured.

(4) They were enforced through a policy of naked economic power and carried out on an arbitrary and unilateral basis.

(5) They were of doubtful constitutional validity.

When the guideposts were first introduced, no exact figures were given. In response to requests for numerical limits, the Council put forth a figure of 3.2 percent. Throughout the mid-1960's, the administration of these guideposts brought the Council face-to-face with many problems, both conceptual and practical. There were many groups in the economy whose income was in no way tied to productivity as usually measured; some workers were engaged in industries which, through exogenous factors having little to do with the workers, were highly productive. In other cases, workers were in areas of industry where, for many reasons, productivity was slow to increase. Participants in wage-price negotiations began to play a numbers game. In early and mid-1966, as labor became restive, the strain on the guidepost concept increased. The President and the Council began to be more and more involved with labor-management disputes and industrial price policies. Naturally, this put the Council on the firing line and exposed it to more critical comment from those segments of the economy who wished to break through the guidepost restrictions. It is impossible under these circumstances to avoid the political implications of the problem. Business argued that the administration was more apt to be looking the other way when labor stepped over the line than it was when business prices were an issue (which may have been true). By mid-1966, with the inflationary settlement of the airline strike, the guidelines reached the end of their usefulness and were, to a degree at least, formally ended in the report of January 1967.

It is in such situations as that described above, where economics and politics merge, where the Council runs grave risks. In effect, the administration was attempting to operate a system of control over wages, salaries, and prices when no formal procedure for control existed. The perils for the immediate administrator of such a policy, in this case the CEA, is apt to garner the wrath of all parties who seek an increase in the price of their goods and services. In a time of rising prices, during which most of the burden of control rested on monetary policy, price increases beyond the limits of productivity were inevitable.

The Council recognized that the figure of 3.2 percent was no longer viable, but the guideposts were considered far from dead. Speaking before the Society of Business Writers in May 1967, Chairman Ackley said:

Is there any hope? Are the guideposts really dead? For my part, I can answer these questions very easily.

I believe that voluntary restraint in the exercise of private discretion will continue because the national leaders of labor, business, and government know that it must. They recognize the problem, and know that the answer does not lie in operating the economy with a wasteful, costly, and unhumane margin of slack; in burdensome, inefficient, and ultimately unsuccessful direct controls; in attempts to atomize private concentrations of market power.

And I believe that this continuing system of voluntary restraint must be based on the productivity principle because no other makes economic sense.

Both the need for restraint and the fundamental importance of the productivity principle were explicitly recognized in a resolution unanimously adopted last August by the President's Advisory Committee on Labor Management Policy:

"We believe that it is essential to the continued economic growth and health of the country that the present inflationary trends be stopped, and that maximum efforts should therefore be made to restrain, through voluntary procedures, unjustified wage or price behavior.

"We believe that the goals reflected in the guideposts as set forth in the 1962 report of the Council of Economic Advisers providing for the alignment of wages and prices with productivity in the economy as a whole need and deserve support."

The Committee reached two further conclusions, with which I think it would be impossible to disagree:

"We also believe that it is impractical if not impossible to translate the goals reflected in the guideposts into formulae for application to every particular price or wage decision.

"We believe that in a free society any policy to achieve price stability will be acceptable and effective only if it bears equitably on all forms of incomes."

In addition, the Committee recommended certain specific procedures designed to develop support of these principles by providing "a more general understanding of why voluntary restraints serve both the national and private interests." The Council met this morning with the Committee in line with the procedures it had suggested.

In discussions of guidepost policy before the Joint Economic Committee and elsewhere, proposals continue to be made for new administrative machinery to help make the guideposts more "effective." The Council would surely welcome new arrangements which would relieve us of our participation in guidepost "administration." But we take an extremely cautious view of all proposals that in any degree tend to move the guideposts closer to the status of direct controls—or that even appear to have that result. However, new techniques for consultation, persuasion, and information to the public and the parties could well be helpful, and should be studied and discussed. [35]

The Joint Economic Committee commented on this matter in the *Statement of Committee Agreement, Minority and Other Views*, in March 1967. The minority noted with approval that the guidepost concept had been abandoned insofar as any specific measure was concerned, but said:

Our pleasure over abandonment of the fixed yardstick is tempered by the administration's apparent intention to continue interference in individual price and wage decisions. The Council admitted that last year it became involved in price decisions in 50 different industries and has stated that its efforts will continue and increase. Some industries apparently are contacting the Council in advance of making price changes. Aside from the fact that such activity can impair the Council's primary function as an advisory body to the President, we think such actions by the Federal Government, particularly without express authorization of Congress, pose serious risks. We would hope that future actions of this kind do not follow the pattern of the steel and aluminum episodes of recent years or of the action taken against the oil industry just last month.

We reject proposals for the establishment of a public Wage-Price-Productivity Board which would review key price and wage decisions in the private economy. The establishment of such a board would be a first step toward control of private

[34]Gardner Ackley, *Address Before the Society of Business Writers*, May 6, 1967 (mimio.).

economic function that changes in wages and prices have in allocating resources to their most productive use.[36]

Thus, Lyndon Johnson had continued, if not expanded, the Council's role in policy. The twnety years from 1946-1966 had been eventful for the Council, with many contrasts in procedure and in philosophy. Yet, as we shall see in the following chapter, there was surprising similarity.

[35]*Statement of Committee Agreement, Minority and Other Views,* Joint Economic Committee, 90th Congress, 1st Session: March 17, 1967, p. 64.

6
ECONOMIC PROBLEMS AND PROGRESS, 1946-1966, THE QUALITY OF ADVICE

The View From "Old State"

The problems of the American economy from 1946 to 1966, with which the various members of the Council were forced to deal in their capacity as advisers, are classifiable as (1) price stability, (2) continued full employment, (3) sustained economic growth. These problems were complicated by the fact that some goals such as continued full employment and price stability are often in conflict with each other, and also by the fact that several major national and international events occurred which were unforeseen and highly disruptive to the course of economic policy.

The immediate problems of the Korean War upset the calculations of the Council and forced Keyserling to retreat in his efforts towards economic expansion. From the end of the Korean War until the recession of 1953-1954, the economy proceeded without major problems. The Administration's measures designed to counteract the recession of 1953-1954 were centered around tax reduction, an easy money policy, and a faith that the built-in stabilizers would be effective. In sum taxes were reduced by approximately $6.1 billion in fiscal 1954-1955. However, there was little reliance on increased Federal spending; instead, the Administration preferred to rely on the antirecessionary effects of the stabilizers, including transfer payments of various types. Federal Reserve easy money policy included reductions in reserve requirements, an increase in the money supply, and lower interest rates. It seems possible that the recession might have been prevented, or at least substantially mitigated if the Administration had taken more account of the effect of the cut in military spending.

The recession was succeeded by a rapid recovery concentrated in the durable consumer and producer goods sectors of the economy, while the agricultural and soft goods industries remained depressed. The economic expansion of 1955-1957 was sectoral rather than general; wholesale prices of durable consumer goods rose at an annual average rate of 5.5 percent, while agricultural prices fell on the

127

average of 1.7 percent. Wholesale prices of nondurables increased at a rate of 1.6 percent, while the general wholesale price index increased 2.1 percent.

These divergent price trends reveal the spotty character of the economy, characterized by "structural" or "sectoral" inflation. [1] Rising prices in machine tools, electrical gear, and related industries spilled over into other sectors, causing an increase in the general price level. The Eisenhower Administration was aware of these facts, but policy was directed more toward general, rather than selective, credit controls, a policy intended to restrain an over-all pull on costs resulting from an excess of demand throughout the economy. No change was made in tax rates; fiscal policy was aimed at securing a cash budget surplus through a reduction in Federal expenditures while maintaining a fixed level of taxes. Since this committed tax policy to maintaining the status quo, the burden of controlling inflation was placed on a monetary and credit policy designed to create credit constraints by raising interest rates, and by controlling bank reserves via open-market operations, thus preventing an increase in the money supply. No attempt was made by the Federal Reserve System to apply selective credit controls in the capital goods sector, the main source of creeping inflation. Thus, general credit controls, which reduced the credit flowing to the consumer sector and residential construction, while failing to have a strong influence on the capital goods market, had the wrong effect under the circumstances.

The capital goods expansion, coupled with a decline in the demand for its outputs, gave rise to a capital goods recession in 1957-1958. [2] Although industrial capacity rose from 1953 to 1957, the index of manufacturing remained almost stable; and idle capacity became a serious problem. The reaction was, of course, a reduction in capital expenditures which, via the multiplier effect, brought declines in national income, personal consumption spending, and expenditures for inventories. GNP fell from a rate of $410.1 billion in the second quarter of 1957 to $393.1 billion in the same quarter of 1958.

---

[1] See Joint Economic Committee, U.S. Congress *Recent Inflation in the United States* (Washington: Government Printing Office, 1959), and "The Postwar Inflation," *Employment Growth and Price Levels,* 1960, Chap. 5.

[2] See *Economic Report of the President,* 1959, "Economic Developments in 1958 and Outlook for 1959," Chap. 3, pp. 7-32.

Although there was some sentiment in favor of remedial tax reduction, the administration did not take any action other than a passive move to extend excise taxes for one more year. Again, hope was pinned on the automatic stabilizers, combined with accelerated governmental expenditures such as the highway program, expansion in the housing program, and increases in certain transfer payments. These fiscal policies were backed by an easy-money policy, reductions in reserve requirements, and open-market operations. Recovery from this recession was never really strong and by late 1960 the economy had lapsed into recession again.

Although the recession of 1957-1958 was brief, it brought to light disturbing trends which were to be troublesome to both the Eisenhower and Kennedy Administrations. The first of these problems was the contrived rise in prices despite the substantial drop in demand. Whereas in the first two postwar recessions prices had remained fairly stable, both wholesale and retail prices rose in 1957-1958. This phenomenon was explained in part by the long-term wage contracts undertaken in 1956 in durable goods industries, and by the shift in the number of nonproduction workers relative to production workers, which increased overhead costs, (cost-push).

A second, and perhaps even more disturbing, fact was the stubborn refusal of unemployment to fall below 5 percent. Even in 1959, when the economy had recovered fully from the recession, unemployment remained high, concentrated to a considerable degree among older and very young workers, unskilled and minority groups. This fact set off the argument between those who adhered to the structural concept (i.e., that unemployment resulted from technological change and regional shift of industry) and those who maintained that there was an insufficiency of aggregate demand. The Eisenhower Administration attacked the problem by technical assistance to depressed areas, programs of vocational training and retraining, and assistance to small business through the Small Business Administration. In its last *Report* (1961) the Saulnier Council, describing the unemployment situation as "the greatest and most complex challenge to public and private policy," recommended legislation to enlarge the existing programs designed to solve structural unemployment. [3] But by the time the Eisenhower Administration ended, little real progress had been made in this sector.

---

[3] *Economic Report of the President,* 1961, p. 36.

Although the Eisenhower Administration came into office with an intent to balance the budget, it eventually accepted the idea that the budget need not be in balance each year.[4] In fact, the Administration was able to secure a surplus in only three of its eight years in office. Likewise, despite the often expressed desire to curb the Federal debt, it increased $20 billion from 1953-1960.

Another troublesome problem was the accelerating drain on gold. Increasing expenditures abroad for various purposes (largely for aid and for the military) reduced gold reserves from $22.8 billion in 1957 to $17.8 billion in 1960. Despite various measures taken to stem this outflow it continued on a large scale.

Not surprisingly, these problems carried over into the Kennedy Administration, and likewise into the Johnson years. The degree of uniformity with which the Burns-Saulnier Council, the Heller-Ackley Council, and indeed, the Nourse-Keyserling Council before them approached these problems is both surprising and encouraging.

Unemployment: The Kennedy Administration continued to be troubled by "sticky" unemployment, and despite its desire to reach the goal of a full-utilization economy, the gap increased between potential and actual output. The Administration estimated that there was a gap of some $40 billion between potential and actual GNP in 1961 ($518 billion as compared to $558 billion)[5] and the administration sought to close it, putting the economy on the historic track of a real increase in GNP of 3.5 percent per year. Although some progress was made, the success in reducing unemployment was modest at best. (See Fig. 6-1.) Unused potential expanded as large numbers of new workers entered the labor market; unemployment remained around 5.5 percent. The Kennedy Council, concluding that the main obstacle to expansion was the tax burden, declared in its 1963 *Report* that:

> For all its advances, the Nation is still falling substantially short of its economic potential. . . . Private initiative and public policy must join hands to break the barriers built

---

[4]The 1961 Report (p. 59) noted: "A tax system must of course, provide the reserves needed to cover governmental expenditures over reasonable periods, though a balance is not required every year. A budgetary surplus in prosperous times helps to curb inflationary pressures, and a deficit during a period of recession may help to reverse the downturn."

[5]*Economic Report of the President,* 1962, pp. 49-53.

up by the years of slack since 1957 and bring the Nation into
a new period of sustained full employment and rapid economic
growth. . . . The main block to full employment is an un-
realistically heavy burden of taxation. The time has come
to remove it. [6]

This move, via increased spending and the multiplier effect, would,
in the Council's words:

yield rich private dividends in higher output, faster growth,
more jobs, higher profits and incomes; and by the same token,
a large public gain in expanded budget reserves. As the economy returns to full employment, the budget will return to constructive balance. [7]

In general, the Kennedy and Johnson Councils continued the wage
and price policies of the Eisenhower years. The unemployment problem was attacked on two fronts, cyclical and structural. The tax
proposals were especially designed to solve the problem of cyclical
unemployment through increasing aggregate demand, and structural effects were approached through such proposals as the Area
Redevelopment Act and the Manpower Development and Training Act.
The various facets of the poverty program were also directed against
structural unemployment. Despite these measures, unemployment
among certain groups remained troublesome.

Economic Growth: The growth issue has been of major concern to
the CEA since its first days. The Truman Council noted its importance in the January 1947 *Report* which, in the long-range program,
intended to keep "our expanding activity in line with our growing
capacities." By 1950 the desirable growth rate was articulated in
quantitative terms when the proposed annual goal was set at three
percent. The Truman Council made long-range projections of GNP
and constructed a five-year national economic budget to be used as
a framework for projecting long-term growth policies.

By the early part of 1950, the CEA had concluded that the distribution of GNP among private consumption, business investment, and
public needs would not sustain a 3 percent annual growth rate. The

[6]*Economic Report of the President*, 1963, pp. ix and xiii.
[7]*Ibid.*, pp. xiv-xv.

1950-1954 economic budget called for remedial measures, but the Korean War caused this goal to be set aside.

The Eisenhower Council, too, recognized the importance of the growth problem, but was reluctant to put the goal into quantitative terms. In 1955 the Council made a ten-year projection of GNP on the basis of an assumed growth rate of 3 percent, but no national economic budget was published. By 1958, the Council had reached the conservative conclusion that "although the rate of economic growth that is best suited to the nation's capacity and requirements cannot be stated precisely, the low current rate would clearly be unsatisfactory as a continuing condition."[8] Although the administration was unwilling to fix what, in its view, would be an adequate rate of growth, it did embark upon many programs designed to enhance the rate. These programs, in the areas of natural resource development, research and development, aid to health and education, small business, and regional assistance, were all designed to aid long-term growth.

The Kennedy Council was deeply interested in growth (which had been much discussed in the campaign), and devoted considerable space to the subject in the 1963 *Report*. The Kennedy Administration reverted to the Truman practice of stating in quantitative terms what would constitute adequate growth, the 1962 *Report* noting that, in view of the rapidly expanding labor force, a rate of 4.5 percent was well within the capability of the economy.

In dealing with these major economic issues the four Councils have displayed a substantially uniform approach. Naturally, everyone is in favor of growth and stability, but beyond this, the twenty-year performance by four administrations reflects a growing tendency for professional economists to view problems similarly. The Burns-Saulnier approach did not differ materially from that taken by Nourse, Keyserling, Heller, and Ackley. Although one must acknowledge differences in each chairman's system of values and scale of priorities, these were largely forced on him by the exigencies of the situation. One former chairman informally expressed the view that, even after full employment is achieved, the Council must face an endless cyclical task of controlling-inflation-caring-for-unemployment-controlling-inflation. One can conclude that, given the nature of the problems, the quality of advice was quite consistent. The Korean War interfered with some of the goals of the Keyserling

[8] *Economic Report of the President,* 1958, p. 3.

Council, as the Vietnam War has forced a realignment of priority
for the objectives of the Ackley Council; but even with these differences in emphasis, the performance has been surprisingly systematic.
One author, commenting on the performance of the American capitalistic system in recent years, said:

> The achievement of economic stability with a higher rate
> of economic growth will present a considerable challenge to
> the American capitalist system. Securing these economic
> goals will require a willingness to experiment with new poli-
> cies and programs. There are many signs indicating that the
> American people are now in a mood for some experimental
> action. Economic and other problems have come to such a
> head that it is clear to the man in the street that the search
> for solutions to these problems cannot be much longer delayed
> if we are to maintain our position as a world leader. Many
> recommendations have come from business, labor, agricul-
> ture, government, and academic groups as to how economic
> instability may be reduced, economic growth may be promoted,
> and capitalism may be made a more workable system in terms
> of the needs of the second half of the twentieth century. It
> remains to test these recommendations in a pragmatic man-
> ner until the policies and programs that are capable of solving
> these problems are found. Since up to now, the American
> capitalist system has displayed a remarkable capacity to ad-
> just to changing economic circumstances, there is good reason
> to believe that it can make the adjustment required for achiev-
> ing the goal of a stable and adequately growing economy. [9]

Tools and Building Blocks

In attempting to reach its goals, the Council has devised and
adapted to its use various concepts, techniques of measurement and
other tools of analysis, many of which have become integrated into
the body of economic theory. Some of these concepts and their use
by the Council are illustrated by exerpts from the 1967 *Economic.
Report:*

[9]Allan G. Gruchy, *Comparative Economic Systems,* (Boston: Houghton-
Mifflin Co., 1966), p. 151.

The United States in 1966 enjoyed the benefits of the fullest
employment in more than a decade. The unemployment rate
reached a 13-year low of 3. 9 percent. At that level, demand
finally matched supply in most labor markets, a situation
which economists define as essentially "full employment. "

Real incomes of all major groups registered sizable gains.
Expansion continued for the sixth straight year. For the third
successive year, growth exceeded 5 1/4 percent, a record
unparalleled in our postwar experience.

By any standard, then, 1966 was a big year for the economy. Gross national product (GNP) expanded by a record $58
billion in current prices and reached $740 billion. As in the
2 preceding years, a major advance in business fixed investment was a key expansionary force. And the rising requirements of Vietnam added $10 billion to defense outlays. State
and local spending and inventory investment also rose strongly.

As a result, 1966 was in some respects too big a year,
especially in the early months. Spurred by the defense build-
up, total demand—public and private—forged ahead at an ex-
traordinarily rapid rate in late 1965 and early 1966. Strains
developed in financial markets. Demand outstripped supply
in several sectors which were already near full utilization.
. . . many of the new orders simply added to backlogs and put
upward pressures on prices. Some of the excess demands
were met by imports, reducing the U. S. foreign trade surplus
and retarding progress toward equilibrium in the balance of
payments . . .

After years of stimulating demand, policy was called upon
to restrain the economy. The need for restraint was recognized at the start of the year. Monetary policy assumed a
restrictive stance. In anticipation of large increases in private expenditures and defense outlays, tax policies were applied to curb private demand. In 1964 and 1965, an expansionary tax policy had stimulated the economy; but in March
1966, restrictive tax changes were enacted at the President's
request. Excise tax cuts were postponed, and income tax payments were accelerated. Moreover, the President's budget

program in January stringently held down nondefense outlays. These measures produced a Federal surplus in the national income accounts budget and a net restrictive fiscal impact in the first half of 1966, despite the strong advance in defense spending.

But the magnitude of the task was not fully appreciated at the beginning of 1966. As private demand and Vietnam requirements exceeded forecasts, policy was adjusted to the new developments. Monetary policy tightened further, causing a major cutback in homebuilding. In September, the President proposed additional selective fiscal measures to alleviate excessive demands for funds and for capital goods.

The initial restraining measures, reinforced by the previously enacted rise in payroll taxes, began to take effect in the spring. By the closing months of 1966, it was clear that the brakes had worked. The economy had shouldered the burden of active hostilities without the need for cumbersome and inefficient controls and without losing its basic health and stability. It was shown that policy could work both ways; it could restrain the economy, much as it had been able to provide stimulus during the preceding 5 years. In particular, the power of tight money as a tool of restraint—as well as its uneven impact—was demonstrated beyond any reasonable doubt.

As 1967 opens, inflationary forces set in motion during the period of overly rapid expansion are still alive, although their strength is waning. But now there is also a renewed challenge to sustain expansion; any further slowdown would be undesirable.

A healthy advance of demand in pace with the growth of potential output would permit gradual restoration of price stability. It would also promote a recovery in our foreign trade balance, thereby aiding the pursuit of equilibrium in the balance of payments. The fiscal program for 1967 is designed to meet these objectives and to assure that the easing of monetary conditions, presently underway, can be extended. [10]

[10]*op. cit.*, pp. 37-38.

Last year's record of economic gains added in length and
strength to the remarkable uninterrupted expansion that began
early in 1961 (Table 1).   This advance can be viewed in many
dimensions.   Presperity has conferred its benefits on nearly
every sector, industry, and region in almost every year.

Employment Gains

Of all its facets, the growth of employment may be of greatest significance.   Increasing numbers of Americans have obtained opportunities to earn secure livelihoods and to contribute
to the material welfare of society.

Employment in 1966

Employment gains in 1966 were the largest of any year in
the expansion.   Civilian employment increased by 1.9 million,
and 400,000 persons were added to the Armed Forces.   The
civilian unemployment rate fell from 4.6 percent in 1965 to
3.9 percent in 1966, the lowest since 1953.   During the year,
the seasonally adjusted rate remained essentially on a plateau,
fluctuating between 3.7 and 4.0 percent.   The number of persons unemployed dropped by 500,000 in 1966.   Nearly all
groups shared in the reduction, the only exceptions being non-
white females in two age groups, 14-19 and 45 years and over.
Although employment in both of these groups expanded, the
increase was not enough to keep pace with the rapid growth
of these groups in the labor force.

The expansion in the demand for labor extended to every
nonagricultural sector of the economy.   The most remarkable
gains were in manufacturing where the number of jobs rose
1 million from 1965 to 1966.   Since most manufacturing employment consists of high-productivity, high-wage jobs, the
gain contributed to a major advance in real income.   Employment in trade and services and State and local governments
also expanded substantially, rising by about 1 1/2 million
workers in 1966.

The mirror image of the rapid increase in nonagricultural
jobs was a remarkable decline of 400,000 in agricultural em-

ployment in 1966. This decrease of 8 1/4 percent was the largest percentage drop on record, as higher-paying nonfarm job opportunities attracted farmers and hired workers out of agriculture. [11]

The Council has adopted the practice of measuring economic performance against economic potential, and thus speaks of a gap between actual and potential performance (Fig. 6-1). In 1966 the economy was operating at full potential for the first time in several years. [12]

THE REALIZATION OF ECONOMIC POTENTIAL

A major economic accomplishment of 1966 is that the United States made essentially full use of its productive potential. Gone were the chronic underutilization of resources, general excess supply in labor markets, and wastefully idle industrial capacity that had blemished the performance of the economy for a decade. Because of the excessive unemployment and idle capital in previous years, the Nation sacrificed the opportunity to consume and invest a large amount of the output that it was capable of producing. At the trough of the recession in the first quarter of 1961, the "gap" between actual and potential GNP amounted to $57 billion (1966 prices). From 1958 to 1965, the cumulative gap totaled $260 billion (Chart 1).

Five years ago, when unemployment was 6 percent of the labor force, there was clearly an excess supply of labor. Nobody could be sure where balance between supply and demand would be reached. The Council of Economic Advisers, among others, judged that an unemployment rate near 4 percent would (with the existing structure of labor markets) yield approximate balance between the supply and demand for labor. Other experts argued, however, that the economy would run into substantial and significant labor bottlenecks when unemployment fell to 5 percent. Another group contended optimistically that

[11]Economic Report, *op. cit.*, p. 38.

[12]Some statistical problems and techniques are discussed in *The Battle Against Unemployment*, Arthur Okun, Ed. (New York: W. W. Norton & Co., Inc., 1965), esp. pp. 13 ff.

FIGURE 6-1

BILLIONS OF DOLLARS* (ratio scale)

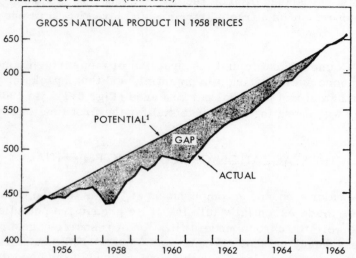

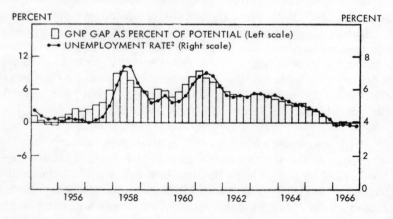

*SEASONALLY ADJUSTED ANNUAL RATES.

[1]TREND LINE OF 3-1/2% THROUGH MIDDLE OF 1955 TO 1962 IV,
3-1/4% FROM 1962 IV TO 1965 IV, AND 4% FROM 1965 IV
TO 1966 IV.

[2]UNEMPLOYMENT AS PERCENT OF CIVILIAN LABOR FORCE,
SEASONALLY ADJUSTED.

SOURCES: DEPARTMENT OF COMMERCE, DEPARTMENT OF LABOR,
AND COUNCIL OF ECONOMIC ADVISERS.

Source: *Economic Report of the President*, 1967, p. 43.

a sufficient expansion of aggregate demand might push unemployment down as low as 3 percent without creating excess demand pressures. The experience of the past year provides a partial answer, suggesting that the 4 percent judgment was nearest to the mark. [13]

If the gap is replaced by a level of production higher than the potential an inflationary condition will persist, until the potential of the economy can be increased. A surge in demand puts pressure on prices and creates serious strains as the economy nears or reaches potential:

STRAINS AND RESTRAINT IN A SURGING ECONOMY

The major theme of recent economic developments is the continuation of progress. But there is also a secondary theme of problems and imbalances, many of which can be traced back to mid–1965, when the sudden increase in defense requirements for Vietnam led to a marked acceleration in economic activity. By the time measures of fiscal and monetary restraint took hold and slowed down the economy, significant problems had developed—an interruption of price stability, a deterioration in international trade performance, acute pressures in financial markets, and sharply divergent movements among the various sectors of the economy.

The Economy in Mid-1965

As of mid–1965, the economy was advancing steadily and healthily toward full employment. GNP had risen by $11 billion a quarter, on the average, for the preceding 2 years; the annual rate of real growth over that period had been 5 1/2 percent. Unemployment was down to 4 1/2 percent of the civilian labor force, and the average operating rate of manufacturing capacity was up to 89 percent. The price record showed few blemishes: average consumer prices in July 1965 were only 6 percent higher than they had been in early 1961, and prices of nonfood commodities had risen by only 3 percent. Prices of manufactured finished products at wholesale had advanced by 1 percent in 5 years.

[13]*op. cit.*, p. 42.

Expansionary fiscal policy had contributed actively to the record of 52 months of advance. The reform of depreciation rules and the investment tax credit, both initiated in 1962, both initiated in 1962, encouraged business to expand and modernize plant and equipment. [14]

The increase in defense spending swelled an already strongly rising tide of business investment expenditures. From the second quarter of 1965 to the first quarter of 1966, business spending for new structures and equipment rose by $9 billion. Defense, investment, and social security liberalization, in combination, speeded the growth of disposable income. Consumer spending responded strongly, growing by $29 billion over this three-quarter interval. All in all, GNP advanced at an average of $16 billion a quarter. Real output grew at a phenomenal annual rate of 7.2 percent, and industrial production rose at an annual rate of 9.7 percent.

Unemployment fell from 4.7 percent to 3.8 percent of the civilian labor force during this period. New orders for durable manufactured goods rose markedly (12 percent), with orders for electrical machinery (20 percent) and defense products (19 percent) increasing especially rapidly.

The surge in demand for goods and labor created pressures on prices in many areas. From October 1965 to July 1966, the annual rate of advance for industrial wholesale prices stepped-up to 3 percent. Prices of industrial crude materials moved sharply upward—at an annual rate of 8 percent from October to April. At the consumer level, demand pressures raised prices of services and nonfood commodities and combined with special supply factors in agriculture to push up food prices. . . . All in all, the economy exceeded reasonable speed limits in the period from mid-1965 through the first quarter of 1966. [15]

The traditional monetary and fiscal controls must be integrated with others to achieve the necessary flexibility of economic policy:

[14] *op. cit.*, p. 45.
[15] *op. cit.*, p. 47.

After years of providing stimulus to the economy, policy changed direction at the turn of the year. Monetary policy accounted for a major share of the restraint during most of 1966. As described in detail below, the Federal Reserve restrained the growth of credit supply in the face of extremely strong demands for borrowing by business. With intense competition for funds, interest rates rose sharply. Institutions which supply mortgage funds to the homebuilding industry lost deposits both to the commercial banks and to the market for new corporate securities. As a result, residential construction was starved for funds, and the sharp decline in this sector was one of the principal moderating influences during the second half of 1966.

Fiscal policy also responded effectively. Although the special defense costs necessarily swelled Federal outlays and were highly stimulative, restrictive actions were taken in other areas Increases in nondefense purchases were held to $300 million from 1965 to 1966. Several restrictive tax measures were proposed in January 1966, and were enacted in mid-March. These included a reinstatement of some of the earlier excise tax reduction, restoring about $1 billion to the annual rate of Federal revenues; and a system of graduated withholding for individual income taxes that drew off $1 1/2 billion (annual rate) from disposable income beginning in May. These new measures followed the $6 billion increase in payroll taxes that took effect at the start of 1966. In addition, revenues were increased in the spring by unusually large payments on 1965 income tax liabilities.

The national income accounts budget for the Federal sector shifted from a deficit at an annual rate of $1 1/2 billion in the second half of 1965 to a surplus at an annual rate of $3 billion in the first half of 1966 . . . (Federal fiscal policy is discussed throughout this Report in terms of the national income accounts budget.)

These monetary and fiscal actions helped to bring the rate of over-all economic expansion in line with the growth of capacity. After the first quarter of 1966, gains in GNP slowed to an average of $12 1/2 billion a quarter, no longer outstripping the growth of potential GNP The unemployment rate leveled off, as employment gains essentially matched the growth of the labor force. Manufacturing output actually rose less than the growth of manufacturing capacity, and average operating rates at year-end were below the 91 percent that had been reached in the first quarter.

The change of pace was first clearly noticeable in the spring. Fiscal restraint appreciably slowed the growth of disposable income in the second quarter and contributed to a marked slow-down in consumer spending. During the summer, consumer demand perked up again. But homebuilding, which had de-clined moderately in the second quarter, was hit hard by the shortage of mortgage financing and took a sharp plunge, hold-ing down the increase in economic activity.

The credit squeeze of 1966 had an impressive and bene-ficial restraining effect on over-all demand. Its side effects were equally impressive but far less beneficial.

These side effects explain in part why relaxation of credit conditions is and has been an objective of policy. The cause of equity was not served by the arbitrary redistribution of in-come produced by very high interest rates or by the adversity experienced in the homebuilding industry. Moreover, the stability of financial markets was at times endangered. While the insurance of deposits and the powers of "lenders of last resort" gave full protection against any recurrence of the financial panics experienced in previous generations, the liq-uidity of portfolios was impaired by rapidly rising interest rates.

Last August, monetary policy was probably as tight as it could get without risking financial disorder. Any further in-crease in over-all demand could not have been effectively countered by general monetary policy. In such a situation, the flexibility of over-all stabilization policy is impaired. It is desirable for both fiscal and monetary policies to be oper-ating from positions where they can move freely either way— toward stimulus or restraint in the event of unanticipated de-velopments.

The main effect of tight money on over-all activity worked primarily through the mortgage market, curtailing home-building and other mortgage-financed construction. In December, expenditures for residential structures were $7 billion (annual rate) below the first quarter level. Homebuilding had been on a plateau during most of 1965 and was rising moderately at the start of 1966. Demand conditions for housing looked fairly encouraging as excess supplies of new housing (especially apartments) that had earlier appeared in certain areas were reduced moderately during 1965. In the absence of tight money, residential construction might have risen slightly further or retreated modestly during the course of 1966; the decline that actually occurred is a reasonable estimate of the impact of the change in credit conditions. By similar reasoning, the performance of commercial and other mortgage-financed types of construction suggests an impact of perhaps $1 billion or more. Monetary restraint probably also had some modest effect on expenditures for producers' durable equipment and consumer durables, but the amount is not evident in aggregate data. [16]

Cessation of hostilities in Vietnam would be the most welcome surprise that could develop in 1967. It would challenge economic policy to smooth the transition—and policy will be ready to meet the challenge. On the other hand, an unexpected increase in outlays required for defense would have important consequences, pointing toward further measures of restraint, particularly from fiscal policy.

A firm set of attainable objectives, a program that fits the present outlook, alertness to changing circumstances, and flexible and well-coordinated use of policy instruments are the necessary means for maintaining full employment and achieving a sustainable advance in 1967.

IMPROVING STABILIZATION TOOLS OVER THE LONGER RUN

The tools of economic stabilization now at our disposal can cope quite effectively with the problems that lie immediately

[16] *op. cit.*, pp. 48-49.

ahead. Over the coming years, however, there is a continuing need to sharpen and improve these policy tools—as well as the institutional framework within which they operate—so that short-term policy can respond efficiently and flexibly to economic fluctuations and simultaneously promote progress along a path of sustainable long-term growth.

Use of Monetary Policy

As a stabilization tool, monetary policy has some distinct advantages. Policy changes can be made quickly in response to changing signals. Furthermore, as was evident in 1966, a restrictive monetary policy can reduce aggregate demand fairly promptly and very sharply.

But there are also distinct limitations on the uses of monetary policy. As demonstrated in 1966 its impact on different sectors of the economy can be highly uneven, both in magnitude and in timing. Moreover, if monetary policy is used repeatedly and in large doses to restrain inflation, it may be difficult to avoid a long-term upward trend in interest rates. And the scope for monetary policy may at times also be limited by balance of payments considerations.

The uneven impact of changes in credit conditions is unavoidable to a certain extent. Monetary policy inevitably has its principal effect on those sectors that are particularly dependent on credit. But the special vulnerability of some sectors to tightening is also importantly related to certain structural characteristics of our financial institutions. Over time, there should be scope for reducing the uneven impact of monetary policy through various modifications in these institutional arrangements. This is particularly true with respect to home-building. [17]

The importance of economic growth was indicated by a chapter (4) devoted to this issue. Education, health, poverty among various age and race groups were discussed at length. The final major element in gauging the welfare of the international economy was treated in Chapter 5, "Growth and Balance in the World Economy. "

[17] *op. cit.*, p. 65.

These are the tools and materials with which economic policy is constructed, and they must be used with care and discretion, since their appropriateness varies from time to time, under differing circumstances. Although the techniques have become standard textbook materials, their successful use involves unique skills and judgment of economic statesmanship. The basic problem is the matter of timing; the fiscal restraint used in the latter part of 1966 was doubtless appropriate then, although there were serious side-effects, whereas it would have been inappropriate in 1952-1953.

Economic growth is an important goal, but it must be pursued with restraint; other matters may arise. The Joint Economic Committee noted in mid-1967:

> All in all, the emergence of rising military expenditures as a phenomenon in the economy creates a heavy responsibility for the administration under the Employment Act of 1946. That act declares it to be the "continuing policy and responsibility of the Federal Government to use all practicable means consistent with its needs and obligations and other essential considerations of national policy * * * *to coordinate and utilize all its plans, functions, and resources for the purpose of creating and maintaining in a manner calculated to foster and promote free competitive enterprise and the general welfare, conditions under which there will be afforded useful employment opportunities, including self-employment, for those able, willing, and seeking to work, and to promote maximum employment, production, and purchasing power. "*

As the committee construes this mandate, it incorporates policies for optimum growth and also for relative stability of prices and wages. A shortfall under either of these objectives would detract from the accomplishment of the act's major purposes.

As a corollary of this, the President has a clear responsibility to take prompt and adequate measures to counterbalance the effects of sudden increases (or decreases) in military requirements. Objectives of growth, full employment, and stability can only be served by timely and adequate action to prepare and recommend policies that are carefully designed to avoid dislocation, and particularly wage-price dislocations.

There should be improved coordination established within the
executive branch to assure these ends, and we commend this
problem to the administration's attention. [18]

For example, in mid-1967 the President recommended a tax surcharge applicable to both corporate and individual incomes, to reduce
the budget deficit and draw off purchasing power, in view of the
unavoidable budget requirements of the war in Vietnam.   Not surprisingly, such a proposal was not popular, and the Congress admon-
ished the administration to reduce domestic spending.   The administration contended such a reduction might impair welfare programs
essential to continued economic growth and social stability.   It is
apparent that the policy questions with which the Council must deal
have many political implications; statistical pitfalls abound, and the
Council's tools are sometimes dull, often fragile, and always dangerous if mishandled.
    The Council faces many difficult tasks, but the first two decades
give cause for encouragement.   Perhaps the most serious challenge
ahead is that the "new economics" has not clearly demonstrated its
ability to handle inflationary problems with the same facility as
deflationary issues.   The second ten years clearly indicate that,
while short-term errors have been made and, in a few cases, the
Council has clearly misread the signs, the over-all record of advice
has been more than satisfactory.   Moreover, in the course of its
lifetime, the Council has made a major contribution to the economist's tool kit which may well prove to be as important as its over-
all operational performance.

[18]*Economic Effect of Vietnam Spending,* Report to the Joint Economic
Committee, U.S. Congress, (Washington: U.S. Government Printing Office,
July 1967), p. 5.

TABLE 1

CHANGES IN ECONOMIC ACTIVITY SINCE 1961

Measure of economic activity	Percentage change per year					
	1961 to 1966	1961 to 1962	1962 to 1963	1963 to 1964	1964 to 1965	1965 to 1966[1]
Production:						
Gross national product, constant prices[2]	5.4	6.6	4.0	5.3	5.9	5.4
Personal consumption expenditures	5.2	4.9	4.4	5.8	6.0	4.9
Business fixed investment . . .	9.7	9.2	4.4	10.6	13.1	11.2
Residential structures	(3)	10.2	4.2	-.8	-2.0	-10.8
Government purchases of goods and services	4.2	7.0	2.0	1.6	2.5	8.0
Federal	3.3	9.9	-.8	-2.9	( )	10.9
State and local	5.2	3.5	5.5	6.6	5.4	5.0
Industrial production	7.3	7.8	5.1	6.4	8.4	9.0
Prices: GNP deflator	1.8	1.1	1.3	1.6	1.8	3.0
Employment:						
Total civilian employment . . .	2.2	1.8	1.4	2.2	2.6	2.6
Nonagricultural payroll employment	3.4	2.9	2.0	2.9	4.2	5.1

[1]Preliminary.
[2]Includes change in business inventories and net exports of goods and services, not shown separately.
[3]Less than .05 percent.

Sources: Department of Commerce, Department of Labor, Board of Governors of the Federal Reserve System, and Council of Economic Advisers.

Source: *Economic Report of the President,* 1967, 1967, p. 39

TABLE 2

CHANGES IN MEASURES OF INCOME SINCE 1961

Measure of income	1961	1965	1966[1]	Percentage change per year[1]	
				1961 to 1966	1965 to 1966
	Billions of dollars				
Compensation of employees	302.6	392.9	433.3	7.4	10.3
Corporate profits:					
Before taxes	50.3	75.7	81.8	10.2	8.1
After taxes	27.2	44.5	48.1	12.1	8.1
Disposable personal income:					
Current prices	364.4	469.1	505.3	6.8	7.7
1958 prices	350.7	530.8	451.5	5.2	4.8
	Dollars				
Farm income per farm:					
Current prices	3,389	4,493	4,965	7.9	10.3
1966 prices	3,684	4,632	4,955	6.1	7.0

[1]Preliminary.

Sources: Department of Commerce, Department of Agriculture, and Council of Economic Advisers.

Source: *Economic Report of the President,* 1967, p. 42

TABLE 3

CHANGES IN GROSS NATIONAL PRODUCT DURING
TWO PERIODS SINCE MID-1965

	Change	
Expenditure category	1965 II to 1966 I	1966 I to 1966 IV[1]
Gross national product	48.3	37.9
Personal consumptions expenditures	28.8	18.8
Durable goods	5.9	-.2
Nondurable goods	12.5	6.8
Services	10.4	12.2
Gross private domestic investment	10.8	3.5
Fixed investment	9.6	-2.0
Business fixed investment [2]	9.1	4.7
Residential structures	.5	-6.7
Change in business inventories	1.3	5.5
Net exports of goods and services	-2.2	-1.2
Government purchase of goods and services	10.7	16.9
Federal	6.3	10.6
National defense	5.5	10.9
Other	.9	-.4
State and local	4.4	6.3

[1]Preliminary.
[2]Nonresidential structures and producers' durable equipment.

Note.—Detail will not necessarily add to total because of rounding.

Sources: Department of Commerce and Council of Economic Advisers.

Source: *Economic Report of the President*, 1967, p. 43

7
THE COUNCIL AFTER TWO DECADES: AN EVALUATION OF FORMAL ADVISERSHIP

Before beginning an evaluation of the Council, it is necessary to examine the organization and mode of operation which have evolved. It is apparent that each chairman has organized the Council in a highly personal way, which is appropriate to an advisory group and has been possible because the Council has remained small and flexible. Throughout its life the Council has followed its original idea of using the services of other Federal agencies and concentrating its own efforts on synthesis and analysis. In recent years the staff has numbered twelve to fifteen persons, a remarkably small number for an agency in operation for twenty years. In addition the Council makes use of part-time consultants (25-30 in recent years), mostly from outside the government.

Staff Qualifications

In most Federal agencies, economists are apt to be oriented towards statistics or empirical economics, their formal training often limited to an undergraduate degree. On the other hand, the Council has maintained high academic standards, while avoiding an ivory tower approach. Apparently, the success of the Council with its professional personnel stems from several factors: (1) The small size and great prestige of the Council makes for a large number of applicants, and the Council can be highly selective. (2) The Council members themselves have many professional contacts, especially in academic circles, and can tap talent nationwide. Almost no one is hired off the street; when a staff vacancy occurs the Council members or staff will usually have a suitable replacement in mind. When a Council vacancy occurs, a list of names is compiled and discussed by the President and the Chairman. The President may make casual inquiries among his contacts and a decision will be reached on the appointment. (3) The academic atmosphere of the CEA makes movement to and from the academic world easier than is the case in most other areas of Federal service.

Obviously, the Council is more than an extension of academic life existing merely for the intellectual pleasure of the staff. It is a

151

pragmatic and hard-working group committed, like all executive branch staff, to long hours and a frantic pace.[1] And the Council must face the frustrations of adjusting its workload to fit the daily or weekly crises facing the Presidency. Although the *Economic Reports* emerge regularly, unforeseen strikes, price incidents, and other emergencies requiring the services of the fire brigade constantly arise. The Council could, of course, assume a minor role in these affairs but the President would lose confidence in it and turn elsewhere for advice. Many have noted that the Council's access to the President is potential, not guaranteed; if the Council wants to be a real part of the operation, its members must undertake a wide range of activities not contemplated by or spelled out in its original mandate.

Presidential Staff Duties

In its early years there was some sentiment expressed that the Council would assume an Olympian, apolitical stance, rendering detached advice upon call. Paul McCracken, a former Council member, has commented on this viewpoint:

> For obvious reasons this was unrealistic. The President's time and energy are two of Washington's most scarce commodities, and a group obviously not a member of the team could hardly expect to get much of the President's time or have much influence on Administration policy. On such a basis, said Roy Blough of Columbia (and a former Council Member) "the influence of the Council might be somewhat above that of a group of university professors with research and publishing facilities, but probably not much above it."[1] On the other hand it was necessary to learn from painful experience that the Council can become too political. In 1952 relations between the Council and the Congress became so strained that appropriations were voted only for operation through the remainder of President Truman's term (January

[1]Several CEA staffers have paid a high price in personal suffering due to the pace and pressure of White House duties.

Roy Blough, "Political and Administrative Requisites for Achieving Economic Stability," *American Economic Review*, Proceedings, (May 1950), p. 176.

1953). Arthur Burns, therefore, actually began his career as an Economic Adviser to the President, and the new Administration then had to take steps to revive the Council. If the Council starts to become too political in the narrow sense of the term, it no longer serves well the Administration or the nation. In a conference with him before I became a member, President Eisenhower said that he wanted from the Council the straight economic advice because otherwise the Administration might start out kidding themselves. This puts very well the danger of the Council's becoming too actively political. Experience has demonstrated that the Council must be on the Administration's team, but it and the Members must preserve their professional status. This is not a wide path, but the Council has successfully kept on it through the Administrations of the last three Presidents.[2]

It is the nature of any organization, governmental or otherwise, to be anxious to extend the scope of its activities. In the White House, where interest in affairs is intense, this tendency is endemic. Consequently, economic activities which, in the Roosevelt days, were carried on by Harry Hopkins, Judge Rosenman, Lauchlin Currie, Isador Lubin, or anonymous White House assistants have fallen into the hands of the Council. Further, the Council, having formulated certain working policies such as the wage–price guideposts, finds itself forced to comment on or defend these policies and thus is more frequently embroiled in day-to-day affairs.[3]

The Council is relatively small and by itself constitutes a modest empire compared to the vast establishments involved in policy creation in the executive branch of the government. On almost every matter of policy there is generally a cabinet officer who is immediately responsible for policy formulation and implementation. Professor McCracken notes that despite this competition the Council is in a strong position:

[2]Paul McCracken, *The Political Position of the Council of Economic Advisors,* address, Western Michigan University, January 19, 1966. (Mimeographed).

[3]Since the guideposts were formulated, the Council has often been involved in wage-price issues. We have seen how the Council played a leading role in the steel price incident in 1962. Since that time, other wage-price issues, such as the New York City transit strike, in 1966 the airline mechanics strike, and steel prices increase also, in 1966, have brought comment from the Council.

The Council is sufficiently well-positioned to have become through the years a major influence on national economic policy. What accounts for this? There are about three major reasons. First, the Council is in the Executive Office of the President, and it reports directly to the President. So long as the President has confidence in the advice he receives, thus having direct access to the occupant of the oval office assures the Council of Economic Advisers an important participation in policy discussions and decisions. Much here depends, of course, on the personal relationship between the President and the Chairman of the Council. Clearly these relationships between Presidents Kennedy and Johnson and Messrs. Heller and Ackley have reflected cordiality and confidence. It was also true for President Eisenhower and Messrs. Burns and Saulnier.

Second, the Members of the Council can meet formally and socially on even terms with other senior Administration officials. This is important. While economists have long been in Government, it was with the Employment Act of 1946 that economists became the Principals of an agency. Thus the wisdom of economics is assured of an opportunity to do its leavening influence in numerous ways. The Chairman regularly attends Cabinet meetings and periodically makes presentations. Members serve on Administration committees, including Cabinet committees. The Chairman and Members of the Council often represent this Government at International meetings. The last Economic Report, in the section reporting on the Council's activities, enumerated at least 47 of these ventures in which Members and staff had been engaged during the year.

Third, the Council has a major impact on policy through its responsibility for the preparation of the Economic Report. This is the Administration's major annual articulation of the case for its programs and policies. And articulation shapes, even makes, policy. Naturally other officials and agencies influence the result, and the Reports inevitably must reasonably reflect the policy posture of the whole Establishment, but there is still a major advantage in holding the pen that is put to paper.[4]

The Council's involvement in current affairs is not without an element of danger: Although the Council must be in the mainstream, when it becomes embroiled in, for example, labor relations commodity price increases, it is open to serious trouble because it is always easier to attack the President's staff than the President himself. In the Roosevelt days, Hopkins, Rosenman and Tugwell were the target of those who did not choose to attack Roosevelt personally. Dr. Steelman absorbed criticism directed at Mr. Truman. Similarly, labor and business leaders who have been reluctant to attack Lyndon Johnson directly have had little hesitancy about attacking the guideposts through Chairman Ackley.[5]

Unfortunately also, the Council like any governmental official or agency can become quickly overexposed. The currency of speechmaking and television appearances is subject to rapid depreciation, and the Council must take care to see that it does not fall into this trap. An additional danger of overinvolvement is that the Council builds up a vested interest and will react subjectively when the almost inevitable opposition arises. All highly-placed officials must guard against this, and the Council is no exception.

The Council and Its External Relations

The pronouncements of the Council and its formal reports have become widely read documents, subject to widespread comment. Council member Arthur Oken testifying before the House Committee on Appropriations noted that sales of the 1965 report amounted to more than 65,000 copies. In 1967 more than 73,000 copies were distributed, and more than 10,000 copies of the monthly publication *Economic Indicators* are sent to members of congress to libraries, and to the general public.[6] Thus, the responsibility of the Council is great and its voice is heard by many.

The Council is again in the limelight when it is called upon for public testimony. It will be recalled that Nourse was reluctant to

[4]McCracken, *op. cit.*
[5]See the Editorial in Fortune, November 1966, "Advisers Should Stick to Advising."
[6]*Economic Report of the President,* 1967, p. 206; 1968, p. 203.

appear before the Congress, but since his day CEA members have often appeared. As their policy-making role has grown, so too has the necessity of defending those policies before Congress and its committees.

The Council has increased its activities also in relation to other Federal agencies. In 1965, for example, it participated in these interagency activities:

Domestic Matters: coordination with Treasury and Bureau of the Budget, and Board of Governors of the Federal Reserve System; participation in a joint effort with the Labor Department, Department of Commerce, and Bureau of the Budget to develop integrated programs on U.S. growth. *International Matters:* the Chairman of C.E.A. served as a member of the Cabinet Committee on the Balance of Payments; The Council was represented on the Trade Extension Advisory Committee, and numerous foreign delegations such as the Organization for Economic Trade and Development (OETD). *Human Resources:* the Council participated in the Economic Opportunity Council, the President's Committee on Manpower, and the Federal Interagency Committee on Education. *Government Statistical Programs:* members of the Council serve on various committees for the improvement of Federal statistical services. In addition, the Council was represented on numerous other bodies interested in defense, consumer interests, and federal credit programs.

In recent years the Council has become much more active in microeconomic matters such as transportation policy which it generally ignored in its earlier years.

In addition to the reports, the CEA has broad public exposure in other ways. Members of the Council appear on television, are the subject of frequent comment in the press, and frequently address professional and business groups. There is no objection to this activity per se, yet there is again, potential danger, and Council members must always be aware of the fact that they wear the Council brand. No matter how much the members emphasized the fact that they speak as individuals, it is evident that this is impossible. Dr. Ackley is identified in the public mind as chairman of the CEA not as a professor of economics at the University of Michigan. His writings prior to the appointment (including a widely-used textbook), are familiar to his professional colleagues, but not to the public. This is even more true of lesser known staff members who have not built a reputation independent of their service on the Council. Dr. Nourse was a man of established reputation within the profession (though not known to the general public) before he was appointed to the Council. Young staff members and some Council members of recent years, although they have high professional qualifications, have no identity outside CEA. Even though an economist may have a professional reputation prior to Council service, his public reputation rests on his Council activities. For example, Arthur Burns, Walter Heller, and James Tobin were well known and highly respected by their fellow economists before their Council service. However, the public and the business community are aware of these men solely in their role as members or former members of the Council. This is, of course, true of all advisers. Paul Samuelson is one of the best known economists in the Country but his *public image* stems from his role as a Kennedy adviser.[7]

A by-product of the high degree of visibility of the Council is the fact that much has been written about it, and this material has been organized to a high degree. In 1956 and again in 1966, on the tenth and twentieth anniversaries of the Act, the professional journals and to a lesser extent, the lay press devoted much space to evaluation and critical analyses of the CEA, the Joint Committee, and the advisory process in general. In 1966 the Joint Economic Committee sponsored a one-day symposium in Washington which featured brief addresses by those who had served on the Council or on the Joint Committee, or who had been instrumental in the passage of the Act. These remarks were printed and circulated. In early fall, a second volume was released, consisting of invited comments on the experience of the Act. In some cases, these were merely comments on what was said in the symposium, although under the title *Directions For The Future*, new ground was broken. Those who appeared at the Symposium were: Congressman Wright Patman, Grover Ensley, Roy Blough, Henry C. Wallich, Leon Keyserling, Arthur F. Burns, Walter Heller, Raymond J. Saulnier, Kermit Gordon, Paul W. McCracken, Bertram Gross, Gerhard Colm, Neil Jacoby, John W. Lehman,

---

[7]Even this fame is, of course, narrow compared to widely-known public figures. A street corner poll would probably turn up only one person out of ten thousand who could identify Gardner Ackley or Walter Heller, as opposed to Frank Sinatra, ZaZa Gabor, or Mickey Mantle!

Edwin G. Nourse, Theodore Kreps, Karl Brandt, George Outland, James Tobin, Stephen K. Bailey, James Stieber, Sidney Konetz, Louis M. Mather, Richard Long, William Freund, James W. Knowles, Senator Paul H. Douglas, and Representative Thomas H. Curtis. All of these men were closely associated with the Act or with its administration by the Council or the Joint Committee. The volume of invited dissertations, on the other hand, contains comments from many outside the circle of active participants, most of whom are academic economists.[8] The analysis of the operation of the Council leans heavily upon these comments.

In general, the Council and the Act were not severely criticized. Many commentators suggested minor alterations or additions to the structure of the Council or Joint Committee designed to improve forecasting or promulgation of policy. For ease of presentation the comments will be divided into two categories: those relating to the administration of the Act as it now exists, and those relating to proposed changes of a more philosophical nature in the structure of the Act.

In the first category, recommendations relate to several facets of Council procedure. Professor Kendrick for example wonders if the CEA should not enlarge its staff and extend its intra-agency contacts.[9] A statistician, Professor Schmidt,[10] notes the importance of improved statistical gathering methods, a point noted also by former Chairman Burns.[11] Very little was said about the administration of the Act per se, and almost nothing about the organization of the Joint

---

[8]These were: William R. Allan, James W. Angell, Joseph Ascheim, William J. Baumol, Nevins D. Baxter, George H. Borts, Walter S. Buckingham, Morris A. Copeland, Elinor S. Daniel, Leo Fishman, William G. Freund, Seymour E. Harris, Water W. Heller, Werner Z. Hirsch, John W. Kendrick, Leon H. Keyserling, C. P. Kindleberger, Philip A. Klein, Stanley Lebergott, Mark W. Liserson, Paul W. McCracken, Stephen L. McDonald, C. A. Matthews, Vernon A. Mund, Hugh S. Norton, Edwin G. Nourse, Frank C. Pierson, Walter S. Salant, Emerson P. Schmidt, Richard N. Schmidt, Martin Schnitzer, Beryl Sprinkle, Herbert Stein, H. Christian Sonne, Philip Taft, William W. Tongue, Robert Triffin, G. J. Viksnins, Jerry Voorhis, Charles E. Walker, Murray Weidenbaum, Leland B. Yeager.

[9]Invited Comments, *Directions for the Future*, Supplement to Hearing, Joint Economic Committee, 89th Cong., 2nd Sess., Washington, D. C. 1966, p. 76.

[10]*Ibid.*, p. 31.

[11]Twentieth Anniversary Symposium, *op. cit.*, p. 32.

Committee. Either these matters are proceeding satisfactorily or they were not considered sufficiently important to merit consideration in light of other more pressing problems.

In the relationship of the Council to other agencies, two major problems were cited. First is the seeming lack of coordination between the Council and the monetary authority; second is the lack of direct reference in the Act to international financial relations. These two problems have assumed major importance in recent years. Both were noted by several commentators: Professors William R. Allen, James W. Angel, Leo Fishman, and Seymour Harris.[12] Especially troublesome was the lack of coordination between the Board of Governors and Administration policy as promulgated by the Council. These problems were by all odds the most serious mentioned.

The problem of Federal Reserve independence is not new and it is only indirectly related to the operation of the Act of 1946. To the degree that the CEA takes part in the administration program, and to the degree that Federal reserve policies inhibit that program, then the Council is involved. It is however, possible (though not probable) that CEA might uphold Federal Reserve policy even in the face of Presidential dissatisfaction since the Council must take Federal Reserve policy into account as part of the total picture.

Matters are somewhat more clear and opinions more uniform in the case of international effects. Given the conditions which existed in 1946, it is understandable that international financial problems of the United States, were expected to play a minor role in the deliberations of the Council. A strong case can be made for incorporating remedial provisions for adequate international economic management into the Act in the near future.

One of the strongest theoretical critics was Leon Keyserling, who questioned present policy in many areas. He found fault with the Council for refusing to take a more active position in promoting issues of policy or politics. In the Keyserling view, economics should "move beyond forecasting toward purposeful policy, and increasingly from defensive to affirmative action." In general he advocates a return to the procedures he himself advocated as Chairman, saying:

> . . . if the CEA is not to lapse into innocuous desuetude in the decade ahead, but instead rise to the full responsibilities of its

[12]Invited Comments, *op. cit.*

key relationship to the Presidency, it needs to move vigorously along these lines:

First, the Council should reinstate its earlier practice of projecting in quantitative terms, needed levels of employment, production, and purchasing power. It must do this, to obey the law. It should do this, because to say we need more jobs or teachers—but not how much more—is no sufficient guide to resource allocation or national economic policy. Second, the Council should set forth and evaluate the Federal budget as an integral part of the Nation's economic budget. Third, the Council's projections should not be limited to the major components of gross national product, but in addition should state quantitatively our basic national priorities and appraise their relative economic cost and necessity. Fourth, the Council should make these projections on a long term basis—5 years or longer—recognizing that we cannot live safely today unless we look ahead. Glowing forecasts for 1965, unaccompanied by indicating the policy road to be traveled year by year to get there, smack of demagoguery rather than leadership. Fifth, the Council should realize that it is not primarily an economic research agency, nor a statistical refinement agency, nor an interpreter of past trends, nor a pure forecasting agency. Drawing of course upon these resources and techniques, it is primarily an agency to help determine needs and evolve policies and programs. . . .

The worldwide situation now is even more parlous than in 1956, and is imposing heavier responsibility upon the U.S. economy for as far ahead as we can see. Deficiencies in many domestic public services and facilities have accumulated further since 1956. Poverty and deprivation among our people have been reduced since 1956 in absolute numbers, but in terms of the new and legitimate expectancies of the victims measured against our rising economic capabilities, the serious problem of 1956 has been converted into the crisis of 1966.

During the 10-year interval, some nations living under the institutions of freedom have done a much better job than we have done, in striking a proper balance between flexibility and planning between individual initiative and public responsibility, between variegated discrete purposes and core national purposes. Above all, some of these nations have done better than we have, in bringing their programmatic efforts closer to their verbal aspirations.

Twenty years after its creation, the Council of Economic Advisers is showing signs of becoming impeded by the inertia and complacency which tend to afflict the relatively elderly Government agencies, instead of recognizing that CEA is still in the infancy of developing the Employment Act into what it was intended to be and should be.

One sign of this premature aging is the propensity of some members of the Council in recent years to publicize how much more attention and acceptance the Council has received in recent years than during its first years. Whether this claim be true or excessive, it is entirely beside the point. The most important test of an agency like CEA is not how smoothly it is getting along, but rather what it is trying to do. I think that the time has come for some to combine more modesty with more enterprise; more testing of what is now being done in terms of what is now needed; and fewer self-serving comparisons between what has happened recently and what happened 20 or 15 years ago.

We live in an age when technology is changing rapidly; when knowledge is growing greatly; when expectancies are rising at a revolutionary rate. Fortunately in the United States, and unlike the situation in some unhappy lands, we have the native endowments and the economic resources to confront these challenges and even to surmount them. But to do so, we must let our minds be bold; and nowhere is this more essential than in the formulation of the national economic policies which encompass perhaps the largest share of responsibility for the future of our Nation and our people.[13]

Keyserling was also concerned with the guideposts, noting that they were apt to slow down the pace of economic progress. Most were

---

[13]Invited Comments, *op. cit.*, p. 84-85.

less critical. Former Chairman Heller has no "burning desire" for change in the formal organization of economic advice in government, although he sees the situation as fluid and is not committed to the status quo.[14]

There was surprisingly little criticism of the structure of the Council and the Joint Committee. Representative Curtis expressed some concern about how those who oppose Council policies can effectively register their dissent, and suggested the establishment of a body to serve as a vehicle for broad-gauge economic analysis and collection of views for various groups.

In terms of fundamental change, a strong case has also been made to amend the Act to take more cognizance of the goal of economic growth. Although the Act of 1946 does not mention growth as a goal, there is no doubt about the priority the Council has accorded growth policies, nor of the importance attached to growth by the profession.[15]

Problems of Staffing and Organization

These problems are somewhat similar to those of the Joint Committee and will be noted in Chapter 8. However, the CEA's problems center more around the pressure of the job and the long hours necessary than the relatively low salaries and inadequate space which vex the Joint Committee staff. The common problems of the two groups will be noted below. It seems more than likely that the prestige which accrues to the professional economist who spends some time on the Council, coupled with the challenge of his assignment, act to overcome the disadvantages cited. No serious staff problems have come to light, and the quality of personnel has remained high.

No doubt the passage of time will bring about changes in the organization of the Council as was done in the case of Reorganization Plan No. 9 which gave the Chairman more authority. New conditions and new personalities will make change necessary.

Some doubt about the ultimate future of the Council has been raised by the proposed merger of the Departments of Commerce and Labor

[14]Heller, *op. cit.*, p. 56

[15]Eg., Herbert Stein and Edward F. Denison, "Economic Growth as a National Goal," *The Goal of Economic Growth*, Edmund S. Phelps, Ed. (New York: W. W. Norton & Co., Inc. 1962).

into Department of Economic Affairs. What will result from this proposal remains to be seen.

In the twenty years of its existence the Council has faced many problems both of philosophy and of organization and while its solutions have seldom met with universal acclaim, the experiment of formal economic advice on the highest level of government has been, on the whole, highly successful. The Council is, as such organizations go, very young. It has been forced to develop its philosophy and its goals as it went along. And it has had to do this, not in the calm of academia, but in the political arena during perhaps the most momentous years in American history. Again, Professor McCracken comments:

> As we look at the Council of Economic Advisers during its two decades of operation, certain conclusions begin to emerge about this aspect of our new venture into the operation of economic policy. The Council of Economic Advisers—obviously operating in a political arena—must be, and be considered, a part of a political team if [Council members] are to influence policy. At the same time they must not become so narrowly political as to jeopardize their status as professional economists, and they may be doing their greatest political service by using their discipline to discourage short-run measures that—whatever their immediate appeal—would only produce long-run economic (and political) problems.
>
> And we must always remember that the Council of Economic Advisers came into being as part of a bold, path-breaking political commitment to give the quality of the nation's economic performance a high priority on the national agenda. We may not thereby have resolved all of our problems, but Beardsley Ruml put it well when he told the Senate Committee that this "statement of the goal and our sincere efforts to attain it will make the reality much closer to the ideal than if the ideal had never been expressed." [16]

The Council in twenty years has done much to make this come to pass.

[16]McCracken, *op. cit.*

8
THE ECONOMIST IN THE CONGRESS AND THE REGULATORY COMMISSIONS

As in the presidency, the economic policy role of the Congress has in recent years become much more demanding. The Congress has not been willing to let the executive take the lead entirely in this regard, and has accordingly expanded its own means for securing advice. In the regulatory commissions, the importance of economic analysis was from the first recognized as an important function, although it has not always been carried out as well as it might be.

Organization of the Congress for Economic Matters

Like other legislative matters, those concerning economics have their origin in the various congressional committees, and advice is generally given, not to the Congress as a whole, but to a committee.

In addition to the committees listed in Table 8-1 there are several special committees oriented toward economics such as The Select Committee on Small Business and, of course, the Joint Economic Committee. Other committees, such as the Joint Committee on Space Sciences, have strong economic influence, although they are organized for other purposes. In addition, the Judiciary Subcommittee on Monopoly, and the Joint Committee on Internal Revenue Taxation fill their parent committee's economic functions.

In both houses there are committees which do not deal directly with economic matters but whose approval is essential for any legislative program. The House Rules Committee may be a key element in deciding a program's future, and in both houses the Appropriations Committees can decide the fate of a program by their action in appropriating funds.

In pursuing its legislative goals, Congress has several procedures which have frequently led to legislation influencing economic policy. Perhaps the most dramatic of these is the *power to investigate*. Congress has often been faced with situations, such as in 1907 when

165

TABLE 8-1
STANDING CONGRESSIONAL COMMITTEES HAVING
MAJOR ECONOMIC POLICY RESPONSIBILITIES

Senate	House
Agriculture and Forestry	Agriculture
Appropriations	Appropriations
Banking and Currency	Banking and Currency
Commerce	Education and Labor
Finance	Interstate and Foreign Commerce
Judiciary	Judiciary
Labor and Public Welfare	Merchant Marine and Fisheries
Public Works	Ways and Means

Source: *Congressional Directory,* 90th Cong., 1st Sess., January 1967.

regulation in the banking and financial field was clearly needed, but considerable information was required before legislation could be approached intelligently. The famous Aldrich Commission was the solution to this problem, providing the basis for the Aldrich-Vreeland Act of 1908, which created the National Monetary Commission and ultimately led to the Federal Reserve Act in 1913. Financial panic, scandal in an industry, or similar disturbances stir the Congress to undertake an investigation.[1] Pure food and drug laws, as well as most of the legislation regarding finance, banking, and labor, have been the fruit of congressional investigation. The investigative power has some advantages other than informing the legislators.

[1]This is a broad hunting license. On occasion, questions have been raised concerning the legislative purpose of an investigation, but in economic matters there has been no major instance where such questions were raised successfully. See Bertram Gross, *The Legislative Struggle* (New York: McGraw-Hill Book Co., Inc., 1953).

It provides a national forum for dramatizing what would be in most cases a dull, disregarded subject; and, while investigations have been known to get out of hand, the net results are probably on the positive side of the ledger.

The *hearing* is the official ear of the legislature and again is part of the learning process. Hearings usually result from the need to explore the desirability of new legislation or the proposed amendment of existing legislation. Most matters coming before Congress are complex and the hearing provides a forum for interested parties to get their views on record, as well as an opportunity for the members to become educated about the problems involved. In 1952, as we have seen, the Joint Committee on the Economic Report undertook to study the problems surrounding the management of the national debt in order to settle the dispute between the Treasury and the Federal Reserve System. The report of this study runs to more than thirteen hundred pages and is a major compendium of opinion of the matter.

To supplement the information generated at hearings, the professional staff of the various committees prepares material and, from time to time, engages special study groups of outside experts to prepare *special reports*. In recent years, an active committee has been the Subcommittee on Antitrust and Monopoly of the Committee on the Judiciary. This committee, under the aggressive leadership of the late Senator Kefauver, published a study on administered pricing which ran to twenty-nine volumes. [2] In addition to the committee's own professional staffs, the members have access to other Federal employees and academic consultants expert in the field. The very quantity of material available might preclude its being read with care, and this is frequently the case. Obviously, the educational process is most often oral and the members sometimes show evidence of being swayed by the rhetoric of a witness in contradiction of evidence which has gone before. Clearly, also, some of the witness testimony will be "chaff" and larded with meaningless platitudes. The special studies and staff reports, on the other hand, are quite likely to be more sophisticated.

A relatively minor device which can occasionally be used to influence policy is the power of the Senate to *advise and consent* with regard to certain Presidentially-appointed officials. Relatively

---

[2] *Administered Prices,* Subcommittee on Antitrust and Monopoly of the Committee on the Judiciary, U. S. Senate, pursuant to S. Res. 57.

little can be done in this manner, but there are infrequent occasions when an agency head who would promulgate an unpopular philosophy may be refused the Senate's approval. The economist has played an increasingly effective role in these procedures, and there is evidence that his role is expanding.

Economic Philosophy of the Congress

Aside from the very broad concepts of private enterprise, economic freedom, etc., Congress as a whole has no consistent economic philosophy. The most important reason for this is the fact that the outlook of the Congress is essentially regional. No Senator, and certainly no Representative, can disregard the basic economic activities of his state or district. Senators from Texas and Oklahoma, for instance, are concerned about oil depletion allowances, though they may be anti-big business on other matters; a Representative from upper Michigan may give much attention to farm problems while his colleague from Detroit is concerned about the effect of automation or import tariffs on the automobile industry.

In addition to this regional orientation, the economic policy which emerges from legislation may bear the personal stamp of those in strategic positions. However, no Senator, even a powerful committee chairman, stands alone, and the essence of legislative procedure is accommodation and compromise. Few bills which concern controversial economic matters emerge from Congress in a form which the sponsor would consider ideal, but he may get all he can reasonably expect. On a few occasions, when some unusual situation has occurred, public sentiment may be so strong that the Congress is almost forced to act, and regional or personal forces count for very little. Usually public sentiment is generated by only the more emotional issues, but the Interstate Commerce Act in 1887 and the securities legislation in 1933 were provoked to a large extent by the opinion of the citizenry.

Legislators, not being economists, are naturally limited in their understanding of sophisticated economic affairs relating to debt management, international trade, budget policy, etc. Of course, most legislators espouse the basic economic prejudices (debt is bad, gold is good, free enterprise should be encouraged, etc.), but thus so lightly armed with theory, most congressmen are strictly empirical economists. Since most men who come to Congress have reached maturity, fundamental change in their economic and social philosophies is unlikely, but there is usually a movement toward a more

worldly view, especially among senators, who must take a more
ecumenical viewpoint. Some members view any departure from
laissez-faire with considerable suspicion, while others favor social
legislation and government activity. However, there is always a
high degree of flexibility to accommodate the facts of political life;
local interests must be looked after, even at the expense of policy.
It is far from unusual to find a liberal, cosmopolitan statesman
taking a rather provincial stance on oil, silver, peanuts, or some
other "essential" product. As Stephen Kemp Bailey has commented:

The fate of any piece of legislation cannot be understood
without an appreciation of the fact that Congressmen are people, with all that that banality implies. Like the rest of us
they become bored by tedious debates, angered by personal
affronts, inspired by the words of leaders they respect, irritated by the weather, confused by technical problems, upset
by domestic misunderstandings or the illness of loved ones.
Like any cross-section of the American public, they have been
molded in their thinking by scores of influences: parents,
teachers, friends, enemies, social status, occupation or profession, personal successes and failures, adult associates,
regional interests, local opinions, party loyalties, and the
general social, economic, moral, and intellectual milieu of
their generation and culture.

The process of personal growth and change continues, of
course, after a Congressman is elected to the national legislature. There he is subject to a series of new pressures and
experiences, and a new perspective is virtually forced upon
him if he remains for any length of time. The interests of
Podunk come to be seen in relation to the interests of a thousand Podunks and a hundred Metropols; the Congressman
meets men of experience and knowledge greater than his; he
finds reinforcement for some of the ideas he holds and lack of
reinforcement for others; he notes consciously or uncon-
sciously the colleagues with whom he feels at ease and whose
judgments he respects; he reevaluates his own capacity for
leadership; he becomes acutely aware of the frustrations of the
legislative process and the few moments in each session when
his decisions may mean the success or failure of a policy
which will affect millions of people. If at times he tends to
overestimate his own importance in the scheme of things, there

are scores of reminders, official and personal, that he is like
the drunken poet who wandered into the zoo congratulating himself on being the highest product of evolution until finally he
became sober enough to recognize that after all he was just 'a
little man in trousers slightly jagged.' Congressional service
is a form of higher education.

But by and large, the basic social philosophy of a legislator
is set before he comes to Congress. It is for this reason that
the study of a legislator from the Washington perspective alone
is bound to be one-dimensional.[3]

Congressional Blocs

Socioeconomic sentiment in Congress divides roughly along the
lines of political affiliation (Republican-Democrat), regionalism
(North-South, urban-rural), and philosophy (conservative-liberal),
but only very roughly. As often as not, a congressman is obliged
to betray one of his loyalties to accommodate another. Thus, a
senator from a large Eastern city might be personally conservative
but vote with the liberal Democrats on some major issues; or a
conservative Southern Democrat may find himself voting with the
Midwestern Republicans more frequently than with Northeastern
Democrats. And aside from these institutional factors, personal
considerations are always potential influences; for example, a senator who nurses Presidential ambitions may vote more liberally
than he did before he became interested in higher office. Although
in rare instances the party leadership may put the heat on, congressional opinion regarding economic matters usually divides along
other than partisan lines.

Economic Pressures on Congress

Like the President, Congress has to deal with pressures; but
unlike his, the pressures are rather direct and specific. The congressman, representing a relatively small area and a narrow consti-
tuency, can usually be certain of the safe position on any question,
but is hence rather bound to that position. A senator's problem is
more complex. Where, for example, both agricultural and indus-

---

[3]Stephen Kemp Bailey, *Congress Makes a Law* (New York: Columbia
University Press, 1950), pp. 190 ff.

trial interests are powerful, a senator will, on many issues, find no position safe. Besides the intrinsic conflict, lobbies and pressure groups will threaten and cajole, attempting to bring pressure to bear. In a day, a senator may talk to a half-dozen groups and get as many viewpoints on how he should vote on a given bill. Many issues, particularly economic issues, cut across party or regional lines, becoming truly national. An excellent example is the debate on price controls immediately following World War II. Some argued that if price controls were removed, goods would quickly become available and prices would fall; other, apparently equally well-informed, held that this process would require so much time that great damage would be done to the economy. Public sentiment did not divide along any traditional lines; strong feeling was evident on both sides of the question; there was no clear-cut, statesmanlike path to follow. This points to the heart of the problem. A member of Congress who is merely a tool of a given industry, who simply goes down the line for his own narrow interests, or who blindly pursues a dogmatic ideology, faces no problem. On the other hand, one who attempts to serve the long-range national interest in economic matters may find no clear-cut course to follow.

Sources of Advice

Congressional committess or individual members seeking economic counsel, may utilize many sources, including friends at home, former business associates and, not infrequently, economists from the staff of Federal agencies. It was not until recently, general practice to keep professionals on the regular staff, other than as committee counsel.[4] The regular committee was seldom organized to handle other than routine matters. However, some extensive, high-level work was performed by special committees or commissions staffed by outside professionals. Notable among these was the afore-

[4]Even in recent years numbers have been small. An informal count in 1962 put the number of economists on committee staff at five, exclusive of the Joint Committee. (See John M. Blair, "Lawyers and Economists in Antitrust: A Marriage of Necessity if Not Convenience." American Bar Association: *Proceedings,* (1962), vol. 20. No doubt members have recourse to advice from economists who are not on any congressional payroll. Often economists from lobby groups play such a role, as do economists from universities and foundations. Quite frequently these economists appear as witnesses in hearings.

mentioned Aldrich Commission study of the money and banking situation, and the famous Pujo Committee which produced the ultimate Federal Reserve Act.

Congressional economic thinking was much stimulated by the market crash and depression in the 1930's. More perceptive members began to reflect on the evolution of the economy since 1920, and the serious lack of pertinent information. Out of this dearth was born the Temporary National Economic Committee in the Senate, which was a minor landmark in the economic history of Congress. Created in June 1938, the TNEC was part of the New Deal campaign against monopoly. Under its auspices, many hearings were conducted into the operation of business enterprise, price policy in industry, and other facets of the economy, attempting to explain price rigidity. Never before had there been such a thorough study of industrial organization. The committee not only influenced congressional economic policy for a number of years, but also had considerable impact upon academic economics (for years, TNEC findings were staple fare for economics textbooks). It served, too, as a springboard for individuals who would later be major formulators of economic policy; Senator O'Mahoney of Wyoming, for instance, a leading figure in the TNEC, later sponsored the Act of 1946. Economists who served on TNEC often showed up in other agencies in later years; others returned to academic life and have made major contributions to the literature on the subject. Those serving were: Oscar Altman, H. Dewey Anderson, Louis Bean, Theodore Bedesman, John M. Blair, Emile Despres, Nathan Engler, Mordecai Ezekiel, Kermit Gordon, Clifford James, Leon Henderson, Edward S. Mason, Robert Mongomery, Saul Nelson, George W. Stocking, Myron H. Watkings, and Clair Wilcox.

The lack of information regarding the causes of the depression also caused Congress to give serious consideration to an economic council, and to hold hearings on S-2309, a bill introduced by Senator Robert M. LaFollette, Jr. Many witnesses appeared; among the notable economists or economic writers who testified were E. A. Goldenweiser, J. M. Clark, Wallace B. Donham, Lewis L. Lorwin, John A. Ryan, George Soule, Leo Wolman, Virgil Jordan, Paul M. Mayer, J. Russell Smith, Walter W. Stewart, and J. Frederick Dewhurst. They were in almost complete agreement about the need for such a council. J. F. Dewhurst outlined in great detail the areas in which lack of economic knowledge was a serious barrier to progress. Professor Clark presented a carefully-formulated plan:

This proposed the creation, by the Federal Government, of a body to gather and analyze economic data and make plans and proposals. To perform this function he suggested that the body be composed of persons "whose qualifications should be defined in terms of things they have expert knowledge about, or experience with, rather than the interests they represent." Since the problems of organization vary between industries, administration should be assigned to industrial councils in each industry made up of representatives of management, labor force, and the consumers of its products. Their duties—

> might run all the way from the mere extension of trade association functions with a more adequate gathering and use of statistical knowledge for the guidance of trade policies, without power to control supply and control prices * * * to setting up consolidated organizations which would have the status of public utilities and be subject to the same kind of control of price and service, or even beyond that. [5]

Obviously Congress was searching for some means of coordinating the economic policy then being carried on by various agencies, but no action was taken until 1946 when the Employment Act was passed.

The Senate also became much concerned about the unemployment problem, and in 1934 the Committee on Education and Labor, aided by the Brookings Institution, investigated the subject of unemployment insurance. Witnesses included industrial leaders and the well-known labor economist, Professor John R. Commons of the University of Wisconsin. TNEC and other undertakings of such scope are rare. An obvious requirement is a Senator or Congressman who has interest in a problem and the power to push it through.

Two fields, monopoly and public finance, have apparently consistently concerned the Congress, provoking more or less continuous research. The Joint Committee on Internal Revenue Taxation has carried on basic research in public finance employing such economists as its influential Chief of Staff, Lawrence W. Woodworth. The Antimonopoly Subcommittee, an offshoot of the TNEC, is directed by John M. Blair, a veteran of long service on Capitol Hill.

[5] Isador Lubin, "The New Lead from Capitol Hill," *The Survey*, March 1, 1932.

As we have noted above, professional economic advice to individual congressmen in the days of small office staffs was a luxury few could afford. An affluent member often acquired additional staff at his own expense, but most members were hard pressed to make do with the funds provided. It was common practice, however, for a member who served as chairman of a committee to carry some of his personal staff assistants on the committee payroll. Thus, a Senator who served as chairman of the Committee on Money and Banking for example, might employ through the facilities of the committee staff an economist as a personal adviser. In the absence of an advisory arrangement, members of Congress usually had to depend upon less reliable sources for information on economic matters, if they were to have any information at all.

The Legislative Reference Service and Other Expert Sources

Since 1946, the Legislative Reference Service of the Library of Congress has been available to Congressmen and prepares brief analyses and reports upon request.[6] The service employs a professional staff including economists who, with the vast facilities of the library behind them, can quickly provide reasonably authoritative information on any subject. For example, in 1964, members of Congress commissioned reports on such economic questions as poverty, public finance, money and banking, international trade and tariffs, labor, transportation and communication, agricultural policy, and natural resources, and on subjects such as Medicare.[7] The L.R.S. is a valuable adjunct to the economic information services available to Congress, but there is no indication that its economists have had a policy role. In addition to this service, the member has access at least in theory to the vast store of expert information in the executive and regulatory agencies. Taken together, the Departments of Defense, Agriculture, Commerce, the Interstate Commerce Commission, etc., have experts in residence on almost every subject of interest to the legislator.

[6]In fact, this service was first made available on a limited scale in 1916, but was formalized and expanded in 1946 (Sec. 203, Legislative Reorganization Act of 1946).

[7]Library of Congress, *Annual Report*, 1964.

Lobby Groups and Advice

Information on various industries is available from the numerous lobby groups who are represented in Washington and many of their activities can qualify as economic research. There are few qualified economists on lobby froup staffs. These groups provide basic data but their interpretation is, of course, not reliable. [8] More unbiased groups such as the National Planning Association are also' available but their staffs are generally too small to perform research tasks on call. However, they are useful for their over-all studies and they are generally unbiased. It is likely that groups such as N.P.A., Brookings, and the C.E.D. have had a greater degree of influence over legislation than appears on the surface. For obvious reasons, the effectiveness of the economist employed by a lobby group is not easily measured. No doubt there have been cases where a well-informed lobby representative has performed an advisery role apart from his other functions, and to this extent he must be considered an adviser, but such cases are rare. A member of Congress must view the advice of the trade association representative with a wary eye and balance it against his other sources of information, *The Joint Economic Committee and Congressional philosophy.*

As we have seen, economic matters fall within the jurisdiction of the appropriate committee and the basic work of economic analysis is performed on that level. Keeping in mind what has been said, let us turn now to the policy role of the Joint Economic Committee. A member of the Congress who aspires to sit on a given committee is generally motivated either by the desire to occupy a powerful position of prestige or by a strong interest in the subject under consideration by the Committee. Appropriations or Foreign Relations are probably the best examples of the first motive; Agriculture, Education, and Labor are typical of the second. Unless his motives are strong, committee service has limited attraction to the member since he must spend long hours in tedious hearings, listening to testimony which is often trivial and repetitious. If he is to be effective. he must spend considerable time preparing himself. In most

[8] A good picture of lobby activities is presented is Lester Milbrath, *The Washington Lobbyists* (Chicago: Rand McNally Company, 1963). One source lists 188 organizations, but this list is not complete. See C. P. Cotter, *Government and Private Enterprise* (New York: Holt, Rinehart, and Winston, 1960), Appendix I. See also, *Congressional Record,* Vol. 110, No. 166, August 31, 1964, 10-80 ff.

cases, the time and energy spent is of little use in directly representing his constituents, unless matters of importance in his state or district are directly related; usually the matters dealt with are too broad to be relevant.

With these thoughts in mind, what of the Joint Committee? First of all, the Joint Committee is unique, since unlike most committees it has jurisdiction over the whole economy. Most (economically-oriented) committees are concerned with some specific phase of the economy (agriculture, transportation, monopoly, etc.). The province of the Joint Committee is the aggregate economy. Consequently the member is concerned with the national interest in the broadest sense, and cannot gain political advantage by pointing to what he has done for potatoes, peanuts, or beef. On the contrary, he has ample opportunity to step on the toes of powerful economic interests. Successful service involves hard work in a difficult area.

> The task of the Joint Economic Committee is as difficult as it is novel in our frame of government. If taken seriously, it entails long and painstaking work and does not carry emoluments of power or prestige (like the Appropriations, Defense, or Foreign Affairs committees). Its requirements are not met by the technical competence of the lawyer or the flair and experience of the politician. It calls for training and practice in the fields on economics, business, finance, and social psychology. The senator or representative who gives the needed measure of time and thought to the work of this committee must not merely curtail to that extent the effort given to legislative work and to rendering personal (and sometimes menial) service to the claims of his constituents or to mending his political fences. Beyond this, he is sure sooner or later, in larger or smaller measure, to find himself, in seeking to advance the national economic interest most soundly, to be refusing support to or actively opposing a pet project of his state or district or of a special interest group that is strongly represented among his constituents. [9]

Service on the Joint Committee presents many problems and few rewards.

[9]Nourse, *Economics in the Public Service,* pp. 429-30.

Fortunately the Committee, particularly in its early years, has had members and chairmen who were deeply interested in its success, and most senior members also serve on other economic committees providing opportunity for considerable cross-fertilization of ideas, (also for some jurisdictional disputes which fortunately have been kept to a minimum). For example, on the original committee, Senator Taft served on Finance, and was chairman of Labor and Public Welfare; Ball was on four committees including Appropriations; Flanders on three including Banking and Currency. On the House side, Patman served on Banking and Currency; Bender on two, including Public Works; and Wolcott was chairman of Banking and Currency. In the early period, there were some problems regarding the relationship of the Joint Economic Committee to those having specific jurisdiction. Former Senator Flanders addressed himself to these problems in 1947, when no specific coordinating procedures had been formulated, and little experience had been accumulated.

While this informal procedure may have been justified during the first year because of lack of staff and in order to allay criticism by the standing committees, it is too piecemeal as a regular proposition. Rather definite procedures should be established whereby an enlarged Committee staff would analyze the principal pieces of legislation which it, or members of the Committee, believe have important economic implications. Following the analysis, a staff memorandum should be submitted to members of the Committee. This memorandum should contain a brief statement of the economic effects of the subject piece of legislation and specific recommendations as to what action the Committee should take. At each meeting the Committee should have a place on his agenda for consideration of these pending bills. Committee action could take the form of a report to the substantive committees including an economic appraisal and recommendations. Alternative Committee action could take the form of a report to the substantive committees containing merely the staff's economic appraisal with no Committee recommendation.

When Committee recommendations are given it may be expected that majority and minority reports could and should be made. The purpose of these reports should be to indicate the economic implications of the pending legislation. Admittedly, other considerations, such as military, ethical, and political, would be involved. All factors, of course, would be weighed by the substantive committee, the majority and minority policy committees, and each individual member of the Congress in taking final action on a bill.[10]

The members of the Joint Economic Committee are, of course, active politicians, whose primary job is to represent those in their state or district, and a member must fit his duties on the Committee into the framework of his routine congressional service. Even if he were vitally interested, he would be able to devote only a relatively small amount of time to the Committee, lest his other responsibilities suffer from lack of attention.[11] In the House in particular, where members face re-election every two years, only a few can overlook the necessity of constantly mending fences. Consequently, a substantial amount of day-to-day responsibility falls on the staff.

The Joint Committee staff is in a somewhat different situation than the Council staff. Council members are themselves professional economists, familiar with the techniques for analysis and interpretation of data. On the other hand, the members of the Committee are not only untrained as economists, but also can give only limited attention to the duties of Committee membership. The Committee staff has more leeway and the staff director or other senior staff members have more control over direction. This is however somewhat balanced by the fact that, while CEA gets its orders from the President, JEC must please many bosses. Another major difference is apparent: the Council staff works for the Council, a body speaking (in public) with one voice, but in the Congress the minority is represented on the JEC, and a staff economist designated as "Minority Economist" is expected to articulate its views.

Due to the fact that the opposite party will be ready to criticize the President's report, fraternization between the JEC and CEA staffs creates some potential problems. The degree to which these

[10] Ralph E. Flanders, "Administering the Employment Act—The First Year," *Public Administration Review*, Vol. VII, No. 4 (Autumn, 1947), p. 226.

[11] The first task of an effective legislator is to be re-elected. There are numerous examples of members who have become influential on the congressional scene in foreign relations, finance, etc., and who have been defeated by a contender who convinced the homefolks that their interests were being neglected. Being a big man on the Washington scene may be the kiss of death at home.

problems may develop depends upon many complex and interacting factors. One important point would, of course, be in the magnitude of difference between the President's policies and those of the opposition party. Also important would be the training and background of the staff. Presumably, professional economists would be able to find more common ground than nonprofessionals.

Differences between the minority and majority members usually reflect differences in the parties or between the Administration and the opposition leaders in Congress.

These differences are minimal as far as popular goals are concerned, but there is much debate about means. Republicans and Democrats alike are opposed to inflation, in favor of economic growth, economic freedom, and the capitalistic system. Such differences as occur are in the method of achieving these goals. The minority will take issue with the President's analysis of events, or with his forecast of the future. Since presumably both CEA and JEC have access to the same basic data, differences in interpretation are all that can occur. But even if there are no basic differences, the fact that the economic report is to be subject to vigorous analysis is salutory. More will be said about the JEC in the following chapter. It has become, without doubt, the most effective channel of economic information available to the Congress.

The Economist in the Regulatory Commissions

In its fundamental role, the regulatory commission performs a specific function which the legislative branch has delegated to it, namely, to regulate particular commercial activities, recognizing that these areas are not self-regulating and require constant attention with a high degree of flexibility that Congress could not possibly undertake. Thus, Congress has created various commissions staffed by professionals who administer day-to-day regulatory policy. [12]

The regulatory body is independent in the sense that it is outside the executive branch and thus outside the direct control of the President; it is a creature of, and reports to, Congress. On the other hand, the President appoints the members and, in some cases,

[12]See Marver H. Berstein, *Regulating Business by Independent Commissions* (Princeton, N. J.: Princeton University Press, 1955). See also the book of readings, Samuel Krislov and Lloyd Musolf (eds.) *The Politics of Regulation* (Boston: Houghton-Mifflin Co., 1964).

designates the chairman. The appointees are subject to statutory control (generally requiring a bipartisan balance) and to the advice and consent of the Senate.

The oldest of the regulatory commissions, and to some degree the prototype of all, is the Interstate Commerce Commission, which began operation after the passage of the Interstate Commerce Act in 1887. The ICC was established as a compromise between legislative and executive administration of the law, an agency which would have quasi-judicial independence. Clearly, Congress could not administer the act itself nor, if the regulatory commission were to be independent, could it turn these functions over to the executive branch of the government. Thus the regulatory commission was created, and it has been called the "fourth branch of government."

Yet, there is a close tie between the independent commissions and legislative branch. The commissions are creatures of the legislative branch and work closely with Congress, and an appropriate committee of Congress maintains a close liaison with the regulatory commission under its jurisdiction. Suggestions for legislation are reported up to the committee and congressional intent flows downward. Quite frequently congressional staff personnel move to the commissions and vice versa.

The regulatory commissions are often congressional scapegoats, as when Congress extricates itself from a crossfire of opinion by assigning tasks to a commission thereby pleasing one camp, but neglecting to provide sufficient authority or adequate funds for enforcement thereby mitigating the displeasure of the other. [13]

Naturally, the work of the regulatory commissions requires that they perform a high degree of economic analysis if they are to function properly. The Interstate Commerce Commission, the Civil Aeronautics Board, the Federal Trade Commission, the Securities and Exchange Commission, and others are constantly engaged in work which will have profound economic effects. Most of the regulatory agencies recognized their research responsibilities at an early date and have engaged in fairly substantial research. However, the quality of work especially in recent years has left much to be desired. The general nature of the work done is statistical; high-level research and effective economic advice have been all too infrequent.

[13]See Louis L. Jaffe, "The Independent Agency, A New Scapegoat," *Yale Law Journal*, Vol. 65 (June 1956).

Some years ago, Charles S. Morgan, who had for many years been closely associated with research in the ICC made comments which, while directed at that body, would apply to most of the regulatory groups. [14]

Several factors can be cited to account for the relatively low level of economic activity that prevails in the regulatory commissions. First, the routine work load is heavy and crash programs are often necessary. Consequently, research work having no immediate application is often shunted aside in favor of more pressing problems. Second, most of the staff has had limited professional training and little contact with outside researchers; budget limitations force use of poorly-qualified personnel. The regulatory commissions often suffer at appropriation time, since unlike "Santa Claus" agencies, they have few congressional champions. Only a few agencies provide for internships or other devices to bring in temporary outside talent. Finally, the fact that this situation has prevailed for some years has given the agencies an unfortunate reputation, and few bright, young, research-oriented economists seek association with them. One would be hard pressed to name a really high-calibre economist who has engaged in research for a regulatory agency since the Second World War.

Undoubtedly a serious obstacle to effective research in the commissions is that they feel their advice will not be taken seriously; a good deal of agency research is merely window dressing, useful only to justify decisions made on other grounds. It cannot be denied that the policies of regulatory commissions are often influenced by factors other than rational economic analysis; indeed, their policies are sometimes contrary to such analysis. [15] This is, of course, frustrating and discouraging to those devoted to scientific analysis. As a result, commission research becomes confined to background studies and statistics-gathering which, useful and necessary as they are to intelligent action, do not give the economist the sense of participation which he finds in other areas of Federal service.

The low budgets of most agencies drastically slow the pace of

[14]Charles S. Morgan, "The Function of Research in a Regulatory Agency," *I.C.C. Practitioner's Journal,* Vol. XXIV, No. 8, May, 1957.

[15]In his book, *The Uses of Economics,* Charles J. Hitch points out that the allocative factors in such matters have been overshadowed by the technical aspects, e.g. concern over television technical regulations has been excessive *vis-a-vis* economic problems.

One further negative influence upon the agency economist is what may be termed the "administration syndrome."[16] Economists entering Federal agencies are assigned civil service rank and salary which roughly correspond to their professional attainment. The ranks offered a young economist in the mid-1960's, generally GS-11 or GS-12 ($9,221 - $10,927), carry comparable salaries to those in academic or business institutions. However, as the career employee climbs the ladder, he usually must become more concerned with administrative tasks, personnel, budgetary decisions, etc. More prestige within the agency and more money usually lie in that direction; consequently, he may become more administrator and less researcher. The upshot of this is that the capable researcher either gives up the battle and becomes a true administrator, or he accepts a reduced salary elsewhere in order to remain an active researcher! [17]

For these reasons, the quality of economic research and advice in the regulatory agencies is generally not as high as it should be in view of their responsibilities. However, a number of outstanding economists have served in these agencies. The ICC in earlier years research so that the conclusions are often made public long after the facts have become common knowledge. Furthermore, researchers are frequently obliged to tread a narrow path among conflicting interests and severely restrict the scope of their work in an effort to avoid disclosure of information or display of partisanship. In some instances commission or departmental research groups submit drafts to industry representatives, ostensibly to check factual matters but, as can be imagined, this often results in a toning down of anti-industry viewpoints. A relatively minor complaint, but one which deserves mention, is that in many agency and commission research groups, the authorship of research papers is attributed to the agency, agency head, or research director, rather than to the researcher who has actually performed the work. For a career Federal employee, authorship may be only relatively important, but to the economist who may wish to move back into academic life, authorship is significant.

[16]This syndrome is by no means restricted to the Federal establishment, but seems to influence most large organizations, public and private.

[17]For the economist of wide reputation, a third alternative exists, namely, resignation to enter academic life or to join a private research group. However, most government economists are not of such repute and would be unable to match their income outside the service. Further, they are inhibited by loss of civil service retirement.

had a very active research program employing such influential
economists as O. M. W. Sprague, W. H. S. Stevens, Ford K. Edwards, Max O. Lorenz, and an economist commissioner, B. H.
Meyer. Much of the ICC's responsibility in the future will be under
the jurisdiction of the new Department of Transportation, which has
encouragingly announced that it will sponsor research on a large
scale, as well as perform in-house research on many problems.

Although the Tariff Commission has long engaged in economic
research work and was once under the direction of F. W. Taussig,
relatively few staff economists have been really influential, perhaps
because the final policy on tariff matters is more often determined
by political expediency than by economic wisdom. There have been,
however, several economist commissioners: Penelope Thunberg,
Ben Dorfman, E. Dana Durand, and the well-known academic economist, Jacob Viner.

The *Federal Trade Commission, Securities and Exchange Commission, Federal Power Commission, Federal Communications
Commission, Tennessee Valley Authority, Atomic Energy Commission,* and others have jurisdiction over very narrow and specific
areas of responsibility; consequently, economists working in these
areas are essentially engaged in technical matters such as the recent
SEC market studies, and their influence as advisers has not been
great. W. H. S. Stevens (also in ICC) was a major figure in the
FTC and Raymond W. Goldsmith was influential in the SEC. [18]

The contribution of the economist in the legislative branch has
been spotty. Generally the Congress has not called upon professional
economists (except for monopoly problems, taxation, and the JEC)
unless a special problem was under study. However when this has
occurred the results have often been outstanding, such as the TNEC
work, the efforts of the Doyle Report on transportation, and the work
of the Antimonopoly Subcommittee.

In the regulatory commissions, the efforts have been more continuous and the results less noteworthy. Given the nature of their
mission, these agencies have not been as successful as they might
have been in carrying on economic research. Much of the research
in the regulatory commissions, though of vital significance in the
general regulatory process, is often ignored at the operating level.

[18] Other economists who served in the regulatory agencies were: George
P. Baker and Paul Cherrington (both now at the Graduate School of Business
at Harvard), Irston Barnes (Yale) and James Bonbright (Columbia).

This problem may be insoluble, but it undoubtedly constitutes a barrier to attracting capable economists into the agencies, where there is a clear need for more high-quality research.

The most influential economists now in the legislative branch are those in the *Joint Economic Committee*. Let us turn our attention to an evaluation of that institution.

9

AN EVALUATION OF THE JOINT ECONOMIC COMMITTEE

As the counterpart of the Council, the Joint Economic Committee occupies a very important place in the advisory structure. But it did not begin its life under very favorable circumstances. Indeed the first report was issued in an atmosphere of acrimony and partisan dispute. The change in political power in the Eightieth Congress made for confusion and the Joint Committee (then the Joint Committee on the Economic Report) began its operations only after some delay. Regarding the membership of the first committee:[1]

Senators	*Representatives*
Taft (R)	Wolcott (R)
Ball (R)	Bender (R)
Flanders (R)	Rich (R)
Watkins (R)	Judd (Herter) (R)
O'Mahoney (D)	Hart (D)
Myers (D)	Patman (D)
Sparkman (D)	Huber (D)

Some comments about the more influential members may be in order.

Robert A. Taft: "Mr. Republican," Ohio. Son of the President, a party and Senate leader. Lawyer by profession, a conservative, but aware of social and economic problems. Interested in the Council from the beginning of the legislation.

Ralph E. Flanders: Republican, Vermont. Industrialist; self-

---

[1]The act originally provided that the Joint Economic Committee be composed of seven members of the Senate and seven members of the House of Representatives. A full committee was appointed late in 1946 but was not active that session. Although Senator O'Mahoney who had been active in the passage of the act had been slated to be Chairman, the election of that year resulted in a shift in the 80th Congress from Democratic to Republican. Senator Taft, who had also been active, thus took over the position of Chairman. Likewise, Mr. Judd resigned in April 1947, and was replaced by Mr. Herter.

made executive (machine tools). President, Federal Reserve Bank of Boston; Chairman of Board, Jones & Lamson Machine Co. Liberal; interested in the original Murray Bill legislation.

Joseph C. O'Mahoney: Democrat, Wyoming. Lawyer, newspaperman. Guiding light in T.N.E.C. hearing. Active in promotion of the Murray Bill. Liberal; long record of interest in social and economic legislation, with a reputation in Congress for economic erudition.

John Sparkman: Democrat, Alabama. Lawyer (later vice-presidential candidate), and congressional leader of the liberals.

Jesse P. Wolcott: Republican, Michigan. Lawyer. Longtime Congressman (seven terms). Chairman of the House Committee on the Banking and Currency.

Christian A. Herter: Republican, Massachusetts. Diplomat (later Secretary of State). High-level Federal service; independently wealthy, "Eisenhower" liberal Republican.

Wright Patman: Democrat, Texas. Liberal of populist sentiments, longtime champion of easy money, and perennial foe of Federal Reserve monetary policy, Lawyer, in Congress since 1928, and ranking House member (1967) of the Joint Economic Committee, and the House Banking and Currency Committee.

The original Committee consisted of eight nominal Republicans, who might be expected to take a hostile attitude toward the concept of economic planning, and six liberal Democrats, who would be expected to take a more benevolent view. However, Taft, Flanders, Wolcott, and Bender had all been involved in the original legislation and were generally favorable toward it. In addition, Herter had a liberal record. Only Rich and Watkins were of doubtful sympathy toward the idea of full employment via planning in the manner contemplated by the Act.

Charles O. Hardy, formerly of the Brookings Institution and the Federal Reserve Bank of Kansas City, was appointed the first staff director. The first *Economic Report of the President* caught the JEC largely unprepared for business. In lieu of a formal report, a two-page statement was issued saying:

These matters are already under consideration by standing committees of Congress which will make a detailed study of each one of them and submit recommendations to the Congress. Most of them are highly controversial. A recommendation from this committee at this time which could only be casual before our studies are made, would not be helpful to the solution of the problems. The committee will proceed to consider these problems with reference to their effect on the maintenance of a stable economy and continuous employment.

The basic problem which this committee has to consider is the method of preventing depressions so that substantially full employment may be continuously maintained. No problem before the American people is more vital to our welfare, to the very existence of our way of life, and to the peace of the world. It is the most complex and difficult of all the long range domestic problems we have to face. It involves a study of price levels and wage levels and their relation to each other, a study of methods of preventing monopoly control in industry and labor from distorting prices and wages, a study of spending for consumption and for capital investment, a study of individual and corporate savings and a study of many other economic forces bearing on a stable economy.

Until we have further studied and analyzed the basic considerations which underlie this problem, we do not feel we should become involved in controversy on current issues which have many aspects besides their effect on the prosperity of the country. [2]

This seemed unsatisfactory to many; former Senator Glen Taylor of Idaho (later to run for Vice-President on the Wallace ticket), an active supporter of the Act, issued a blistering statement criticizing the Committee for not rendering a report, saying that Taft had offered instead "a series of excuses."[3]

The midyear *Economic Report* (July 1947) was given only passing attention, but in late July the JEC undertook an extensive study of food prices and followed this with a special study on the cost of living.[4] As elaborate procedure was used, including public hearings held under subcommittees in various parts of the United States.

---

[2]Originally mimeographed, but later printed as S. Doc. No. 11 (80th Congress, 1st Session).

[3]Nourse, *op. cit.*, p. 187.

[4]*Senate Report* 1565, June 9, 1948, 80th Congress, 1st Session.

Late in 1948 the Committee also began a series of hearings on the President's message on inflation.[5]

All in all, though a disappointment to some, performance during the first year of the JEC's existence was reasonable. After this somewhat slow start, the Committee began its second year of operation on a rising plane and has been quite active since.

Performance of the Joint Committee

As we have seen, Nourse's policy was to avoid legislative testimony; thus Committee-Council relations had been distant, though cordial, from the first. Nourse (though not Keyserling and Clark) had on several occasions been reluctant to appear before the Committee and had been cautious of too close relationship. Generally, Keyserling, though more than willing to appear, did not achieve a harmonious relationship with the Congress.

Burns followed somewhat the same philosophy and in general "played close to his chest," although as we have seen modified his stand and was generally willing to testify. To what degree this situation influenced the work of the committee is difficult to say. Heller took steps in 1961 to bring Council-Committee relations somewhat closer together.

By its nature, the Committee is in a position to "second-guess" the Council; that is, it can examine the reports, call either friendly or hostile witnesses, and has, to some degree, the benefit of hindsight because time will have elapsed since the data upon which the report is based were collected. Upon occasion the "unfriendly" witnesses can ask embarrassing questions. Consequently, caution on the part of the Council is understandable. To be sure, one of the functions of the Joint Committee is to force the Committee to be rather beholden to the Congress, a factor very much in the minds of those who drafted the original legislation. Especially when the situation under discussion is fluid and controversial, the questioning can become rigorous.[6] Yet, no one can read the hearings without becoming fully aware of the two-way educational process which

---

[5]U. S. Congress, "The President's Program to Deal with the Problems of Inflation," 80th Congress, 1st Session, *Senate Report* 809.

[6]See the questioning of Dr. Ackley by Representative Thomas B. Curtis, *Hearings on January* 1965 *Economic Report of the President,* 89th Congress,

takes place. Nor can one escape the fact that the members involved have most often spent considerable time with their "homework. " The Committee has the benefit not only of the views of the Council, but also of the large number of distinguished economists who are invited to testify. In the 1965 hearings for example, Seymour Harris, John Kenneth Galbraith, Raymond Saulnier (a former CEA Chairman), and others joined in the exchange. In addition, Secretary Dillon and Chairman Martin of the Federal Reserve, appeared as witnesses. It cannot be expected that every member of the Committee has the time or inclination to absorb and digest the vast amount of complex information (the 1965 hearings ran to 494 pages), but over-all the value of the procedure is beyond calaculation.

Having seen committees at work on complex economic matters, a cynical observer might be excused if he had little faith in the JEC. To be sure, the Committee has not been beyond reproach, but its performance has been most rewarding over the years.

Not only have the committee's studies affected a broad range of legislation but their direct influence, both current and long range, on the actions of executive agencies has been impressive. Today's concerns over restoring excise tax cuts and increasing tax rates remind us of the Joint Economic Committee's unanimous resolution in July 1950 calling for an immediate increase in taxes to finance the Korean war on a pay-as-you-go basis and how it changed current policy of that time. There was the Treasury- Federal Reserve "accord" which came out of the Subcommittee on Monetary Policy's studies and hearings—and the new or improved statistics initiated as a result of the studies of the subcommittee working so intensively in that area. Studies of balance of payments and foreign economics bore fruit in the Trade Expansion Act and some of the corrective measures involving the balance of payments. The Agriculture Subcommittee's presentation of alternative agricultural programs also shows how hearings and reports lay the ground for executive as well as legislative action.

We could go on through study after study to illustrate in depth this role the Joint Economic Committee had in the early identification of public economic problems and in the long, ofttimes repetitive process of public education so essential to the acceptance of an idea. As Walter Heller noted, we could document the development of the 'New Economics' of last year's tax cut in the studies of the Fiscal Policy Subcommittees, in the 'Study of Employment, Growth, and Price Levels,' and that 1954 best seller, 'Potential Economic Growth in the United States in the Next Decade.'[7]

The range of subjects covered in the hearings is illustrated by the names of witnesses appearing. At the 1965 hearings on the economic report (February 1965), in addition to the members of the Council, others who appeared were Secretary Dillon (Treasury), Kermit Gordon, (Director of the Bureau of the Budget), economists Seymour Harris, John K. Galbraith, Raymond J. Saulnier, William Mc. C. Martin, Jr. , (Chairman, F.R.B.), Jerry Voorhis (former congressman and Director of the Cooperative League of the U.S.A.), Leon H. Keyserling, Walter P. Reuther, (United Auto Workers), Carl H. Madden, (U. S. Chamber of Commerce), T. O. Yntema, (Committee for Economic Development), Grover Ensley, (National Association of Mutual Savings Banks and a former staff director of JEC), and representatives from the Federal Statistics Users Conference, Independent Bankers Association, Machinery and Allied Products Institute, National Association of Manufacturers, National Farmers Union, The National Grange, and the United Mine Workers.

Probably the most worthwhile result of the JEC has been its role as educator. Lehman's comments are again pertinent:

[Who would have foreseen]
that the committee would bring the kind of reciprocity between academe and the Congress that would prompt a reference shelf writer 18 years later to say that—
" 'The Joint Economic Committee is the nom de plume of the world's largest class in economics, in which astute and overworked Congressmen and Senators take turns being pupils and instructors to most of the Nation's economists.'
"The committee surely was not set up to be the voice urging and defending adequate and proper economic statistics, but it has been and it continues to be, in the clearest of tones."
Nor did anyone, I suspect, ever anticipate that the Joint Economic Committee would virtually have to invent a hearing

[7]John W. Lehman, "Administration of the Employment Act," *Twentieth Anniversary Symposium*, p. 89.

format and method in order that the wide-ranging views of many kinds of witnesses could be fairly and effectively present-ed. The use by the Joint Committee and other congressional groups of the roundtable, seminar-type hearing, and the com-pendium of witness papers prepared and distributed in ad-vance is so common now as to make us forget their origin.

Or who would have thought in 1946 that an experimental hearing, bringing together physical and social scientists in 1955 for a discussion of 'Automation and Technological Change,' would have highlighted the need for improved educational stan-dards at all levels, 3 years before the traumatic impact of Sputnik I? And it was the Joint Economic Committee which about that same time began the series of pioneering studies that have led us through the maze of economic statistics we must tread if we are to understand comparative rates of growth between the United States and the Soviet Union.[8]

As Lehman implies, the growth of the educational role of the Com-mittee has been accidental, but it is nonetheless real and viable.

The Committee has been educator not only to Congress, but also to the general public and the economics profession as well. Its al-most four hundred publications include studies on virtually every facet of the economy. In recent years for example, the Committee has published volumes on *Automation and Technology in Education* (1966), *Fiscal Policy Issues of the Coming Decade* (1965), *Measuring the Nation's Wealth* (1965), *New Approach to United States Inter-national Economic Policy* (1966), *Economic Impact of Federal Pro-curement* (1965), *Economic Policies and Practices* (1965), *The Im-pact of Government-Generated Cargo on the U.S. Flag Foreign Trade Fleet for Calendar Year 1964* (1965), *The Federal Reserve Portfolio* (1966) and *Economic Effect of Vietnam Spending* (1967).

These publications have been broadly distributed, and one would be hard pressed to think of any organization with comparable re-search resources and equal capability in the distribution of its re-sults. So the usefulness of the information to business, research and academic groups can hardly be overestimated, and it is clear that Joint Committee efforts have greatly increased economic un-derstanding both in the Congress, and in the country at large.

[8]Lehman, *op. cit.*, p. 91.

Committee Membership and Staff

As we saw, the original membership of the committee was some-what a mixed bag with, by good fortune, a cadre of interested members. Over the years this general pattern has been followed.

Senator Goldwater, candidate for President in 1964, served two terms on the committee. A liberal, Senator Proxmire of Wisconsin, joined the committee in the Eighty-seventh Congress and served as Chairman in the Ninetieth Congress. Two members, Senator Sparkman and Representative Patman, have served continuously. Senator Douglas served on the committee from the 81st Congress until his defeat in 1966. Another member, Representative Bolling of Missouri, has served continuously since the Eighty-second Congress.

As of 1966, the Joint Committee has been a going concern for ten Congresses. Service on the Committee in five or more Congresses might be considered evidence of considerable interest, assuming of course that the member lived and was elected to five Congresses. Those who meet this test, including the charter members Sparkman and Patman are:

Ten Congresses:
Sparkman
Patman
Nine Congresses:
Douglas
Eight Congresses:
Bolling

Seven Congresses:
Fulbright
Six Congresses:
O'Mahoney
Watkins
Five Congresses:
Wolcott

Several major differences are evident between the staffs of the Joint Committee and the Council. Perhaps first is that the staff of the JEC is likely to have more leeway professionally than that of the CEA, because the CEA staff reports directly to a group of professional economists. The JEC staff on the other hand deals with a group which includes professional economists only by chance, although to be sure, the committee members may be very knowledgeable. Further, the members of the Committee have many other pressing matters to attend to, whereas Council members are fully occupied with matters of economic analysis. While it is extremely hard to generalize, it is probable that the staff members of the Committee have been a shade less distinguished in the eyes of their fellow economists than is true of their counterparts on the Council. Perhaps this is an illusion caused by the fact that the Council staff has had more of an academic orientation.

The Committee staff has remained small and has made considerable use of the resources available to congressional staffs like the Legislative Reference Service of the Library of Congress and employees of executive branch agencies and other congressional committees. Like its CEA counterpart, the JEC staff has made frequent calls upon economists outside the Government.

The JEC staff also has more variety in its scope of work. The Council must in general direct its effort towards turning out the Economic Report on schedule. On the other hand, the Committee staff can respond to the reports as the Committee sees fit. Also, subject to agreement with the committee concerned (e.g., Banking and Currency) the JEC staff can range far and wide in special studies.

The Committee has been fortunate in having had able staff directors, but the rate of turnover has been higher than one would wish. The longest service was that of Grover Ensley who served from April 1957, only four months short of six years. In the two decades from March 1947 to March 1967, ten men have served. Since Ensley's service accounted for almost one-third of the total, the average time for the others was about one and one-half years. (There were three months when no one occupied the office.) It would seem desirable to have somewhat longer tenure in an office of such importance.

Executive Directors of the Joint Economic Committee 1947-1967

Charles O. Hardy, staff director . . March 1947-November 1948.
Fred E. Berquist, acting staff
  director . . . . .December 1948-August 1949.
Theodore J. Kreps, staff
  director . . . . .August 1949-March 1951.
Grover W. Ensley, staff
  director . . . . .April 1951-December 1955.
  Executive director* . . . . .December 1955-July 1957.
John W. Lehman, acting
  executive director . . . . .August 1957-March 1958.
Roderick H. Riley, executive
  director . . . . .March 1958-December 1959.
John W. Lehman, acting
  executive director . . . . .January 1950-February 1961.

Wm. Summers Johnson,
  executive director . . . . February 1961–February 1963.
James W. Knowles, executive
  director . . . . February 1963–January 1967.
John R. Stark, executive
  director . . . . February 1963–January

*This title was changed from staff director to executive director on adoption of the rules of the committee in December 1955.

MEMBERSHIP, JOINT ECONOMIC COMMITTEE
1946–1967

Seventy-Ninth Congress (1946)

Senate	House of Representatives
Joseph C. O'Mahoney of Wyoming	Edward J. Hart of New Jersey
	Wright Patman of Texas
James M. Tunnell of Delaware	George E. Outland of California
Abe Murdock of Utah	Walter B. Huber of Ohio
Francis J. Myers of Pennsylvania	George H. Bender of Ohio
Robert A. Taft of Ohio	Walter H. Judd of Minnesota
Styles Bridges of New Hampshire	Robert F. Rich of Pennsylvania
Robert M. La Follette, Jr. of Wisconsin	

House Members were appointed on March 11, 1946, and Senate Members on July 1, 1946. No business was transacted in the 79th Congress. From the 79th through the 85th Congresses the majority party was represented by four Senators and four Representatives and the minority party by three Senators and three Representatives.

Source: *Employment Act as Amended, With Related Laws,* Joint Economic Committee (Washington, D. C., U. S. Govt. Printing Office, 1966), p. 17.

Eightieth Congress (1947-48)

Senate	House of Representatives
Robert A. Taft of Ohio, *Chairman*	Jesse P. Wolcott of Michigan, *Vice Chairman*
Joseph H. Ball of Minnesota	
Ralph E. Flanders of Vermont	George H. Bender of Ohio
Arthur V. Watkins of Utah	Robert F. Rich of Pennsylvania
Joseph C. O'Mahoney of Wyoming	Christian A. Herter of Massachusetts
Francis J. Myers of Pennsylvania	Edward J. Hart of New Jersey
John Sparkman of Alabama	Wright Patman of Texas
	Walter B. Huber of Ohio

Representative Herter was appointed on April 17, 1947, to fill the vacancy created by the resignation of Walter H. Judd from the Joint Committee on the same date.

Note.—The following were appointed as temporary members of the Joint Economic Committee to assist in the hearings on high prices of consumer goods pursuant to Senate Concurrent Resolution 19, agreed to July 16,1947:
    Eastern Subcommittee:
        Senator Raymond E. Baldwin of Connecticut
        Representative Clarence E. Kilburn of New York
    Mid-Continent Subcommittee:
        Senator James P. Kem of Missouri
        Representative Henry O. Talle of Iowa
    Western Subcommittee:
        Senator Zales N. Ecton of Montana
        Representative Walt Horan of Washington
        Representative Norris Poulson of California

Eighty-First Congress (1949-50)

Senate	House of Representatives
Joseph C. O'Mahoney of Wyoming, *Chairman*	Edward J. Hart of New Jersey, *Vice Chairman*
Francis J. Myers of Pennsylvania	Wright Patman of Texas
John Sparkman of Alabama	Walter B. Huber of Ohio
Paul H. Douglas of Illinois	Frank Buchanan of Pennsylvania
Robert A. Taft of Ohio	Jesse P. Wolcott of Michigan
Ralph E. Flanders of Vermont	Christian A. Herter of Massachusetts
Arthur V. Watkins of Utah	Robert F. Rich of Pennsylvania

Source: *Ibid.*, p. 11-16.

Eighty-Second Congress (1951-52)

Senate	House of Representatives
Joseph C. O'Mahoney of Wyoming, *Chairman*	Edward J. Hart of New Jersey, *Vice Chairman*
John Sparkman of Alabama	Wright Patman of Texas
Paul H. Douglas of Illinois	Richard Bolling of Missouri
William Benton of Connecticut	Clinton D. McKinnon of California
Robert A. Taft of Ohio	Jesse P. Wolcott of Michigan
Ralph E. Flanders of Vermont	Christian A. Herter of Massachusetts
Arthur V. Watkins of Utah	J. Caleb Boggs of Delaware

Representative McKinnon was appointed on June 3, 1951, to fill the vacancy created by the death of Frank Buchanan, April 27, 1951.

Eighty-Third Congress (1953-54)

House of Representatives	Senate
Jesse P. Wolcott of Michigan, *Chairman*	Ralph E. Flanders of Vermont, *Vice Chairman*
Richard M. Simpson of Pennsylvania	Arthur V. Watkins of Utah
Henry O. Talle of Iowa	Barry Goldwater of Arizona
George H. Bender of Ohio	Frank Carlson of Kansas
Edward J. Hart of New Jersey	John Sparkman of Alabama
Wright Patman of Texas	Paul H. Douglas of Illinois
Richard Bolling of Missouri	J. W. Fulbright of Arkansas

Senator Carlson was appointed September 29, 1953, to the existing vacancy due to the death of Senator Taft, July 31, 1953.

Eighty-Fourth Congress (1955-56)

Senate	House of Representatives
Paul H. Douglas of Illinois, *Chairman*	Wright Patman of Texas, *Vice* Ch *Chairman*
John Sparkman of Alabama	Richard Bolling of Missouri
J. W. Fulbright of Arkansas	Wilbur D. Mills of Arkansas
Joseph C. O'Mahoney of Wyoming	Augustine B. Kelley of Pennsylvania
Ralph E. Flanders of Vermont	Jesse P. Wolcott of Michigan
Arthur V. Watkins of Utah	Henry O. Talle of Iowa
Barry Goldwater of Arizona	Thomas B. Curtis of Missouri

Source: *Ibid.*, p. 11-16.

Eighty-Fifth Congress (1957-58)

House of Representatives	Senate

Wright Patman of Texas, *Chairman*
Richard Bolling of Missouri
Hale Boggs of Louisiana
Henry S. Reuss of Wisconsin
Henry O. Talle of Iowa
Thomas B. Curtis of Missouri
Clarence E. Kilburn of New York

John Sparkman of Alabama, *Vice Chairman*
Paul H. Douglas of Illinois
J. W. Fulbright of Arkansas
Joseph C. O'Mahoney of Wyoming
Ralph E. Flanders of Vermont
Arthur V. Watkins of Utah
John D. Hoblitzell, Jr. of West Virginia

Representative Boggs was appointed on January 27, 1958, to fill the vacancy created by the death of Augustine B. Kelley, November 20, 1957.

Representative Reuss was appointed on February 17, 1958, to fill the vacancy created by the resignation of Wilbur D. Mills from the joint committee on January 27, 1958.

Senator Hoblitzell was appointed on March 10, 1958, to fill the vacancy created by the resignation of Barry Goldwater from the joint committee on the same date.

Eighty-Sixth Congress (1959-60)

Senate	House of Representatives

Paul H. Douglas of Illinois, *Chairman*
John Sparkman of Alabama
J. W. Fulbright of Arkansas
Joseph C. O'Mahoney of Wyoming
John F. Kennedy of Massachusetts
Prescott Bush of Connecticut
John Marshall Butler of Maryland
Jacob K. Javits of New York

Wright Patman of Texas, *Vice Chairman*
Richard Bolling of Missouri
Hale Boggs of Louisiana
Henry S. Reuss of Wisconsin
Frank M. Coffin of Maine
Thomas B. Curtis of Missouri
Clarence E. Kilburn of New York
William B. Widnall of New Jersey

Representative Coffin was appointed on February 18, 1959, and Senator Kennedy on March 19, 1959, under the provisions of Public Law 85-1, approved February 17, 1959, which increased the membership of the joint committee from 14 to 16.

Source: *Ibid.*, p. 11-16.

Eighty-Seventh Congress (1961-62)

House of Representatives	Senate
Wright Patman of Texas, *Chairman*	Paul H. Douglas of Illinois, *Vice*
Richard Bolling of Missouri	*Chairman*
Hale Boggs of Louisiana	John Sparkman of Alabama
Henry S. Reuss of Wisconsin	J. W. Fulbright of Arkansas
Martha W. Griffiths of Michigan	William Proxmire of Wisconsin
Thomas B. Curtis of Missouri	Claiborne Pell of Rhode Island
Clarence E. Kilburn of New York	Prescott Bush of Connecticut
William B. Widnall of New Jersey	John Marshall Butler of Maryland
	Jacob K. Javits of New York

Eighty-Eighth Congress (1963-64)

Senate	House of Representatives
Paul H. Douglas of Illinois,	Richard Bolling of Missouri, *Vice*
Chairman	*Chairman*
John Sparkman of Alabama	Wright Patman of Texas
J. W. Fulbright of Arkansas	Hale Boggs of Louisiana
William Proxmire of Wisconsin	Henry S. Reuss of Wisconsin
Claiborne Pell of Rhode Island	Martha W. Griffiths of Michigan
Jacob K. Javits of New York	Thomas B. Curtis of Missouri
Jack Miller of Iowa	Clarence E. Kilburn of New York
Len B. Jordan of Idaho	William B. Widnall of New Jersey

Eighty-Ninth Congress (1964-65)

House of Representatives	Senate
Wright Patman of Texas, *Chairman*	Paul H. Douglas of Illinois, *Vice*
Richard Bolling of Missouri	*Chairman*
Hale Boggs of Louisiana	John Sparkman of Alabama
Henry S. Reuss of Wisconsin	J. W. Fulbright of Arkansas
Martha W. Griffiths of Michigan	William Proxmire of Wisconsin
Thomas B. Curtis of Missouri	Herman E. Talmadge of Georgia
William B. Widnall of New Jersey	Jacob K. Javits of New York
Robert F. Ellsworth of Kansas	Jack Miller of Iowa
	Len B. Jordan of Idaho

Source: *Ibid.*, p. 11-16.

Ninetieth Congress (1966-67)

Senate	House of Representatives
William Proxmire of Wisconsin, *Chairman*	Wright Patman of Texas, *Vice Chairman*
John Sparkman of Alabama	Richard Bolling of Missouri
J. W. Fulbright of Arkansas	Hale Boggs of Louisiana
Herman E. Talmadge of Georgia	Henry S. Reuss of Wisconsin
Stuart Symington of Missouri	Martha W. Griffiths of Michigan
Abraham Ribicoff of Connecticut	William S. Moorhead of Pennsylvania
Jacob K. Javits of New York	Thomas B. Curtis of Missouri
Jack Miller of Iowa	William B. Widnall of New Jersey
Len B. Jordan of Idaho	Donald Rumsfeld of Illinois
Charles H. Percy of Illinois	W. E. Brock 3d of Tennessee

Source: *Ibid.*, p. 11-16.

Members have been exceptionally influential in the Congress and in national affairs; Taft, Sparkman, Patman, Herter, Goldwater, and Douglas have been household words.   The 1968 membership includes the chairman of that Senate Foreign Relations Committee (Fulbright) and a former candidate for Vice President (Sparkman). A member of Congress cannot confine himself to one intensive activity and survive politically, but must operate on many fronts and provide a wide variety of services to his constituents.   A Congressman who must support interests in welfare wool, copper, silver, peanuts, or automobiles may have problems if he endorses some view of the Joint Committee.   The point is that the Joint Committee transcends regional interest and focuses instead upon national interest.   It would be naive to believe that when a member enters the committee room of the Joint Committee, he sheds his State or district interests, or forgets his inherent, parochial, and perhaps incorrect economic beliefs.   However, service on the Joint Economic Committee has been a form of higher economic education, and the Committee and its staff have rendered a valuable service to the Congress and to the Nation.

What is the picture of the Joint Committee which begins to take shape after two decades of development?   Perhaps first and foremost is that the Committee has become a tremendous force for economic education.   Secondly, it is an invaluable vehicle for the coordination of legislation relating to economic affairs. And third, it serves as a forum for the disparate economic views of those who appear before it. The level of sophistication at which it generally operates is illustrated by an exchange between Senator Douglas and Chairman Ackley:

Senator Douglas. Let me ask what would you say to an antitrust policy of reducing prices to match purchasing power instead of trying to pump purchasing power up to the level of prices?

Mr. Ackley. I certainly am a strong supporter of antitrust policy. I think it is a major element in our economic structure, an important one which helps account for our general economic success. However, I rather doubt that antitrust policy could or should be used as a major weapon of redistributing income from corporations to individuals.

Senator Douglas. Well, if we had a competitive economic system would we have these difficulties which we are trying to remove?

Mr. Ackley. It is very difficult to imagine what a purely competitive economy would look like in the textbook sense of the term. It would be a very different economy. It would have many advantages. But perhaps it might also have some disadvantages. I think the kind of economy that our antitrust laws try to promote is not really the purely competitive economy described in textbooks.

Senator Douglas. Well, not in the sense of an infinite number of producers each producing an infinitesimal fraction of the total supply. That, of course, is true. But is it not true also that the attempt to cure unemployment by fiscal means is apt to push into the background any emphasis upon antitrust policies as a means of increasing competition and getting prices reduced?

This is the way that I have always felt Keynes was generalizing and giving a false interpretation of what was happening in Great Britain. Great Britain ran for almost 15 years with high unemployment, and Keynes described various reasons which were monetary and fiscal in character. But all the English economists disregarded the fact that right under their eyes England was becoming cartelized. In industry after in-

dustry cartels would be formed. There would be complete
monopoly—Imperial Chemicals and the rest; and as a result
the competitive price structure was disappearing in England.
They emerged after World War I with only five banks, for all
intents and purposes.

Keynes assisted in cartelizing industry, and making industry less competitive. Robbins and Keynes—you never could
get them to admit that monopoly or quasi-monopoly was a
cause of continued unemployment, and they turned continuously
to fiscal policy and monetary policy as a means of offsetting
this weakness in the society about them.

And if monopoly is inevitable—if you cannot do anything
about it—then I would welcome these compensatory movements.
But I would want to be pretty certain that they do not push into
the background efforts to introduce a greater degree of competition.

Now I wonder what your comments would be on that.

Mr. Ackley. I would merely express the hope that pre-
occupation with fiscal and monetary policy to maintain high
employment would not divert attention from the structural
problems of our economy, one of which is the problem of competition. I think the British economy today undoubtedly suf-
fers from the stagnation of innovation, from rigidities, and
from a nonprogressive structure which, at least in part, are
attributable to the high degree of concentration in British industry. [9]

or between Chairman Ackley and Representative Griffiths:

Representative Griffiths. You say that, although we have
acted too slowly in checking past declines in demand, we shall
act more promptly in the future. Does this reflect better
warning, improved forecasting, or the institution of procedures for taking fiscal policy actions with greater alacrity,
or both?

Mr. Ackley. I think the word was not "shall" but "should"
act with greater speed. I think that all of these things you

[9]"Fiscal Policy Issues of the Coming Decade," *Hearing,* Subcommittee
on Fiscal Policy, JEC, 89th Congress, (July 1965), p. 27.

have mentioned are important in improving our ability to act quickly.

Certainly improving our forecasting, perhaps being more forthright as to what we think is going to happen. I believe that in the past, when even within the Government recessions were foreseen as a strong possibility, the administration has not always been fully frank in communicating to the Congress the possible need for action.

I think one requirement is that the administration first forecast as best it can, then recognize the requirements and make its recommendations to Congress. Hopefully, Congress can perhaps improve its procedures for acting quickly when such recommendations come forward.[10]

These excerpts are fairly typical of the level of discourse at JEC hearings. More technical matters raise the level of sophistication, as when Professor Ray Blough, Senator Javits of New York, and Senator Proxmire of Wisconsin, discussed international economic policy:

Mr. Blough. There can be no question, Senator, that $10 billion makes more impact on the economy than $2 billion makes. However, I believe there is considerably more incentive involved in $2 billion of investment credit than in $2 billion of increase or decrease in taxes.

Senator Javits. And isn't it a fact that this is a critically important incentive money, because what is happening to you is that you need to increase productivity? It may be that you can leapfrog this whole situation, if you had some unbelievable burst in activity.

For example, it is analogous in my mind to what might happen to Britain, which is in terrible trouble, if this North Sea gas find should really be the tremendous asset which it might turn out to be. So that really it has two difficulties. It is too small, it is too late—and it may be very well counterproductive, going completely down the wrong road under present circumstances.

Mr. Blough. May I respond, Senator. I think that the

[10]*Ibid.*, p. 33.

counter-productiveness is almost altogether based on the question of timing, and whether we have hit the wrong time for it. But, certainly, the big increases in capacity——

Senator Proxmire. I just can't resist asking if you will yield? That was the reason I expressed the National Industrial Conference Board finding and the lag which the best expert we could get at that time said was involved in this thing. It takes a year, and in a year industry may be cutting back anyway.

Mr. Blough. If you decrease somebody's burden and then try to put it back on him again, you have troubles, but if you put a burden on him and find that it is too much, it is not dificult to take it away quickly.[11]

Or again a question by Representative Ellsworth to Professor Despres of Stanford University:

Representative Ellsworth. Let me ask a question to clarify something in my own mind. Would you explain to me or attempt to, so that even I can understand it, what exactly is the direct link between our having a deficit in our balance of payments on the one hand, and on the other hand our ability to engage in this financial intermediation function that you have talked about as a direct investor and as a lender.

Mr. Despres. Yes.

Representative Ellsworth. In other words, why is it necessary for us to have a balance-of-payments deficit in order for us to perform that function?

Mr. Despres. The United States typically has a surplus on current account, net exports of goods and services. If our lending and investing abroad precisely equaled the surplus on current account, then one could say that the function of the lending and investing was exclusively to effect real transfer of goods and services to other countries and one could call this, if one wanted, a position of balance.

What I am really saying is this: that American lending and investing abroad performs two functions. One, it finances

[11]"New Approach to United States International Economic Policy, " *Hearing,* Subcommittee on International Exchange and Payments, JEC, (Sept. , 1966), p. 21.

real transfer of goods and services. Two, it is a trade on financial assets. It enables foreign countries to get financial claims of the type that they desire, while we provide financing to permit investments that go forward abroad. We not only export a part of our savings to the rest of the world but our financial markets help other countries to mobilize their savings for investment use.[12]

The value of this type of discourse to both member and witness is obvious; before the Joint Committee was created, it was rarely found.

Problems of Staffing and Organization

As was noted in Chapter 5, the Joint Committee and the Council share several problems in this area, and their general nature will be further discussed here. Those peculiar to the Joint Committee are salaries allegedly lower than those available in the executive branch, rather poor physical working conditions,[13] and lack of continuity in that chairmen are apt to change with elections. (The Chairman generally names the staff Director). The CEA can hire staff who report to one person, the JEC must satisfy several, majority, minority, chairmen of other subcommittees, and so on. This makes hiring very difficult and tends to increase staff turnover. Despite these serious problems, the committee has so far operated with efficiency and surprising harmony.

The Joint Committee is by no means alone in some of its problems. The staff of the Antimonopoly Subcommittee works under similarly unsatisfactory physical conditions as do a good many people on Capitol Hill. Adequate space seems to be a constant problem throughout the Federal establishment. While lack of space, salaries lower than those of comparable jobs, and other disadvantages have no doubt increased job turnover, there is little indication that there has been a noticeable decline in the quality of personnel who staff the Joint Committee. The likely upshot is that a steady supply of

[12]*Ibid.*, p. 31.

[13]The Joint Committee staff is housed in very crowded conditions in the New Senate Office Building, with several people farmed out in the Rayburn Building. Senior staff people are in cubicles separated only by bookcases, and in other ways the physical conditions are poor.

talent might be attracted but that a relatively low number of these would be career people. The task of working for the Joint Economic Committee is attractive from many standpoints. The opportunity to rub elbows with national figures and to take part in national affairs (even on a low level) is attractive to many. Unfortunately, the glamour may fade rapidly as frustrations mount and other opportunities present themselves. In any event, from the record, turnover has not been a major problem. Since 1946, a total of twenty-one economists have served (including the staff of seven in 1967). Over the years, the staff has ranged between four and seven, exclusive of consultants. Thus a total of twenty-one over a twenty-year period is a reasonably good record. Also, while turnover presents problems, it has some positive advantages in that fresh viewpoints are available, an advantage which many Federal agencies lack. The staff, like the Committee members, can cite many reasons against staying on, but the number who do so is surprising in both cases.

By 1967 (Ninetieth Congress), the Joint Committee had published almost four hundred studies and held countless hearings. The level of discourse has been generally high, and the value of the educational role both in the Congress and in the nation at large is incalculable. Whatever the future of economic advisorship, it is clear that the function of clearinghouse and sounding-board must be continued in some form.

10
THE EMERGING PATTERN
THE IMPACT OF THE ACT OF 1946

In evaluating the impact of the Act of 1946, one must first recall the lukewarm reception which the Act received. Not much was expected from the battered piece of legislation which emerged from Congress weakened by compromise and diluted to offend the minimum number of people.

Professor Galbraith has written recently:

> One wonders whether, on preliminary form there was ever a more unpromising piece of legislation than the Employment Act of 1946. The title itself was a hedge; reference to full employment was too controversial. Any mention of methods by which employment would be sustained was avoided. To have hinted at deficit financing would have been fatal. Three economic advisers were provided which, it could be foreseen, was a certain formula for endless disagreement. They had no visible executive authority. A Congressional Committee was authorized but with no legislative powers, a point emphasized in its original name. As a substitute for solid function, an impressive system of reports was provided for. I remember discussing the legislation in 1946 with Milton Gilbert who was one of its architects. We agreed that it was principally a gesture though probably a useful one. He thought it more useful than I did.

Yet in retrospect the Employment Act appears as the most important single piece of economic legislation of the postwar years. The Council of Economic Advisers which it created has, a few early months apart, functioned harmoniously as a powerful general staff on economic policy. It has far outstripped the Secretary of Commerce and the Federal Reserve Board in influence. Probably it is now more powerful than the Treasury. The Joint Economic Committee, as it has been retitled, if a less spectacular success, is the most respected forum for economic discussion in the Congress. How did it come about?[1]

By almost any measure, the Council has performed more effectively than most observers would have forecast in 1946. Several circumstances seem to account for this success. First, the Council has not had to cope with a major economic downturn; indeed, the Council's actions have helped to prevent a major breakdown. To what degree the Council would have been effective in 1929, given the philosophy of the Hoover Administration, is a matter of speculation. The Council faced and passed a severe test in 1953-54 and again in 1960-61. However, an economic breakdown of the magnitude of 1929 has not occurred; and to that degree, the Council (along with other such devices) remains untested.

Second, the Council has both benefited from and contributed to the increasing acceptance of economic analysis in government and business. The performance of economists during the Second World War and in the quarter century since has been creditable and the usefulness of economic analysis at high levels of business and government has been proven. Finally, and of most importance is the acceptance of the Council function by the President who is, of course, the key to the process. Without such acceptance, the Council would have had, at least in the early years, no real purpose. Perhaps now that it has become firmly established, it would be very difficult for the President to ignore it. President Truman, while supporting the Council idea, was apparently unwilling to use it to its full potential. The record indicates that he looked upon it as essentially a political device. This judgment may be harsh, but it seems to be supported by the historical facts. Mr. Eisenhower, after a somewhat tenuous beginning, became an enthusiastic supporter of the Council, though it would likely have perished in 1952 had not bipartisan congressional support saved the day. Burns's great contribution was that he established the Council's reputation for usefulness in an administration not generally thought to be sympathetic to economic planning and research. President Kennedy was known to be an enthusiastic supporter of the Council with some personal interest in research methodology. Mr. Johnson, although more in

[1] Review by John Kenneth Galbraith, "Economic Advice and Presidential Leadership," Edward S. Flash, *American Economic Review*, December 1966, p. 1249.

the Truman mold, has continued the Kennedy activist tradition as far as the Council is concerned.

A third factor in the success of the Council has been the good fortune in choice of chairmen.   All six men have in different ways performed in admirable fashion, although, to be sure, their modes of operation have been widely different.   Professor Saulnier served the longest term, four years, one month; with Burns second at three years and ten months; followed by Heller, only one month less, by Nourse (three years, four months); and Keyserling (three years, one month).   No chairman has served the full term of his President with the exception of Heller whose term overlapped the Kennedy-Johnson years; but all have remained for more than three years.[2] The change from Nourse to Keyserling was a shift both in mode of operation and in economic philosophy.   The Burns–Saulnier shift was only mildly noticeable in the area of operating technique, as was that from Heller to Ackley.   It is notable also that in every case when a chairman has resigned during an administration his replacement has come from within the Council.   No President has gone outside the Council to replace the chairman, and in several instances staff members have been promoted to Council membership.   When Johnson succeeded Kennedy, he made no change until Heller resigned in November 1964.   The Council members have been orthodox professional economists; although they represented varying views, none has been an adherent to "far out" schools of thought such as those which flourished in the 1930's.

While twenty years is a short time in the life of a Federal agency, the Council seems firmly established and has indeed become a strong competitor with the older agencies for influence on economic policy. Even if the Council should itself be eliminated, the function of formal advice seems well enough established to survive in another framework.

Impact of the Council on Other Agencies

Not surprisingly, the Council has had substantial influence on the agencies with which it has been associated.   The relationship of greatest significance has, of course, been with the Joint Com-

---

[2]As this is written, Chairman Ackley has been in office slightly more than three years, and his resignation has been announced to take effect shortly.

mittee. Although this might have been a delicate situation, it has for the most part been amicable and naturally beneficial. Similarly, the presence of the Council has been conducive to interest in economic research in other agencies. We have seen that CEA has depended upon various Federal agencies for information, not building up a large research staff.

Located in the White House, the Council enjoys substantial prestige and public exposure not available to other research organizations. In part, it has shared this standing with other research groups and gives these organizations a sense of participation at the White House level which was seldom experienced before 1946. Also, the Council has concentrated attention on statistical gaps and on lack of uniformity in reporting information, thus making more effective the process of data collection and analysis on the Federal level. The movement of Council staff to and from other agencies has also been important in unifying economic advice.

However, despite the Council's successes, several minor shortcomings or potential problems can be observed. The most serious problem which has resisted solution since the Council's formation is that of independence from full commitment to the administration program while enjoying the confidence of the President and participating in the administration's general policy. It seems more than likely that no wholly satisfactory solution will be found. Nourse, Keyserling, Burns, and Ackley have all laid down precedents which will be helpful to future chairmen; yet each chairmen will face unique problems and personalities and the relationship between Council, President, and Administration will repeatedly need to be re-established. Again we must remind ourselves that two decades is a brief time in the life of an agency. With the passage of time, the Council will acquire a patina of tradition which will be more difficult to break through. One of the major advantages of the Council has been its flexibility; it would be unfortunate if in gaining maturity and stature, it also acquired rigidity.

Changing Goals

There can be no question that the Employment Act of 1946 has been a success in the first two decades of its existence. From the uncertain years of 1946 to the end of the Truman Administration through the years of confidence in the Kennedy and Johnson Administrations, the Council has had its troubles and triumphs, but the

general course has been upward. There seems to be no serious
opposition to the Council as an institution. The Council and its
counterpart, the Joint Committee, have reached a high level of influence in national affairs. The paucity of suggestions for improvement put forth in the *Twentieth Anniversary Symposium* of the Act
in 1966, is symptomatic of the general esteem in which these agencies
are held. We must, however, remember that the years since 1946
have presented economic problems resulting mainly from inflation.
Thus, the major objectives of the Employment Act, although somewhat altered to be sure, have been relatively within reach. Less
success has been achieved with the objectives of price stability and
growth which also come within the purview of the Act as now inter-
preted. Much credit is due other Federal agencies and the business
community which like the Council have become more sophisticated
in their formulation of economic policies. Obviously, the CEA and
the Joint Committee, essentially coordinating agencies, would not
have been able to carry out their programs unaided.

The question of success or failure must in the end be answered
in relation to the objective of the organization in question. It is
obvious that the goals of the Employment Act have shifted since 1946.
The original objective of the Act was to prevent a major postwar
depression or a sliding back into the slough of 1937-1939, a more
than remote possibility in the eyes of many people. For many reasons
this has not occurred and over the twenty years which have elapsed
the original goal has been replaced by the dual objectives of economic
stability and economic growth. What began as defense against the
enemy of deflation became largely a battle against inflation.

One must also note that what was a suitable objective for the
Council two decades ago is hardly adequate today. In 1946 Mr.
Truman gave the Council its "sailing orders," namely to keep the
national income up to $200 billion![3] It was then $180.9 billion, and
first exceeded $200 billion in 1948; by this measure it had achieved
its objective within two years. Likewise it has done its job in
preventing a major depression. The recessions of 1948-49, 1953-54,
1957-58, and 1960-61 have been mild. In no case did employment
exceed 8 percent nor GNP fall by more than 3.7 percent; in every
case, the reversal in trend took place within at the most thirteen
months. In a sense, the Council has been the victim of its success.
Not satisfied with the prevention of catastrophic depression, the

---

[3]Nourse, *op. cit.*, p. 109.

increasingly demanding public has charged the Council with prevention of unwelcome price increases and the promotion of growth. Within a decade, the goal of a national income of $200 billion had jumped to $350 billion (1956) and by 1966, anything less than $600 billion would have been considered a poor performance. Economic growth, not even mentioned in the original act, has become an objective of major interest.

Along with growing responsibility, the Council has acquired increasingly effective tools and techniques to cope with its problems. As one cannot compare the performance of the Council except in relation to the changing objectives and problems which it faced over time, neither can one compare the effectiveness of the various Councils except in relation to the problems faced by each. Nor must we overlook the fact that each Council built upon the experience of its predecessors: Nourse fought battles which Keyserling did not have to refight; Burns benefited from the trials of Keyserling; Heller enjoyed a heritage from Burns, and passed benefits on to Ackley. Like the Presidents they served, the Councils must be evaluated not so much as against each other, but in terms of the problems they faced and the goals they attempted to reach with the tools at their disposal. In an earlier chapter it was pointed out that the overall approach of the Councils to their problems was surprisingly uniform, given the general orientation of the Administrations of which they were a part. Nourse, as befitted the first chairman, attempted to maintain an objective and scientific approach. Keyserling on the other hand, as an unreconstructed New Dealer, maintained a much more activist tradition. Burns, as part of an administration dedicated to reducing the area of governmental influence, acted more as a consultant to the President or a doctor of economic ills on call. Saulnier faced new problems of controlling inflation. Heller was the prototype of the modern economist and confidently extended the influence of the Council into new areas.

Although the basic approach to major economic problems has been consistent, the Council has, partly by design and partly by fortune, remained a small, highly-personal, noninstitutional organization. One can speak in meaningful terms about the "Burns Council" or the "Heller Council," whereas one would not speak of a "Benson Department of Agriculture," or a "Dillon Treasury." The personal nature of the Council-President relationship has been much more significant than one would have expected it to be. To what degree the Council has been forced to remain small because of budget limitation design is difficult to say, but the important point is that it has remained small and informal in its organization. Reorganization Plan No. 9 has had the happy effect of providing a direct and formal channel of communication to the President without binding the Council in red tape.

The generally academic tone of the group, and especially under the Heller chairmanship the frequent use of temporary consultants has helped to diminish isolation and bureaucracy. Only a handful of the staff have been realtively permanent; the rest have come and gone with considerable frequency. The this-is-the-way-we've-always-done-it syndrome has largely been avoided, and the Council's tie with the academic and business communities has remained viable. Numerous Council alumni (both members and staff) are now leaders in academic life, research groups, and business.[4] These alumni have retained their Council interests and often returned for short stints. Thus, the Council has a constantly enlarging group of knowledgeable, dedicated friends who provide it with useful contacts on many levels.

On the other hand, senior staff members from both the CEA and the JEC have expressed concern about lack of staff continuity. As one senior staff member of the Joint Committee expressed it: "No one stays long enough to know where the bodies are buried." Several problems have arisen from this situation, such as wasted effort in duplication of exploratory work already done before the staff member's arrival and the need of constantly renewing personal contact among the agencies. The high rate of turnover has been attributed to relatively low salaries; the pace maintained in both JEC and CEA, which creates serious personal problems for the staff members; and poor physical working conditions, especially in the Joint Committee. Of these, both JEC and CEA staffers were especially concerned about the workload which involved routinely working on Saturdays, holidays,

---

[4]Although the large majority have returned to academic life, increasing numbers are making high-level business connections or moving into research groups. Of the living Council members who had completed service in 1967, twelve had returned to academic life, one had entered business, two were retired, and one had gone into private practice as a consultant. All were still alert to Council problems and active as writers and commentators on Council activities and related problems.

and in the evenings.[5] Obviously, this condition cannot be maintained for an indefinite period of time. One staff director had been somewhat successful in reducing overtime by careful organization, but the nature of the operation makes this very difficult. On the other hand, both the JEC and the CEA offer prestige, challenging situations, and other attractions which partly overcome these disadvantages.

The Council has over the years been in competition with other agencies and organizations and with individuals as the source of economic advice to the President, who is served by a multiplicity of advisers in the field of economics. As *the official* adviser to the President, and the agency bearing responsibility for the economic report, the Council cuts across jurisdictional lines. However, the President must decide how much and what type of use he wants to make of the Council. In any organization, there is potential conflict between staff and line organizations as far as their influence upon the decision-maker is concerned.

What lines were to be drawn regarding jurisdiction over these matters and who was to draw them? In the labor field, for example, Secretary Goldberg and his successor Secretary Wirtz (who were directly responsible for labor matters), were active in impressing upon President Kennedy the importance of full employment policies. Even when other advisers press for the same policies as the Council, they are in competition with it. When they put forth opposing advice the President must then decide which course of action to follow. In many cases the advice offered or the policy championed by a cabinet officer has an atmosphere of urgency (such as Agricultural or Civil Rights policy) or a patina of personality (e. g. , Humphrey) which forces the President to give it unusual consideration.

In evaluating the competitive aspects of advice one must consider also the fact that though there is no direct conflict with Council economic views, there may be strong noneconomic aspects—military or social factors—which must be considered or perhaps given priority. Above all and perhaps most important is the sheer demand made on the President in terms of his available time and energy. Neustadt has described this daily pressure:

[5]On one occasion, the author interviewed a staff member at 2:30 P. M. , at which time the staff member had not yet had lunch. He was still on the job at 8:30 that evening.

A President's own use of time, his allocation of his personal
attention, is governed by things he has to do from day to day:
the speech he has agreed to make, the fixed appointment he
cannot put off, the paper no one else can sign, the rest and
exercise his doctors order. These things may be far removed
from academic images of White House concentration on high
policy, grand strategy. There is no help for that. A President's priorities are set not by the relative importance of a
task, but by the relative necessity for him to do it. He deals
first with the things that are required of *him* next. Deadlines
rule his personal agenda. In most days of his working week,
most seasons of his year, he meets deadlines enough to drain
his energy and crowd his time regardless of all else. The net
result may be a far cry from the order or priorities that would
appeal to scholars or to columnists—or to the President himself.[6]

The Council must compete for the President's time with cabinet
officers, senators, delegations from home, visiting heads of state,
4-H Club champions, war heroes, and countless others. Even a
superhuman appetite for data, memoranda, and advice would be
satiated by the offerings of the multitude of advisers.

The formal power structure (Treasury, Defense, etc., with many
serious problems all calling for immediate solution) is a formidable
competitor. No Council has, or is likely to, interpose itself between
the President and these old line agencies. Heller for all his influence
could not have displaced Dillon, nor did he try to do so. In competing
for the President's ear, the Council must remain largely passive.
It can pass him memoranda, but he cannot be forced to read them.
The Council must wait until the President asks for its services. It
may "assist and advise," "analyze and interpret," "develop and
recommend." It has no executive power. The Council has no field
staff, no clientele like USDA, no power to involve itself in programs
comparable to those of the Bureau of the Budget; no congressional
champions like those who safeguard the Air Force and the Navy.
The Council must rely on what reflected glory it can attract from
its position close to the President and its reputation for integrity

[6]Richard E. Neustadt, *Presidential Power* (New York: John Wiley and
Sons, 1960), p. 155.

and expertise. It has always faced the necessity of creating a demand for its services and, in doing so, has performed its major function.[7]

Despite a lack of formal power and notwithstanding its host of competitors, the Council is more than a façade concealing an empty structure. First and foremost, the Council is the visible symbol of the Presidential responsibility for economic welfare, but it is more than a symbol. The Council has performed very tangible and very important services for the Presidency which to a high degree are unique. The Council, as *the* expert group on economic matters, serving the President on a highly personal basis, provides him with a vehicle by which he can take the initiative in the continuous power struggle with the Congress and with the independent agencies and executive departments. The Council has been able to coordinate and synthesize the views of the various specialized expert groups within the executive branch. The Council gives him not only expert economic advice in private but also backs his authority with professional expertise in public. It can be useful in this way, thanks largely to the battle for professional objectivity fought by Nourse and his successors. Over-all, the Council has acquired a reputation for being as objective as it can be under the circumstances. Thus it is useful to the President as it never would be if it were thought of as a "rubber stamp" organization. How much weight the Council carried in back-stopping the President in his dispute with the steel industry, for example, cannot be determined, but there is no doubt that its moral force was useful to him as he injected himself into a complex argument involving such matters as price increases, productivity, and other esoteric economic issues. The Council, through either its report or oral testimony, is a useful channel for bringing matters before the public or the Congress, matters which the President may wish to ventilate, but does not care to make a formal part of his program. The Council, like any good staff arm, can take the blame if such matters prove to be embarrassing. In fact, the Council may serve the President as well in defeat as it does in victory. Rejection or apparent rejection of the Council viewpoint may mean not that its economic advice has been found defective, but that more serious

---

[7]Council staff people have pointed out to the author that Heller's success in involving the Council came from his persistence in bringing memoranda to the attention of the President. One staffer said, "Heller spent half his time in the West Wing."

problems have intervened or that different values have been forced upon the President for consideration. The Council's strength lies in the fact that the President is not required by law to accept its advice or indeed even to listen to it. Its success has come when it was needed and its advice asked for.

The value of the Council and the Joint Committee as educational agencies to both the President and the Congress has been commented upon and needs no further elaboration. The Council and the Joint Committee have together increased the awareness of economic matters in the public mind.[8]

The educational role has, of course, strengthened the public interest in and intensified the President's responsibility for economic activity, thus providing feedback to the Council itself. As Flash puts the matter:

> The Council has supplied information and analysis, but even more it has articulated the concepts needed for determination and defense of policy. The value of such an organization has been gradually recognized and accorded legitimacy by politician and bureaucrat, by economist and layman. [9]

The impact of the Act of 1946 has been immense. It has created not only a new mechanism for dealing with or viewing economic problems, but also a continuing awareness of what must and can be done to influence the course of economic events. Begun almost solely as a device to prevent depression, the Act has become much more, an economic gyroscope acting to stabilize the entire economy. It has created a viable force for economic education and a meaningful framework for economic discourse both within and without the government.

Though the Council and the Joint Committee have discharged their advisory functions with considerable success in the past two decades, it may be that the present arrangement will pass out of existence. Some years ago, Professor Blough suggested that the Council might, like its members, be expendable. No government agency is immortal.

[8]See Arthur F. Burns, "Progress Toward Economic Stability," *American Economic Review* (March 1960), pp. 1-19.

[9]Flash, *op. cit.*, p. 325.

Recently, suggestions have been made that the Department of Commerce and Labor be combined into a Department of Economic Affairs. If this comes to pass, it is likely that pressure will arise to include the Council or a similar organization within the scope of that Department. If this were done, the President might acquire a staff economist, and the Council would report to the President, only through the Secretary of the new Department. This would appear to be less satisfactory than the present arrangement. It seems clear from what has been said that a very important aspect of economic advice on high level is the degree of rapport between the adviser and the official concerned. Moving the Council out of the Executive Office Building both organizationally and physically would severely reduce the opportunity for frequent face-to-face contact. Further, it would very likely subject the Council to considerably greater likelihood of creeping bureaucracy, and, buried in the new department, subject to organizational rules, the Council would soon lose the status it now enjoys as part of the White House establishment.

It seems unlikely that the functions of the Council and the Committee be entirely dispensed with. In two decades the advantage of a group advising the President and a comparable group acting as a sounding board in the Congress have become obvious. Likewise, the degree of Federal involvement in the economy has become more pronounced and seems destined for even greater growth.

It is clear, however, that this function cannot be effectively performed under any and all circumstances. Form and organization are important. Several requisites for effective advice seem to emerge.

(1) The advisory agency must be independent of other established executive departments in order to remain objective in its views.
(2) The agency must remain relatively small and informal in organization.
(3) Though it must have a degree of organizational stability to function effectively, it must also remain flexible with a maximum interchange of ideas and personnel between itself and other organizations, both in and out of government.
(4) It must retain its standards of professional competence.
(5) It must remain close to the President both in terms of organization and physical location.

(6) It must be subject to comment by a comparable body in the
      Congress (now the Joint Economic Committee) in order for
      executive and congressional views to mesh with the maximum
      effect. The relations between these bodies must be close and
      friendly, but at arm's length.
(7) The Agency should involve itself in the President's program
      but avoid commitment to the point of losing objectivity.
(8) It seems desirable to have a resident economist in the White
      House to field the wide variety of economic issues which a-
      rise, and to bridge the gap between the President and the Ad-
      visory Group. Care must be taken, however, to see that he
      acts as a bridge not a barrier.

If it adheres to these principles, the name of the agency or in fact
its organizational status will be of minor import. The Act of 1946,
after two decades, has established a successful pattern and the principles outlined above seem to contain the formula for future success.

Almost half a century has elapsed since 1920—one of the most
eventful social and economic periods in the nation's existence. The
economist in government has increased his role both in the numbers
and level of his participation. Economic advice on the Presidential
level has become a formal responsibility. Two decades have elapsed
since that time and the previous chapter has examined the impact of
that development in some detail. In a broader sense, the role of the
economist in government has undergone marked change. Much of
this change has resulted from developments which came about in the
profession itself.

In 1920 the American Economic Association had slightly more than
two thousand members. In 1967, the figure had risen to more than
fifteen thousand. An increasing number of these persons were engaged in full-time research and advisory activities in either government or business. The reasons for this increasing participation are
diverse. The increasing complexity of the economic system and the
growing interdependence of government and business are clearly the
major factors. Fortunately, there has been increasing ability in the
profession to deal with these problems and to teach others to deal
with them in a systematic fashion. This is a recent development;
it seems very doubtful that if the CEA had been established in 1926
rather than in 1946, it would have been possible to staff it, despite
the limited needs of the day. The foundations of the present day

system of economic analysis and advice were laid in private research organizations and governmental agencies in the years from 1930 to 1945. The National Bureau of Economic Research, the Department of Commerce, OPA, and the Defense Department were coeval with the universities as the training schools for the new economics. This change has been so marked that probably few people other than professional economists appreciate its magnitude. National income analysis, input–output analysis, and other tools of modern economic policy were to all intents nonexistent before the Second War. The critical need for rational wartime planning intensified their development. The contribution of the economist in the stress of the war years assured his participation in the postwar era. The increasing involvement of government in business and in society since 1945 has made much the same type of economic analysis mandatory from the standpoint both of the government and those subject to governmental policy. (It is not coincidence that the older regulatory agencies have been engaged in economic research for many years.)

Fortunately for the profession, economists have been able to respond to these needs in contrast to their pedestrian performance in the field of public policy during the depression years. The response of the economist after the crash of 1929, for example, was not encouraging. When one considers that the professional economist in some form had been in existence for almost half a century by 1935, it would appear that the profession was woefully short of practical solutions to real life problems. Yet in a span of a few years, it apparently was able to make a satisfactory contribution. What was the cause of this change? Was the "Keynesian Revolution" such a mighty force as to change the outlook and ability of an entire profession?[10]

---

[10] The overthrow of Say's Law by the wide acceptance of Keyne's *General Theory* was to be sure a powerful factor in the acceptance of a greater degree of responsibility on the part of the state for assuring full employment. This, in turn, was a factor leading to the need for planning which lead in turn to a need for economic analysis, but it would be difficult to assign such weight to this factor. See Paul Baran, "National Economic Planning," *A Survey of Contemporary Economics,* Vol. II, (Homewood: Richard D. Irwin, American Economic Association, pp. 354 ff.) For a fine brief analysis and appraisal of Keynesian economics and its influence on policy after thirty years, see Alvin Hansen, "Keynes After Thirty Years, (With Special Reference to the United States)" *Welt Wirtshaftlicher Archives,* Band 97, Heftz, 1966.

Were the problems of wartime economics, although tremendous in scope, more easily approached than those of depression? It cannot be denied that the wartime problems were more closely within the competence of microoriented economists than were those of the depression. Likewise, since 1940 the body of economic doctrine has become more cohesive, more standardized, and more systematized. In short, economics at least in its academic branches has become more of a science. Yet on the higher levels of advice, it must clearly remain in large part an art form. Granted that economics has since 1920 or even 1940 made progress toward the goal of status as a systematic science, granted that the increasing sophistication of mathematics has to a degree made it more exact and increased the usefulness of the tool kit, granted that the economists who reach the high levels of advice are often the most able in the profession, do these factors explain the increasing success and prestige of the economist as an adviser and, more precisely, do they explain the change which seemingly took place in a short period of the decade, 1935-1945? Apparently they do when one considers that they were acting in concert. No doubt the Keynesian influence was the major factor, but the concurrence of other factors was important in the dramatic shift in the status of the economist which took place in a short time.

Despite these impressive gains, some question arises as to the future of economists in their role as advisers and participants in the public policy area. It has been noted on several occasions in this book that the level of economists' technical competence had increased in the years since the Second War and that they seemed better prepared to deal with real-life problems. To a degree this is true, but it requires qualification. Many of the economists who were active in the Roosevelt years and those who were then students, were enticed into economics by the fact that serious social problems existed, and they viewed economics as a way in which these problems might be studied and solved. Critical domestic problems of this magnitude have not existed in such a dramatic fashion since the end of the Second World War. Young economists who have been trained in the past two decades are proficient in model building and mathematical manipulation. They are often overimpressed with the apparatus and somewhat inclined to be disdainful about empirical applications. If one is impressed by social and economic issues, then clearly economics is a field of study which has great appeal and, in order to be successful, the analytic tools must be mastered. If, on the contrary, one is fascinated by methodology and by manipulation of data per se, he might be equally as interested in theoretical physics or astronomy as in economics. The profession must take care that it does not train economists who are more concerned with the apparatus used than they are with the results obtained, nor must it become dedicated to a single method of approach to economic problems. The complexities of policy formulation will require all the talents available.

Qualities of the Adviser

From time to time, mention has been made of the necessary personal and professional qualities of the adviser. In his book, *New Dimensions of Political Economy,* Walter Heller outlines these qualities as follows:

. . . in regard to the question of advocacy that "It raises no insoluble problems of integrity and few of objectivity (though silence may occasionally be golden. . .)"

The adviser must be prepared to serve as lightning rod [citing several of his experiences under Kennedy].

The adviser must maintain objectivity and perspective. . . .

He must be modest, and recognize the limitations of his tools, the role of luck, and the role of the private sector. . . .

[One must recognize] . . . the value of judgment, good nerves and "above all" good luck. [He attributes the success of the 1964 tax cut to a large share of luck and timing.]

. . . economic advisers have sometimes been "accused of acting as though they alone were carrying and balancing economic expansion on their shoulders." [He argues that this charge is wide of the mark, but does admit that on occasion the "view from the third floor of the Executive Office Building does not always have the private economy in sharp focus." In fact, Heller's book seems to underrate the private sector.]

Lastly, the economist on the policy firing line has fewer options than his academic counterpart, being circumscribed by political reality, public understanding, and institutional rigidity, as well as the limits of his scientific knowledge. [11]

---

[11] *New Dimensions in Political Economy, op. cit.,* pp. 18 ff.

Professional Pitfalls

The adviser who hopes to succeed at his trade must take care to avoid some serious pitfalls. Those who shuttle back and forth between academic life and government are less susceptible to these problems than those who are career government employees, although they are by no means entirely immune. The first of these dangers is that of passing from economic adviser or economic analyst to bureaucrat. The bureaucrat is more concerned with paper work and empire building than with economic analysis. There is nothing reprehensible about being a bureaucrat, but a talented economist who becomes one is wasting his resources. A second and indeed more seriously dangerous malady is that of the economist who desires to seize power in order to remake the world.[12] The worst aspect of this ailment is that it flourishes in secret and may be hard to detect until it has reached a serious stage. An economist who wishes to seek office can of course do so but he should do so openly and not attempt to exercise power through those whom he advises. Relatively few have held high office but those who have done so have generally done well.

One senior economist with some thirty years of policy level experience in the government expressed the view that the influence of professional economists had been considerably overrated and that the profession had been in recent years guilty of self-congratulation. In his view, the major changes in policy which have taken place since 1920 would have in large part taken place anyway. After hearing this opinion, the author was at pains to seek out the reactions of others. In general, his view was not supported, although there was some feeling that more humility might not be amiss. One with a sense of irony might speculate as to the immense prestige of the broker-banker in the late 1920's, in their role as guardians of prosperity and the rapid decline which took place!

It was also pointed out that the role of the economist has been especially effective in the area of micro-economics as opposed to macro-economics. Most economists might not subscribe to this opinion. Some good work has been done in the antitrust field, but

---

[12]Several economists who have reached high levels have been accused of this fault by others contacted by the author, in several cases, no doubt, with justice.

work in the regulatory agencies has been sadly neglected since the 1920's. Policy in agriculture has been largely shaped at micro level by economists, but the effects have been somewhat overcome by the political aspects influencing macro level policy, and in any event agricultural policy over-all can hardly be cited as a satisfactory example of economic policy-making.

Heller notes that in some quarters there has been some fear of a "technicians take-over," but he discounts this view noting that "the President's advisers cannot wrap themselves in their professional cocoons and hope to be effective. . . The political economist who advises presidents not only has to operate within the bounds of the possible, but has to help the President push out those bounds." In Heller's view, the technician can only achieve success by making his product salable to his number one customer, and also to the Congress, the press, and the public.[13]

Professors Jöhr and Singer point out that there are several dangers inherent in the advisory process. Among them, the tendency on the part of the economist to engage in an excessive amount of methodological study in the face of practical problems:

> However, from the point of view of basic research there are still unsolved problems the solution of which would be desirable for the purpose of determining economic policy. But quite often there is no time for this: if we try to solve them, we are in danger of delaying too long our judgment on the problem of economic policy. We behave like a doctor who, discovering that one of his patients is suffering from cancer, informs him that the causes of cancer are still unknown, but that he will straightway begin to investigate them. This doctor may have the luck to discover, after decades of research, what causes cancer. But the patient has died long ago. This, however, might have been avoided. The doctor might have cured him by an operation or by the use of rays. . . .[14]

These authors also note the importance of the comprehensive picture which may include noneconomic, political or social factors

---

[13]Heller, *op. cit.*, p. 51.

[14]W. A. Johr and H. W. Singer, *The Role of the Economist as Official Adviser* (London: Allen and Univin, Ltd. , 1955), p. 24.

of great importance. Public officials may, for example, issue statements for public consumption which, though not sound in terms of economic analysis, are useful for the purpose and should be accepted by the economist though they may offend his professional sensibilities. [15]

Also of great importance is the economist's breadth of experience; he must be able to adopt the viewpoints of others and be wise to the ways of the world, having a close acquaintance with all levels of income and practices of industry, in order to avoid the myopia of the academic theoretician. This work includes a passage worth quoting by way of summary of the intangible qualities essential to the adviser.

> In judging practical problems of economic policy so many difficulties pile up that the economist may well feel reluctant to devote himself to their solution. But if he is one who is touched by the privations and sufferings of certain classes and nations, if he recognises that the shaping of the economic order is a life and death problem for western society, and if, an an economist, he feels that he shares responsibility for its fate, he will not shrink from the difficulties which rise in his path when he sets out to judge problems of economic policy. [16]

Professor Ackley strikes a note in favor of an active role for the adviser, and he does not feel that the economist should shrink from value judgments:

> Any discussion of the role of economists in policy-making would be incomplete without some reference to the problem of value judgments.
> I referred a while ago, for instance, to the goals of employment growth and price stability as at least partially competing, and I pointed out that different people value these objectives differently. So far, I have only argued that policy choices involving them could be more intelligently made if we knew more about the tradeoff between them.

[15]*Ibid.*, pp. 89 ff.

[16]*Ibid.*, p. 94.

But I have not asked what kind of policy advice an economic adviser should give assuming he knows what the terms of trade are. Should he tell his principals (in this case): a bit more restraint will produce greater price stability but higher un-employment—you must choose which you want; that is a political not an economic question? Should he express his own tastes, though labelling them as such? Or is this presumptuous, since, in matters of taste, his views should count no more than those of any other citizen who has no access to the ear of high officials?

Frankly, I believe that these often discussed problems are largely false problems. As an economic adviser, I do not feel that I should hesitate to express my views on questions of this sort. Those in authority get plenty of advice from others who show no great delicacy in distinguishing technical questions within their competence from questions of values. The President hears from other members of his Administration, from businessmen, from labor leaders, from journalists— yes, from economists. If his economic adviser refrains from advice on the gut questions of policy, the President should and will get another one.

Moreover, in practice, most attempted distinctions between questions of technical economics and problems of values break down on examination. Price stability, for example—even full employment—is surely not an ultimate value. Price stability is a desirable and urgent goal of public policy primarily because its absence creates economic dislocations and strains. There is an element of truth in the view that attempts to increase employment in a given year at the cost of inflation really mean that policies will be necessary later on that will reduce employment in some future year. [17]

Robert D. Caulkins warns of the gap between professional and public understanding in the formulation of policy, and notes that as economics becomes more technical and economists more highly skilled, they must not neglect public education. [18]

[17] Gardner Ackley, "Contribution of Economists to Policy Formulation," *Journal of Finance,* Vol. XXI, No. 2, May 1966, p. 176.

[18] Robert D. Caulkins, *Economics As an Aid to Policy,* Graduate School of Business Administration, University of Southern California, Report to Management #9, (August, 1963).

Like economic advice itself, the adviser's role is seen from diverse viewpoints, yet the degree of uniformity is substantial and rewarding.[19]

Economists in their role as analysts and advisers have come far since 1920. These eventful years have witnessed major wars, a great depression, and the continued growth of Federal economic involvement. It has also been a time of undreamed-of growth in the private sector of the economy. Economists have been fortunate enough to participate in this process and to make a modest contribution to the public welfare. Their skills as well as their opportunities have increased in the half-century now nearing its end. Like most professionals, economists are anxious to use their training in the public service and to see meaningful results. Thus, the esteem they presently enjoy is a source of satisfaction to them. However, many difficult tasks lie ahead; the success enjoyed in recent years must breed a renewed dedication to the future.

[19]An excellent discussion demonstrating keen insight, and generally in agreement with others, is found in the brief article by James Tobin, "Academic Economists in Washington, " *National Economic Policy* (New Haven, Yale University Press), 1966, Chapter 18.

APPENDIX A

Economists in the Executive Branch

In addition to the economists mentioned in the text of chapter 3, numerous economists have been cited by their associates as having played an important role in formulating policy, or in aiding others on the policy level. These include both academic economists and career civil servants. Many of them served in various agencies. Those who were in the executive branch and the war agencies include: M. A. Adelman, Sidney Alexander, Jack Alterman, James W. Angell, Melvin Anshen, Robert Anthony, H. B. Arthur, Warren Ashby, Martin Bailey, Harold Barger, Harold Barnett, Lewis V. Bassie, Francis Bator, Theodore N. Beckman, Eugene Birnbaum, Richard Bissell, Roy G. Blakey, Lawrence N. Bloomberg, Betty Bock, Francis M. Boddy, Howard Bowen, Raymond Bowman, Ward S. Bowman, Gerard M. Branon, Daniel Brill, Andrew Brimmer, Henry Brodie, Edgar Brossard, Philip S. Brown, Weir M. Brown, Ralph E. Burgess, Arthur R. Burns, Eveline Burns, Norman Burns, Louise Butt, Miriam Camp, William Capron, Deane Carson, John M. Cassels, James Cavin, Vincent Checchi, Hollis B. Chenery, Benjamin Chinitz, J. M. Clark, H. B. von Cleveland, Frank V. Coe, Samuel Cohen, Wilbur Cohen, Emilio Collado, Walter W. Cooper, Morris Copeland, John H. Cover, Dewey Daane, Arthur Dahlberg, Edmund Day, Jack de Beers, Joel Dean, Charles L. Dearing, Louis Dembitz, Edward Denison, Ralph L. Dewey, Robert Dorfman, Evsey Domar, John Dunlop, Edgar Dunn, Jr., James S. Early, Laszlo Ecker-Racz, George Eddy, Lynn R. Edminster, Henry H. Edmiston, William J. Elliott, Stephen Enke, W. Duane Evans, Solomon Fabricant, Marvin L. Fair, Rashi Fein, Alan R. Ferguson, Frank A. Fetter, Ernest Fisher, Bertrand Fox, Manuel A. Fox, Isaiah Frank, Irving Friedman, Milton Friedman, Irwin Friend, Walter Gardner, Frank Garfield, Oscar Gass, Edwin B. George, Milton Gilbert, Henry Glass, Harold Glasser, Richard Goode, Lincoln Gordon, Robert A. Gordon, Henry Grady, Leo Grebler, Howard C. Greives,

Everett Hagen, John Haldi, R. L. Hale, Bernard F. Haley, Roy A. Hall, Simon Hanson, C. Lowell Harris, Bray Hammond, George Hass, H. G. Hayes, Richard Heflebower, Arthur Hersey, A. Ford Hinrichs, Fred S. Hoffman, Michael Hoffman, Edward D. Hollander, Richard Holton, Paul Homan, Harrison F. Houghton, Don D. Humphrey, George R. Jacobs, George Jaszi, Griffith Johnson, Homer Jones, Weldon Jones, Edward Kalachek, Mortimer Kaplan, Alfred Kahn, Dexter M. Keezer, John W. Kendrick, Joseph Kershaw, Lucille Shepard Keyes, Albert Koch, Nathan Koffsky, Martin Korst, Frank J. Kottke, Murray Latimer, Edmund P. Learned, Walter Lederer, William Levin, Robert Levine, Harold Levinson, Sar Levitan, Ben W. Lewis, Walter Liebenberg, D. Philip Locklin, Samuel M. Loescher, Louis L. Lorwin, David Lynch, Edward Lynch, August Maffry, Wilfred Malenbaum, Arthur Marget, Jesse Markham, Stacy May, Paul W. McGann, Glenn McLaughlin, Joseph M. Meehan, David Meislman, John Myer, Max F. Millikan, Edwin S. Mills, George Mitchell, Frederick T. Moore, William H. Moore, Charles S. Morgan, Loyle A. Morrison, Chandler Morse, Jacob L. Mosak, Willard F. Mueller, Henry Murphy, James C. Nelson, Norman Ness, William A. Niskanen, John H. Nixon, David Novick, J. G. Noyes, Eugene Oakes, Oscar Ornati, F. Taylor Ostrander, Jr., Alfred Oxenfeldt, William N. Parker, Anthony Pascal, Leo Pasvolsky, Charles A. Pearce, Merton Peck, Henry M. Peskin, Howard S. Piquet, Samuel Pizer, Kenyon Poole, Lee Preston, Edward W. Prokter, Alfred Reifman, Stuart A. Rice, Charles F. Roos, Martin Rosen, Morris Rosenthal, Henry Rowan, Oscar Ryder, William Salant, R. Duane Saunders, Orvis Schmidt, Ira O. Scott, Lawrence H. Seltzer, Thomas C. Schelling, Eli Shapiro, Julius Shishkin, Sumner Slichter, Irving H. Siegel, Edward K. Smith, Mark Smith, Henry Solomon, Robert Solomon, Henry Spiegal, Harold Spiegel, Herbert Stein, George Steiner, Leroy Steinbower, W. H. S. Stevens, George Stigler, O. C. Stine, G. W. Stocking, Herbert Striner, Allan R. Sweezy, Paul Sweezy, Boris Swerling, Philip Taft, Henry J. Tasca, Amos E. Taylor, Merlyn Trued, Beatrice Vaccara, Lawrence Vass, Raymond Vernon, William Vickrey, William A. Vogley, Donald H. Wallace, W. Allen Wallis, Clark Warburton, Forrest G. Warren, Murray L. Weidenbaum, David Weintraub, Simon Whitney, Aryness Joy Wickens, Walter F. Wilcox, E. H. Williams, Jr., Faith Williams, Vladimir Woytinsky, Dwight Yntema, Charles Zwick.

APPENDIX B

Personnel of the Council

Members, Council of Economic Advisers
1946 – 1967

Name	Position	Oath of Office Date	Separation Date
Edwin G. Nourse	Chairman	August 9, 1946	November 1, 1949
Leon H. Keyserling	Vice Chairman	August 9, 1946	
	Acting Chairman	November 2, 1949	
	Chairman	May 10, 1950	January 20, 1953
John D. Clark	Member	August 9, 1946	
	Vice Chairman	May 10, 1950	February 11, 1953
Roy Blough	Member	June 29, 1950	August 20, 1952
Robert C. Turner	Member	September 8, 1952	January 20, 1953
Arthur F. Burns	Chairman	March 19, 1953	December 1, 1956
Neil H. Jacoby	Member	September 15, 1953	February 9, 1955
Walter W. Stewart	Member	December 2, 1953	April 29, 1955
Joseph S. Davis	Member	May 2, 1955	October 31, 1958

Source: Economic Report of the President, January, 1965, p. 175.

231

Name	Position	Oath of Office Date	Separation Date
Raymond J. Saulnier	Member	April 4, 1955	January 20, 1961
	Chairman	December 3, 1956	January 31, 1959
Paul W. McCracken	Member	December 3, 1956	January 20, 1961
Karl Brandt	Member	November 1, 1958	January 20, 1961
Henry C. Wallich	Member	May 7, 1959	July 31, 1962
James Tobin	Member	January 29, 1961	December 27, 1962
Kermit Gordon	Member	January 29, 1961	November 15, 1964
Walter W. Heller	Chairman	January 29, 1961	August 31, 1964
John P. Lewis	Member	May 17, 1963	
Gardner Ackley	Chairman	November 16, 1964	
Otto Eckstein	Member	September 2, 1964	
Arthur M. Okun	Member	November 16, 1964	
James S. Duesenberry	Member	February, 1963	February, 1963

Economists associated with the Council either as staff or as more or less continuous consultants are:

Henry J. Aaron
Ascher Achinstein
Shirley M. Almon
W. H. Locke Anderson
John J. Arena
Kenneth J. Arrow
Robert E. Asher
Richard Attiyeh
Jarvis M. Babcock
Richard M. Bailey
G. Paul Balabanis
Bernard S. Beckler
Barbara R. Bergman
Eugene A. Birnbaum
Guy Black
Stanley W. Black
James T. Bonnen
W. G. Bowen
Harold F. Breimyer
Michael F. Brewer
Harold F. Breimyer
Henry W. Briefs
Martin Bronfenbrenner
David B. Brooks
Cary Brown
Samuel L. Brown
Benjamin Caplin
William M. Capron
Jack W. Carlson
Susannah E. Caulkins
Richard Caves
Lowell J. Chawner
Benjamin Chinitz
Robert C. Colwell
Charles A. Cooper
Richard N. Cooper
Donald E. Cullen
John C. Davis

Hamilton Q. Dearborn
Melvin G. de Chazeau
George H. Deming
Robert Dorfman
John W. Dorsey, Jr.
Rosalie K. Epstein
Rashi Fein
Joseph L. Fisher
Peter C. Fousek
Karl A. Fox
Stanley L. Friedlander
Catherine H. Furlong
Theodore J. Goering
Stephen M. Goldfield
Leo Grebler
W. Lee Hansen
Dale E. Hathaway
Catherine A. Heitzman
Bert G. Hickman
Edward Hollander
Paul Homan
Edgar M. Hoover
Francis M. James
Myron L. Joseph
Alfred E. Kahn
Edward D. Kalacheck
Marshall Kaplan
E. Gordon Keith
Peter B. Kenen
Saul Klaman
Burton Klein
David T. Kresge
Edwin Kuth
Robert Lampman
Hal B. Lary
Susan J. Lepper
Harold Levinson
Wilfred Lewis Jr.

John V. Lintner, Jr.
Clarence Long
David W. Lusher
Paul W. MacAvoy
Donald D. Martin
Daniel Marx, Jr.
Timothy W. McGuire
John A. Meek
John R. Meyer
Raymond F. Mikesell
Edwin S. Mills
Cary P. Modlin, Jr.
Theodore Morgan
Richard A. Musgrave
James R. Nelson
Richard R. Nelson
Saul Nelson
Robinson Newcomb
William H. Nichols
Frank E. Norton
Benjamin A. Okner
Theodore K. Osgood
Joseph A. Pechman
George L. Perry
Lee E. Preston, Jr.
Frederick Q. Raines
Albert E. Rees
Alfred Reifman
Kenneth D. Roose
Melvin Rothbaum
R. Robert Russell
Vernon W. Ruttan
Walter S. Salant
William A. Salant
Virgil Salera
Paul Samuelson
Paul S. Sarbanes

Raymond J. Saulnier
Frank W. Schiff
John A. Schnittker
Charles L. Schultze
Martin Segal
Louis Shere
George P. Shultz
Norman J. Simler
Mary Smelker
Warren L. Smith
Robert Solomon
Robert M. Solow
Lewis J. Spellman
Walter F. Stettner
Collis Stocking
Boris C. Swerling
Charles A. Taff
Paul J. Taubman
Lester D. Taylor
Philip E. Taylor
Nancy H. Teeters
Penelope H. Thunberg
Lester C. Thurow
Robert Triffin
Lloyd Ulmann
Haskel P. Wald
Joseph J. Walka
Donald Wallace
Charles B. Warden, Jr.
Robert Warren
F. V. Waugh
Leroy S. Wehrle
Burton A. Weisbrod
Betty J. Willis
Sidney G. Winter, Jr.
Ramsay Wood

(Source: *Economic Report of the President,* 1946–1967.)

APPENDIX C

Staff Members and Consultants, Joint Economic Committee, 1946-1967

Professional Staff

Barber, Richard J.
Berquist, Fred
Boggs, Thomas H., Jr.
Brown, Samuel L.
Ensley, Grover
Hardy, Charles O.
Henderson, John B.
Iden, George R.
Johnson, William Summers
Knowles, James W.
Lehman, John W.
McClung, Nelson D.
Moor, Roy E.
Moore, William H.
Murray, Alan P.
Obal, Thaddeus J.
Pollack, Gerald A.
Reilly, Roderick H.
Stark, John R.
Ture, Norman B.
Webster, Donald A.

Economic Consultants for study of Employment, Growth and Price Levels

Abramovitz, Moses
Bernstein, Edward M.
Beza, Sterie T.
Bleile, George W.
Brower, Michael J.
Chandler, Lester V.
Conrad, Alfred H.
Eckstein, Otto

Eisner, Robert
Fand, David I.
Fisher, Joseph L.
Fromm, Gary
Frucht, Padraic
Harris, Seymour E.
Hirsch, Werner Z.
Kareken, John H.
Kaysen, Carl
Kuh, Edwin
Lampman, Robert J.
Lebergott, Stanley
Leiserson, Mark W.
Levinson, Harold
Musgrave, Richard J.
Redford, Emmette S.
Schultze, Charles L.
Selden, Richard T.
Shuman, Howard E.
Smith, Warren L.
Snodgrass, Donald R.
Suits, Daniel B.
Taylor, George R.
Topping, Frances K.
Tryon, Joseph L.
Warden, Charles B., Jr.
Wilson, Thomas

Other Economic Consultants

Allen, Julius W.
Allen, Robert Loring
Bean, Louis H.
Billings, Elden E.
Brandow, George E.
Darbyshire, Bernard N.
Darling, Paul G.
Dawson, Harris P., Jr.
Dechert, Charles R.
Despres, Emile

Diamond, Arnold H.
Ettin, Edward C.
Forbes, John Van Gelder
Geiger, Theodore
Gilfillan, S. Colum
Gurley, John G.
Halvorson, Harlow W.
Handler, A. Benjamin
Hathaway, Dale E.
Hendrix, William Elbert
Houthakker, Hendrik S.
Humphrey, Don. D.
Hunsberger, Warren S.
Ladd, David L.
Lutz, Friederich A.
McCabe, Ralph
Manning, Raymond E.
Massel, Jean M.
Meltzer, Allan H.
Mikesell, Raymond F.
Mund, Vernon A.
Murphy, Henry C.
Peck, Gustave
Piquet, Howard S.
Pisar, Samuel
Popkin, Joel
Rose, John Kerr
Redding, A. David
Schnittker, John A.
Schnitzer, Martin
Scoll, David E.
Sheldon, Charles S.
Shimkin, Demitri
Snyder, Eleanor
Snyder, Eugene E.
Von der Linde, Gert
Tarshis, Lorie
Ward, Ray
Weidenbaum, Murray L.
Weintraub, Robert

Welch, Charles A.
Wilcox, Walter W.
Zwick, Jack

BIBLIOGRAPHY OF MAJOR SOURCES RELATING TO ECONOMIC ADVICE IN GOVERNMENT

The subject of economic advice in government has been quite thoroughly explored in recent years. Since 1946 various participants have documented the work of the Council. Before that, references to economic advice are more often included as part of general accounts, biographies of public figures, etc. In these cases, the reference to economic advice is generally brief and must be searched for diligently.

Marriner Eccles's *Beckoning Frontiers* (New York: Alfred A. Knopf, 1951) is an excellent source of information on economic policy in the mid-New Deal years. The landmark work on the Roosevelt era, *The Age of Roosevelt* by Arthur M. Schlesinger, Jr., (Boston: Houghton, Mifflin, 1955), is invaluable, especially in the volumes, *Crisis of the Old Order* and *The Politics of Upheaval*, which relate to the early New Deal and the preceding era.

Portions of Rosenman's book are very informative with regard to the brain trust, as are portions of Moley's work: Rosenman, Samuel I., *Working With Roosevelt* (New York: Harper & Row, 1952); Moley, Raymond, *After Seven Years* (New York: Harper & Row, 1939). For the most part, general accounts, biographies, etc., relating to the Presidency make only the most casual reference to economic policy and advice, and are not rewarding as sources of data, except in bits and pieces, and for general background.

A good early source is Goldenweiser, E. A., "Research and Policy," *Federal Reserve Bulletin,* 30: 1-6 (April, 1944).

Several general works dealing with the Presidency touch upon the economic powers and obligations of the office; eg. Neustadt, Richard E., *Presidential Power, the Politics of Leadership* (New York: Wiley, 1960), and Rossiter, Clinton A., *The American Presidency*, 2d ed. (New York: Harcourt, Brace and World, 1960, Professor Flash includes many sources in his bibliography relating to the administrative aspects of the Employment Act: Flash, Edward S., Jr.,

239

Economic Advice and Presidential Leadership (New York: Columbia
University Press, 1965).

Accounts dealing with the Council and its activities have multiplied
in recent years. The first chairman, Dr. Nourse, recounted the
early years in Nourse, Edwin G., *Economics in the Public Service*
(New York: Harcourt, Brace and World, 1955).

Other valuable sources of information dealing directly with the
Council and the Advisory function are:

Burns, Arthur F., *The Management of Prosperity* (Pittsburgh: The
    Carnegie Institute of Technology, 1966).
Burns, Arthur F., "An Economist in Government, *Forum I* (Winter,
    1957).
Canterberry, E. Ray, *The President's Council of Economic Advisers*
    (New York: Exposition Press, 1961).
Hansen, Alvin, *The American Economy* (New York: McGraw-Hill,
    1957), esp. Ch. 5-7.
Harris, Seymour E. ,*Economics of the Kennedy Years*, (New York:
    Harper and Row, 1964).
Heller, Walter W., *New Dimensions of Political Economy* (Cambridge:
    Harvard University Press, 1966).
Tobin, James, *National Economic Policy* (New Haven: Yale University
    Press, 1966).
Tobin, James, "The Intellectual Revolution in U. S. Economic Policy
    Making," *Noel Buxton Lecture*, University of Essex, England,
    Jan. 18, 1966. (Mimeographed).
Saulnier, Raymond J. , *The Strategy of Economic Policy* (New York:
    The Fordham University Press, 1962).
Silverman, Corrine, *The President's Council of Economic Advisers.*
    The Interuniversity Case Program. (University: University of
    Alabama Press, 1959).
Wilkins, B. H., and Friday, C. B., eds., *The Economists of the New
    Frontier* (New York: Random House, 1963).

On the general role of the economist, the article by Gardner
Ackley, "Contributions of Economists to Policy Formation," *Journal
of Finance* (Vol. XXI, No. 2, May 1966), is excellent.
Bounding, Kenneth, *The Skills of the Economist* (Toronto: Clark,
    Invin, 1958).
Economics and Public Policy (Washington, D. C. : The Brookings
    Institution, 1955).

Also useful are:

Hitch, Charles J. "The Uses of Economics," Brookings Dedication
    Lectures, *Research for Public Policy* (Washington: The Brookings
    Institution, 1961).
Jöhr, W. A., and Singer, H. W., *The Role of the Economist as Offi-
    cial adviser* (London: Allen and Univin, 1955).

The numerous publications of the Council and the Joint Committee
are, of course, an invaluable source of information. The two volumes
issued on the twentieth anniversary of the Act are especially useful:
U. S. Congress, *Twentieth Anniversary of the Employment Act of
1946, An Economic Symposium,* and *Supplement to Hearing Before
the Joint Economic Committee, Invited Comments on Directions for
the Future,* 1966, Joint Economic Committee, 89th Cong. , 2d Session (Feb. 23, 1966).

An excellent analysis of the first decade appears in Gerhard Colm,
*The Employment Act, Past and Future: A Tenth Anniversary Sym-
posium,* (Washington: National Planning Association, 1950).

Although general in nature, Theodore Sorenson's *Kennedy* and
Schlesinger's *A Thousand Days* contain a substantial amount of
information relative to the economic policy of the Kennedy Administration:

Sorensen, Theodore C. , *Kennedy* (New York: Harper and Row, 1965).
Schlesinger, Arthur M. , *A Thousand Days* (Boston: Houghton-Mifflin,
    1965).

The leading source of information on the events leading up to the
passage of the Employment Act is Stephen Kemp Bailey, *Congress
Makes a Law* (New York: Columbia University Press, 1950). See
also his article, "Political Elements in Full Employment Policy,"
American Economic Review, Papers and Proceedings (May, 1955),
pp. 341-350.